VIOLENT EMOTIONS

VIOLENT EMOTIONS
Shame and Rage in Marital Quarrels

SUZANNE M. RETZINGER

SAGE Publications
International Educational and Professional Publisher
Newbury Park   London   New Delhi

For information address:

 SAGE Publications, Inc.
2455 Teller Road
Newbury Park, California 91320

SAGE Publications Ltd.
6 Bonhill Street
London EC2A 4PU
United Kingdom

SAGE Publications India Pvt. Ltd.
M-32 Market
Greater Kailash I
New Delhi 110 048 India

Printed in the United States of America

Library of Congress Cataloging-in-Publication Data

Retzinger, Suzanne M.
  Violent emotions : shame and rage in marital quarrels / by Suzanne M. Retzinger
      p.   cm.
  Includes bibliographical references and index.
  ISBN 0-8039-4183-8 (cl.). — ISBN 0-8039-4184-6 (pb)
  1. Marriage. 2. Interpersonal conflict. 3. Shame. 4. Anger
I. Title.
HQ734.R374   1991
306.81—dc20   91-3310
                                                                                CIP

93 94 15 14 13 12 11 10 9 8 7 6 5 4 3 2

Sage Production Editor: Diane S. Foster

Contents

Preface

Mary Anne Fitzpatrick

The main reason for reading a preface is to find out what the book has to say. Suzanne Retzinger has done such a fine job of presenting her theory and research that a detailed description by me of this book would be redundant. Consequently, after a cursory treatment of the main points of Dr. Retzinger's argument, I will try to indicate the importance of this book by placing it within the context of the work concerned with communication in the family across a number of social science disciplines. These last are fields with which I am familiar, but they are relevant beyond that fact. A communication theory of the family must account for emotional processes, and Dr. Retzinger's research moves the field in an important direction in that regard.

According to Dr. Retzinger, connection with others is the primary motive in human behavior and is accomplished through communication. Central to her theory is the idea that social connections or bonds between people are at risk in all encounters: If they are not being built, maintained, or repaired, they are being damaged. Within her framework of human sociability, an important source of conflict and aggression between intimates becomes reactions to lapses in important social bonds. A perceived attack by one partner on the bond between partners causes rage and shame and hence conflict escalation.

Dr. Retzinger presents a powerful theory of emotional processes and conflict escalation in intimate relationships. In testing her theory of protracted conflict, she employs complex verbal and nonverbal coding schemes, identifies specific emotions within the context of marital quarrels, and isolates recurring patterns preceding the escalation of a quarrel. She provides exemplars of how this theory works through the intensive analysis of segments of conflict exchanges in four couples. The reader will come to know Rosie and James, David and Colleen, Roxanne and Brian, and Randy and Karin very well by the end of this book. I suspect that many researchers, teachers, and therapists will turn to the vivid descriptions and transcripts the author provides to illustrate important points about communication in intimate relationships.

If Dr. Retzinger had accomplished only these feats in her book, it would be an important addition to the literature. She has, however, done much more. I hope to show the extent of her contribution by discussing the fault lines dividing the research on family process, the central role of affect in understanding conflict dynamics, and how this theory can benefit other major lines of investigation in the family area.

THE EPISTEMOLOGICAL FAULT LINES

The study of marital and family interaction cuts across disciplinary boundaries. Researchers are housed in a variety of disciplines, including communication, psychiatry, social work, sociology, and clinical, social, and developmental psychology. Each discipline approaches the study of family interaction somewhat differently. Some of the differences come from the weights that each discipline assigns to the various levels of analysis from which an examination of the family can proceed (Fitzpatrick & Wamboldt, 1990); some come from the quantitative versus qualitative fault line that splits family communication researchers.

This book and the way Dr. Retzinger approaches her research may keep the fault line from becoming a chasm. She heavily references and relies on both quantitative and qualitative work to build her argument, displays great sensitivity about how the "other side" may view the importance of case studies, and is extraordinarily careful in documenting her arguments about sequence and pattern in these dialogues. In other words, within a conversation, Dr. Retzinger compares the presence or absence of shame and rage and its relationship to escalation, and justifies her conclusions with empirical evidence. It is up to the reader to decide the degree to which the method of proof used in this book defends against alternative explanations. But the same holds true for the reader of a piece of communication science research in family interaction (Jacobs, 1988).

Dr. Retzinger and I are on opposite sides of this epistemological fault line; whereas she may be considered a discourse analyst who uses a case study method, with its focus on intensive analysis and in-depth exemplars, I am a communication scientist who studies family communication processes by employing large-scale data sets and quantitative techniques to examine sequence and pattern in couple communication. According to the usual logic of these positions, the methods of argument and the standards of proof differ so radically that little can be learned from the writing generated on the other side of the fault line. Like children at parallel play, work on family dynamics proceeds along similar tracks within each camp, yet is rarely acknowledged outside of the group. Panel discussions at academic conventions sometimes give lip service to how much we all have to learn from one another. The political fact, however, is that researchers and theorists working in what might be called discourse-analytic approaches versus communication science approaches to communication in the family rarely read or cite each other's work, appear in each other's edited volumes, or review each other's books.

As a communication scientist, I see Dr. Retzinger operating within the context of discovery in that she has carefully outlined a theory that can be (and is) operationalized and tested. The assumptions behind her theory as well as her propositions are unambiguously presented to the reader. Communication scientists, working within a context of justification, may want to demonstrate the relative frequency of occurrence or the situational variability of the emotional patterns that Dr. Retzinger has discerned in her four conversations. Indeed, I believe that important research in communication science can be generated from the theory presented by Dr. Retzinger on how couples and other intimates escalate conflict by attacking the social bonds. Those workers in communication science interested in third-party intervention and mediation may find exactly the theoretical stance they need on conflict in intimate relationships in Dr. Retzinger's theory (Donohue, Lyles, & Rogan, 1989).

THE ROLE OF AFFECT IN INTIMATE CONFLICT

Few would argue with the commonsense notion that emotion in families and close relationships is an important area of study. Many would be surprised to find that until recently little attention has been paid to this area of study. Within the last decade, however, given the work of a number of fine investigators, it has become the accepted view that the emotional climate of a distressed and conflict-ridden marriage includes both more negative affect and more reciprocation of negative affect than that of a nondistressed marriage. This finding has been replicated in different laboratories and cultures and appears to show strong cross-situational consistency within a given couple. In addition, the causal effect of such negative affect cycles has been demonstrated in longitudinal designs (see decade review by Noller & Fitzpatrick, 1990). If this is the accepted view, what information do we gain about affect by reading the work of Dr. Retzinger?

Two answers to this question immediately spring to mind. The most obvious answer is that the strength of this theory is that it unpacks the construct of negative affect so that we may examine it more closely. Rage and shame are given central theoretical focus as the causal mechanisms responsible for marital conflict escalation. Anger alone is not the villain, but the accompanying shame that comes with an attack on the marital bond. A less obvious, yet far more important, answer is that the author presents an interactional theory of affect (also see Gottman, 1990). Family communication theorists often decry the scarcity of relational-level terms in both naive language and scientific writing. Within the theoretical tradition that attempts to keep concepts and inferences at the relational level, and thus rejects individual-motivational terms, affect has long been suspect (Raush, Greif, & Nugent, 1979). Within this decade, negative affect reciprocity has joined this construct class, yet still other relational-level affect descriptors for interaction are needed. In a field still weak in language to describe process, Dr. Retzinger introduces social emotions or emotions that operate to regulate the bond between people in order to ensure the survival of connections between intimates.

Aside from the theoretical importance of this language, it has pragmatic value as well. By the end of this book, Dr. Retzinger is able to give pragmatically oriented readers advice about short-circuiting dysfunctional communication patterns. Rather than making generic statements about being more positive and less negative, she shows the reader actual ways to derail the rage-shame interact, and accompanying conflict escalation, either within one's own interaction or when observing that of a third party.

RELATIONSHIP TO OTHER RESEARCH

One of the major ways that scientific research is judged is the degree to which it complements other research endeavors. The working assumption for those who research intimate relationships is that embedded patterns of interaction between partners cannot be successfully hidden but are revealed through a close examination of how couples communicate. Dr. Retzinger's research is clearly within this tradition: It should set to rest the doubts anyone might have about the willingness and ability of couples to engage in conflict with one another while being videotaped in a scientist's laboratory (I refer skeptics to Karin and Randy).

In reading the intensive analysis of the dialogues of Retzinger's couples, I was struck by the similarity of the conflict patterns she uncovered to those I have seen in my laboratory (Fitzpatrick, 1988, 1991). From both the presentation of psychological information about the couples and their standard dialogic patterns of engagement and avoidance of marital conflicts, I would like to speculate as to the definition of the marriage held by each couple. The definition that each couple holds concerning their marriage incorporates three dimensions: ideology (e.g., relational beliefs, values, and standards), interdependence (e.g., degree of connectedness), and expressivity (e.g., views on conflict avoidance/engagement). I would argue that the definition that couples hold about their marriage is one way to describe in detail the kind of bond that couples have. This description may help to predict a priori which messages would be more likely to be an assault on the bond for given sets of couples and, considering the degree to which this theory complements my own work, will allow me to make more substantive and theoretical statements about conflict escalation in various types of marriages (for an attempt, see Burrell & Fitzpatrick, 1990).

Rosie and James have conventional marital and family values, yet also they privilege their individual freedoms over the maintenance of the relationship. This couple is not very companionate, and they share little with each other, trying to maintain a psychological distance in their relationship. Rosie and James might describe their communication with each other as persuasive and assertive, yet they collude in avoiding open conflict. One partner may display outright hostility yet retreat quickly if the partner disagrees. In my terminology, Rosie and James are Separates.

Roxanne and Brian share nonconventional values about relationships and family life, yet are very open and companionable with one another. This couple is constantly renegotiating their roles, and disagreements are a fundamental part of their relationship. Because they tend to engage in conflict very openly, Roxanne and Brian are Independents.

In my terminology, David and Colleen are a mixed type, in that he appears to have an independent view of the marriage whereas she has a separate definition. Mixed types are noted for their disagreement on fundamental issues in the relationship as well as their different ideologies and views about connectedness. David and Colleen are Independents/ Separates.

Although the definitions of their marriages held by the first three couples seem to fall clearly into patterns I have previously uncovered, I am loath to speculate about Randy and Karin. Not only is there less information given about the values and levels of interdependence in this marriage, but this couple seems to be in severe distress after the loss of two children. Whereas the other three couples enacted protracted yet manageable conflict escalation, the nature of the conflict interaction in Randy and Karin's marriage is severe and intense. This couple may be an Independent couple who, although previously able to control their angry exchanges, have now escalated their conflict out of control.

Concern for saving the face of the partner and preserving the bond in the marriage is a major feature of the final major type of couple I have isolated in my research, the Traditionals. Traditionals do not appear in this book about rage and shame in the escalation of marital quarrels. It may be that Traditional couples use the conflict deescalation techniques suggested by Dr. Retzinger in the final section.

CONCLUSION

The theory and research presented in this book pass what I think of as David Reiss's (1981) three-point heuristic test of a model of family processes. To have lasting effects, a work on family process must be found to be (a) plausible and familiar, (b) robust enough to stand revision and tinkering, and (c) capable, with some additional work, of greatly expanding our understanding of family process. Dr. Retzinger's model of conflict escalation through the emotional displays of rage and shame has this heuristic power.

Acknowledgments

This book proposes a theory and method for understanding conflict in relationships. Primary emphasis is placed on the importance of the social bond; lapses in the bond are precursors for conflict. Alienation and emotion usually precede disruption. Although it is common knowledge that anger is involved in conflict, the important role that shame plays in perpetuating anger is not as well understood. I use the information from many fields in a microscopic approach to understanding conflict

Writing this book took several years of hard work and help from many people: Financial support was provided by the Patent Fund and the Humanities/Social Science Research Grant at the University of California, Santa Barbara, and by Sarah Scheff.

Parts of this book were based on three of my articles: "The Role of Shame in Marital conflict," in *Perspectives on Social Problems* (parts of Chapters 4-7); "Shame, Anger, and Conflict: Case Study of Emotional Violence," in *Journal of Family Violence* (part of Chapter 7); and "Shame-Rage Spirals: Videotape Studies," in H. B. Lewis (Ed.), *The Role of Shame in Symptom Formation* (1987). Permission to reprint this material is gratefully acknowledged.

I thank Lawrence Erlbaum Associates for permission to reprint tables from the article "Shame and Guilt in Neurosis," by

H. B. Lewis; and W. H. Freeman for permission to reprint a figure from Close Relationships, edited by Harold H. Kelly et al.

The following persons gave helpful comments: Gale Miller (*Perspectives on Social Problems*) and Michel Hernsen (*Journal of Family Violence*). I am indebted to Robert Levenson for granting permission to use one of his videotapes for this study.

Many thanks to Bert Adams for his comments on an earlier draft; Anthony Giddens for his long, detailed review; and Don Brown. Mary Ann Fitzpatrick and John Braithwaite have also been most helpful. Thanks go also to Lori Terry for her secretarial assistance and to D. J. McLaren, who provided construction of Figures 2.1, 2.2, and 2.6. I am grateful to Catherine Welles for her conversations that contributed to Chapter 2, on social distance and boundaries. I also thank Melvin Lansky for his comments, clarification of ideas, and continued support.

I am indebted to those who have been a source of support throughout this project: Richard Applebaum, John Baldwin, and Dorothy Kreuger. Each helped by offering emotional and intellectual support, editing, comments, varying perspectives, and suggestions.

I am grateful to my children, Jennifer, Thomas, and Lydia, who have provided a haven of retreat, kept me in perspective, and were patient and responsible throughout this project. I have learned an immense amount about human relationships from them.

My debt to the late Helen B. Lewis cannot be expressed easily. She was my adviser and role model; her support and loving care will be difficult to match. Her *Psychic War in Men and Women* provided the seed for this book; I express my sorrow for the loss of a great woman. I extend my gratitude to her husband, Naphtali Lewis, for his continued encouragement.

My greatest debt is to my friend and colleague Thomas Scheff; we explored ideas about the social bond and emotions together. His insight into human nature provided a point of departure; his tolerance made my exploration possible, allowing me to try out new ideas. He has relentlessly read and reread earlier versions of this book and has been my most important editor and critic. He has been an unending source of emotional

and intellectual support and encouragement. I extend my most
abundant appreciation.

Finally, I wish to thank the couples who volunteered to be a
part of this study. They are true pioneers who enabled me to
map a passage into an unexplored territory

—Suzanne M. Retzinger

Introduction

The Godhead is broken like bread.
We are the pieces. ("Herman Melville",
W. H. Auden)

Randy and Karin, like many couples, have been arguing about the same topic for years; they can't seem to connect with each other:

10:13.50 K: ya but the support doesn't come in telling me not what
to eat but realizing that I have some problems an I'm
internalizing them is where the support an YOU should
come in
23.34 R: ya but I can't get into your mind

Although the primary topic of their argument is the weight Karin has gained, they go from topic to topic. They are alienated and feel hopeless in the situation; they blame each other for the problems:

13:53.00 K: . . . that sex isn't the greatest, could any of it be your
fault?
R: NO
56.62 K: NONE of it?

R: uhuh
K: none of it in BED was your fault, it was all my fault that
    it wasn't the greatest (1.8) you see what you're saying
R: ya I do ( ) and that's what I'm saying
    . . .
14:10.00 K: wel-I mean but lets be honest about it ( ) I'm THAT
              horrible in bed and you're that exciting ( ) is that what
              you're saying
          R: umhmm

Blame only makes the situation worse. Change of topic does
not get them any further in resolving their issues, but leads
them further into entrenchment; they move to another topic,
and the vehemence between them rapidly increases. To observ-
ers their topics often seem trivial:

54.40 R: . . . I mean it used to be that you had some actual lips ( )
           NOW::you're there's-ther there's very
17:01.31 K: (interrupting R) [you don't have any upper lip]
          R: little definition
          K: don't talk about my lips

Randy and Karin might be any of us. Although the topic may
be different, many couples can recognize the beat of the drums
in their own relationships. The topic could be body weight,
money, sex, the division of household duties, or the way the
kids are raised. Although topics may change, giving the appearance of a new quarrel, the beat goes on. Some couples end in
divorce, some live with conflict and violence, others lead lives
of quiet desperation; some actually resolve their conflict.

The questions I raise are these: How is it that the same quarrel
can continue for years on end, even with great effort to resolve
it? What are the driving forces beneath the quarrel that give
seemingly trivial topics a powerful life of their own? What roles
do emotions play? How can conflict be self-perpetuating?

Although this book is about couples, it may also have implications for other forms of conflict. Conflict is a fundamental
problem facing our society. It is clear that conflict is endemic,
as suggested by even the most casual glance at present world
conditions. Evidence for conflict can be found in all areas of

modern civilization; so little seems to change—wars rage on, violence continues among family members, races, classes, and religions. All the expert systems and advanced abstract knowledge have not seemed to help.

Dahrendorf (1965) implies that conflict is a basic human element when he argues that "wherever we find human societies there is conflict. Societies . . . do not differ as to the presence or absence of conflict, but rather to the degree of violence and intensity" (p. 171). Simmel (1955) suggests that "a certain amount of discord, inner divergence and outer controversy, is organically tied up with the very *elements that ultimately hold the group together*" (p. 18), conflict can be important for *group cohesion*.

If one assumes an innate propensity for conflict, this assumption might lead to the belief that conflict is a predominant motive of human behavior. On the other hand, if human beings are thought to be fundamentally social creatures, maintenance of social contact would be primary. One question to ask is, If conflict is fundamental to human societies, what is it that holds the group together?

Marx (1844/1964) and Simmel (1955) suggest the underlying function of conflict—restoration of social bonds and group unity. The implication of this perspective is that human behavior is not primarily conflictful, competitive, or aggressive, but rather social; conflict is an attempt to restore bonds—the social bond being the glue that holds the group together.

Marx began his analysis with concern for communal bonds, assuming connectedness (solidarity) among its members. In his view, communal bonds were being replaced by alienation in the Industrial Revolution; with the emergence of modern industrial society, community had declined. Marx's writings represent a plea for community, and the hope that eventually conflict would restore community. Simmel (1955) takes a similar view: "Separation does not follow from conflict but, on the contrary, conflict from separation" (p. 47). Although both Marx and Simmel propose that the function of conflict is to restore group cohesion or unity, other theories are permeated with the assumption that aggression and conflict are primary.

A rapidly changing world can lead to breakdown in community (bonding between identified persons). Community is replaced by society—where persons are "arbitrarily and artificially united by promise and contract" (Scheler, 1961, p. 166). Where relationships once were immediate, with rapid changes in time and space, they are becoming increasingly more abstract and distant (Giddens, 1989). Social relationships are being lifted out of the present. In an alienated society there is danger of excessive conformity to symbolic values in an attempt to reestablish community. In the process of overconformity, certain aspects of the self are in danger of being lost; the result can be alienation from self.

Recent studies by Lewis (1976), Bowlby (1988), Ainsworth (1989), and others suggest that sociability and affectionateness are primary to bonding; conflict seems to arise only under specific conditions, such as thwarts, threats, or damage to social bonds (i.e., loss of face). A glance at the earliest behavior of human beings finds clutching and clinging rather than fight or flight. Sociability and affectionateness seem to occur prior to aggression; connection with others can be a goal of even conflictful behavior.

I chose to study conflict escalation in marriages for several reasons. First, broken family bonds can be one of the most intense sources of conflict. For example, in some child custody disputes, two otherwise rational people seem to become temporarily insane. Each partner becomes violently reactive to the slightest gesture of the other; the two cannot disentangle themselves emotionally from each other—the level of conflict can increase virtually without limit. Another reason to study marriages is that a precise method can be used that captures moment-by-moment escalation: videotapes of actual quarrels.

The integration of diverse approaches to conflict is the foundation for this book: couples conflict, community conflict, communication theories, large-scale warfare. Conflict theorists have discussed the importance of the social bond, but recent work on marital and family conflict, based primarily on atheoretical observations, has virtually ignored this aspect of human behavior. Few have dealt with sequences of events that occur during escalation.

Relationships among social bonds, shame, and conflict are proposed. <u>Protracted conflict is marked by social-emotional separation and unacknowledged shame, leading to anger, which in turn is expressed with disrespect, which leads to further separation, and so on.</u> The role of *hidden alienation and shame* as the source of repetitious cycles of conflict is investigated.

This book is divided into three parts that present theory, case studies, and conclusions. Part I reviews studies from the different disciplines, and provides a background for a new theory (Chapter 2). An integrative method (Chapter 3) has implications for theory building, research, and practice; it is applied to four cases.

Chapter 1 covers theories and research from large-scale conflict, marital disputes, and communication processes. Sociological theories provide a wide-angle view of basic variables that underlie conflict. However, they deal mainly with abstract explanations; few provide concrete empirical examples.

Unlike their sociological cousin, recent psychological approaches to marital conflict deal with emotions and communication patterns between persons. Although they deal with emotions, very few address specific emotions or the function of emotion during conflict; emotions are usually clumped into two categories, positive and negative. In studies that do specify emotions, behavior and emotion are often confused. The implications of such groupings are important for understanding conflict.

Work on marital conflict has also dealt with concrete behavioral patterns, but lacks a theoretical backdrop—it does not tie into any of the existing theories of conflict, and does not build theory from the findings. Rather than dealing with conflict per se, these studies are concerned primarily with the comparison of functional and dysfunctional marriages—that is, understanding what distinguishes distressed from non-distressed, satisfied from dissatisfied. Few have attempted to expand the traditional theories or to spell out dynamics of escalation. Much can be learned from integrating findings from various approaches.

Another problem with many of the conflict studies is that only aggregate data have been used. While useful in describing patterns of conflict and prevalence, they lose some of the richness found in qualitative studies; aggregate studies do not lend themselves to a dynamic theory of conflict escalation.

There are few theories of conflict escalation compared with studies of conflict in marriage; some mention escalation in passing and, like other research on conflict, touch only the surface of the problem. Escalation as yet has not been adequately explained.

Chapter 2 outlines a theory of conflict. Social bonds are vital to community as well as to individual relationships. Conflict is discussed in regard to threatened and broken bonds. I suggest that the emotion of shame plays a particularly important role in the structure and process of bonding, and therefore in conflict. A new theory of escalation is described: Escalation of conflict occurs when there is alienation and shame is evoked but not acknowledged.

Chapter 3 develops a method that has implications not only for understanding escalation, but also for resolution of conflict (i.e., repair of the bond). It integrates visual, verbal, and paralinguistic methods. Applied intensively to case material, this method may help to advance our knowledge of conflict.

Case studies with sequential analysis are not without limitations. They are time-consuming and expensive to conduct. Intensive investigations also do not provide information about prevalence, but gain in advancing knowledge for understanding *sequences* of behavior that would otherwise remain invisible. Intensive research can reveal nuances of behavior that hide underlying similarities, and lends itself well to application to practical problems.

Part II presents four case studies of marital quarrels. Each couple is introduced with an explanation of their background. Each couple is unique, and on the surface they all look very different. Hidden beneath surface differences are similarities, however. As each couple quarrels, escalation is observed, moment by moment. Underlying the vast differences, similarities emerge—patterns that lead to escalation: the role of unacknowledged alienation and shame in the generation of anger or silence. Because of the complex and detailed nature of the analysis, only a short segment of each couple's argument is analyzed in detail.

Part III addresses repairing the bond and presents some propositions and conclusions. Chapter 8 deals specifically with repair and implications for resolution. The dynamics of resolution are based on an inverse view of the new theory and findings on conflict, as well as on observations of actual instances of deescalation. Practical implications are also reviewed. The last chapter reviews patterns that emerge from the four cases, develops propositions, and discusses the ambiguity of communication and problems of translation.

PART ONE

Theory

1 Theoretical Perspectives on Conflict

> Things are in the saddle. (Ralph Waldo Emerson, "Ode Inscribed to W. H. Channing")

Sociology has the oldest research tradition in the study of conflict; it arose out of the intention to reform. Marx was perhaps the first conflict theorist, as he addressed the struggle between classes—"the property owners and the propertyless workers." One result of the struggle between the haves and the have-nots was that "the increasing world of *things* proceeds in direct proportion to the devaluation of the world of men" (Marx, in Tucker, 1978, p. 71). Objectified labor becomes an "alien, hostile, powerful object independent [of the person, and whose] position towards it is such that someone else is the master of this object, someone who is alien, hostile, powerful, and *independent* of him" (p. 78). In Marx's view, the processes of objectification and alienation go against the very social nature of the human being. The value of *things* over others alienates human beings from nature, self, and others, transforming social beings into isolated individuals.

One result of alienation, according to Marx, is protracted conflict. When the tension became too great, Marx predicted, revolutionary conflict would restore community—communism was his solution. With the integration of the social being to roots in community, the age-old conflict between the individual and society would be resolved. Although Marx's notion of communism was vague, he may have been pointing to an important issue. Communism, community, communion, and communication have common roots. Each is a social phenomenon; each suggests a bridge between persons—the *social bond*.

In his work on conflict, Simmel (1955) proposes the idea that conflict follows separation, rather than separation being a result of conflict. He describes an integrative process, noting that hatred is caused by hurtful feelings generated by rejection. Although Simmel began describing the most fundamental aspects of conflict, he never tested his ideas empirically, or spelled them out explicitly.

Many sociologists and psychologists, working with varying perspectives, have since focused on conflict (e.g., Bateson, 1972; Boulding, 1962; Brockner & Rubin, 1985; Coleman, 1957; Collins, 1975; Coser, 1956; Dahrendorf, 1965; Deutsch, 1969; Gelles, 1987; Gelles & Straus, 1979b; Kreisberg, 1973; Raush, Barry, Hertel, & Swain, 1974; Simmel, 1955). Theorists generally agree that conflict is inevitable, although they do not always agree about its function. Some view conflict as functional, while others view it as dysfunctional. Coser (1956), Marx (1844/1964), Sumner (1906), and Simmel (1955) do not regard conflict as inherently destructive. Each believes conflict has positive functions. According to Simmel, conflict "resolves divergent dualisms; it is a way of achieving some kind of unity" (p. 13). Simmel, like Marx, views certain types of conflict as adaptive.

Coser (1956) suggests that conflict stimulates interest and curiosity, prevents stagnation, is a medium through which problems can be aired, is the root of personal and social change, and builds group cohesion. Like Simmel, Coser states that under certain conditions conflict can be functional; it is dysfunctional when "there is . . . insufficient toleration. . . . What threatens the equilibrium . . . is not conflict as such, but the *rigidity itself which permits hostilities to accumulate* and to be

channeled along one major line of cleavage once they break out into conflict" (p. 157; emphasis added). Boulding (1962) also contends that tragic consequences resulting from conflict are dependent on the rigidity of the system and not the conflict itself; both Coser and Boulding posit that the more intolerance there is to conflict and the more hostility that is repressed, the more dangerous the ultimate conflict.

While some view conflict as serving the function of readjustment, social change, and cohesion, others, such as Parsons (1949) and Rosenstock and Kutner (1967), view conflict as inherently dysfunctional. Although Parsons sees conflict as endemic, he also considers it a disease or sickness in the system. Being primarily interested in the conservation of existing systems, he disregards the possibility of positive functions of conflict. Like Parsons, Rosenstock and Kutner view conflict in itself as destructive, evoking rigidification and withdrawal between parties.

Deutsch (1969) makes a distinction between destructive and constructive conflict. He agrees with Simmel and Coser about the positive functions, but says: "Destructive conflict is characterized by the tendency to expand and to escalate. . . . such conflict often becomes independent of its initiating causes and is likely to continue long after these have become irrelevant or have been forgotten" (p. 11). Things move from bad to worse: Tactics become extreme, the number of issues increases, motives become adversarial. Deutsch, following in Simmel's footsteps, notes that a quarrel between husband and wife may clear up unexpressed misunderstandings and lead to greater intimacy, but may also produce bitterness and estrangement.

Conflict can be either constructive or destructive. Conflict does not always resolve differences, unify persons or groups, or result in constructive change; sometimes it is destructive, erodes relationships, and ends in violence. Not all conflict strengthens solidarity in communities, groups, or individuals. When further alienation rather than unity occurs it can be destructive.

Studies by Coleman (1957) and Kreisberg (1973) also have addressed conflict in light of the social bond. Coleman found patterns in the initiation of dispute that imply the importance of the social bond: Alienation and polarization of opposing factions leads to intensified conflict—that is, there is little identification with the opponent and lack of close and continued relations. Coleman suggests that future studies investigate the strength of attachments between persons and to community affairs.

Most studies in the sociology of conflict have dealt with such issues as social bonds and function—that is, unification and social change. The same amount of attention has not been given destructive forms of conflict in community settings or in intimate relationships. What happens when conflict creates further alienation rather then solidarity? What if the change created by conflict is genocide or the destruction of the planet? Are there general societal trends toward intense, destructive conflict or periods in history when conflict is more constructive? (Nazi Germany in the 1940s marks a particularly destructive era.) Many of these questions, of course, are beyond the scope of this book.

The problem of protracted or escalating conflict and its relationship to unity—the social bond—is the foundation of this book. If some of the precise dynamics can be located, perhaps they can be generalized and applied to large-scale conflict. What has not been described adequately is how and why some conflict escalates or becomes destructive and other conflict does not.

THEORIES OF ESCALATION

Researchers from several disciplines have dealt with conflict escalation and protracted conflict from various perspectives (Brockner & Rubin, 1985; Deutsch, 1969; Johnston & Campbell, 1988; Kreisberg, 1973; Lansky, 1987; Peterson, 1983; Pruitt & Rubin, 1986; Retzinger, 1991a, 1991c; Scheff, 1987; Watzlawick, Beavin, & Jackson, 1967). Some theories of escalation concern communities or groups of people; others involve individuals in various settings. Several mention escalation, but only abstractly and/or in passing, and many have focused on "investment," or material objectives. Others have described factors that produce underlying hostilities, but from material or external perspectives (cost and benefit), and not from a focus that involves the process underlying actual quarrels.

Escalation has also been observed through communication patterns that elicit reciprocation during conflict (Barnett & Nietzel, 1979; Bateson, Jackson, Haley, & Weakland, 1956; Kelley et al., 1983; Raush et al., 1974; L. Rubin, 1983; Scheflen, 1960; Sillars & Weisberg, 1987; Stuart, 1980). While reciprocation can begin to explain prolonged, unresolved conflict, it does not explain how the reciprocal behavior in itself arose, and how it led to protracted dispute.

In their book on conflict escalation, Brockner and Rubin (1985) focus on entrapment as an important determinant in escalation. These researchers define entrapment synonymously with escalation: "a decision-making process whereby individuals escalate their commitment to a previously chosen, though failing, course of action in order to justify . . . prior investments" (p. 5). Although they imply that entrapment is a cognitive process, they go on to explain that entrapment resides not only in the situations, but in reactions to the situations. *Face-saving*, they say, is an important variable in escalating processes; people tend to become more entrapped when they need to save face. Face-saving involves *feelings*; people do not consciously and rationally get themselves entrapped. Entrapment, like face-saving, is an emotionally charged process.

Kreisberg (1973) found that adversaries in conflict tend to become increasingly isolated from each other; communication barriers increase. Anger increases, and perceptions of the other side become increasingly inhuman. The basic condition that affects escalation is the way parties interact: with over- or underreaction. Patterson's (1982) work also mentions that social isolation makes escalation more likely.

Several commentators note the use of threats and coercion, which they say are likely to generate counterthreats and aversive behavior that contribute to escalation (Coser, 1956; Deutsch, 1969; Kreisberg, 1973; Patterson, 1982; Raush et al., 1974). Threats, according to Coser (1956), involve the core symbol of the relationship, and in doing so *weaken the forces that bond the spouses together*. When threat is used, the attacked individual feels forced to behave in a more menacing manner in order to save face (Goffman, 1959, 1967). Threat induces defensiveness and reduces tolerance of ambiguity, as well as openness to new and unfamiliar ideas (Deutsch, 1969).

Brockner and Rubin (1985) deal mainly with cognitive/material determinants of entrapment, skimming the surface of emotion. They use experimental, game-playing methods, and only touch on underlying dynamics: Commitments deepen, rationality decreases, emotional involvement increases, and people get caught in dysfunctional behavioral patterns. The *hows* of commitments deepening, rationalities decreasing, and emotional involvements increasing are not described.

Pruitt and Rubin (1986) also deal with escalation. They note that bonds are weaker in larger communities, which makes members more prone to conflict. Coleman (1957) has also noted that in larger communities there is enough contact, but no bonds to protect people from escalation. Pruitt and Rubin note two types of bonds: group membership and dependency—that is, too weak a bond or too strong. "False cohesiveness" may give the appearance of group membership (Longley & Pruitt, 1980); conformity may be an attempt at belonging—the bond is weak. Pruitt and Rubin go on to note that weak bonds, as well as those that seem to have too much dependency, are at risk for escalation; the more dependent persons are on others, the more prone to escalation they become.

Although Pruitt and Rubin show the importance of the social bond and mention dominant underlying variables such as emotions of "anger, fear, and wounded pride," they never make connections among the variables. They say that the emotions result from escalated tactics, but do not make it clear how or why the tactics escalated. Their explanation, like that of others, is a black box, never revealing its contents.

The vulnerability to violent escalation by dependent people is supported by Shupe, Stacey, and Hazelwood (1987) in their study of family violence: "The more violence in the relationship, the more dependence there was" (p. 36). Dependent men had poor skills for communicating emotional needs and frustrations, as well as beliefs about dependency as a feminine trait.

They attempted to drive off the very affection they sought, which made them vulnerable to the slightest threat. Bowlby's (1988) work also gives support to the dependency hypothesis. He found the dependency needs in violent mothers to be especially strong; these mothers were unable to make close relationships at the same time they had a great need for them. Lansky's (1987) work also indicates that violent men are very dependent but cannot express this need.

In his formulation of destructive conflict, Deutsch (1969) notes that "both rage and fear are rooted in the sense of *helplessness* and *powerlessness*: they are associated with a *state of dependency*" (p. 35); he says that rage and fear often make it impossible to communicate a message. Deutsch believes that rage leads to destructive conflict, that fear weakens the commitment necessary to induce change, and that rage is more useful than fear and less damaging to *self-esteem*. Why do rage and fear make it difficult to communicate and how do they increase? What are the relationships among inadequate bonds, rage, and fear? Although Deutsch's observations are especially significant, as they stand they do not explain the dynamics involved in escalation.

Peterson (1979) used couples' written accounts of their daily interactions in an attempt to understand escalation. The four conditions he describes that perpetuate conflict are criticism, illegitimate demands, rebuff, and cumulative annoyance. But criticism, for example, does not lead to escalation in all cases; each of us is subjected to criticism in some form daily. We all have illegitimate demands made on us; we have all experienced rebuff. Under what conditions do these variables lead to escalation? What are the hidden emotions behind these behaviors?

The work of Katz (1988), Lansky (1987), Retzinger (1987, 1991b), and Scheff (1987) suggests that emotions are central to escalation. In Katz's studies of crime, he includes the extreme end of the spectrum of conflict—homicide. He points out the quick development of rage in case studies. Although a given argument may have been about paying the bills, he concludes that the killing was not really about who would pay the bills. Underlying the external topics are *moral implications* and *humiliation*.

The *topics* of conflict (e.g., money, sex, power, roles, responsibilities, jealousy) represent the cognitive components. Knowing the topic of the conflict reveals little about the dynamics of escalation; *anything* may become an issue. Searching for issues or topics may be an unrewarding way of explaining conflict. The topic is often forgotten or ceases to be an issue as conflict continues.

Scheff, Lansky, and Katz have independently detected shame and humiliation during intense conflict. They use case studies; in one study, Scheff (1987) uses characters from a drama involving love relationships to illustrate interminable quarrels and impasses; he has also reported a real quarrel between therapist and client (Scheff, 1990). Lansky's cases involve violent husbands and couples in a VA hospital setting. All these researchers identify shame as crucial in protracted and destructive conflict.

COMMUNICATION THEORIES

Communication is an important issue in escalation: Human relationships exist and develop through communication. Society exists only in mutually concerted action; the structure of society exists and is maintained through processes of communication. Mead (1934) assumes that communication produces social organization. Cooley (1909/1962) considers it so basic that he asserts that studying changes in communication patterns is the best way to understand social change. Communication is also central to understanding escalation.

Communication involves the mutual coordination of actions of participants, which results in the flow of information between them (Condon & Ogston, 1971; Duncan & Fiske, 1977; Kendon, 1967; Raush et al., 1974; Scheflen, 1973; Stern, 1977; Tronick, Als, & Adamson, 1979; Watzlawick et al., 1967). Because language has a common surface and private base, it is both very easy and very difficult for people to understand one another. "Language makes man at home in the world, but it also has the power to alienate" (Steiner, 1981, p. 82).

Jackson (1965b) defines communication as "behavior in the widest sense: words and their non-verbal accompaniments, posture, facial expression, even silence. All convey messages to another person, and each are subsumed in the term 'communication' " (p. 7). The single most important point on which there is agreement is that communication is essential; it is an integral part of all relationships (Bateson et al., 1956; Cooley, 1909/1962; Dewey, 1925/1958; Mead, 1934; Satir, 1967; Scheflen, 1974; Watzlawick et al., 1967).

Goffman's (1967) work has focused on gestures; he sees deference and demeanor as means of communication. People communicate to each other through their dress, grooming, posture, movements, and glances, every time they come into the presence of others, with or without awareness. "It is these covert forces of self-evaluation and other-derogation that often introduce a dreary compulsive rigidity to sociable encounters, and not the more bookish kinds of social ritual" (Goffman, 1959, p. 191).

Deference and demeanor involve *manner*. Manner goes beyond speech in defining relationships and is essential for understanding conflict escalation. Every word, gesture, facial expression, action, and implication gives some message to the other about social worth (Goffman, 1967). All interaction involves obtaining respect and avoiding what Goffman calls "embarrassment" or loss of face.

Through observing *manner* each person monitors the amount of respect received; each is acutely sensitive to receiving either too much or too little. The manner of communication informs participants of their roles vis-à-vis the other, status, emotions, immediate intentions, degree of dominance, deference given, and intensity and intimacy of the relationship; it organizes the flow of interaction—when to speak, when to listen, and when to end. It involves posture, gesture, facial expression, voice inflection, sequence, rhythm, cadence of words, and so on. *Manner defines the relationship* by establishing the frame for interaction, and provides cues to regulate its progress.

The manner in which we communicate can have more emotional impact than anything we actually say. Manner carries more implication than words, because it is about the immediate relationship between persons. Although both words and gestures carry emotion, words emphasize *information*, cognitive content, while gestural communication emphasizes *feeling* (Archer & Akert, 1977; Mehrabian, 1972).

Words are inherently ambiguous. Implications of words are potentially infinite, depending on the manner in which they are presented. Teenagers' use of language provides hundreds of simple examples of this. Depending on the context, the word *bad*, for instance, can mean "really good, better than good—this is IT; this is where it's at." To an unsuspecting parent it may seem to mean the opposite. Any word or phrase can have multiple implications, depending on the accompanying gestures and context.

Family therapy literature provides examples of the incongruity between verbal and bodily gestures (e.g., Satir, 1972). A woman may say to her husband, "I love you." The words alone do not tell much—the gestures that accompany the words give clues to what is implied. What is the intonation, the cadence, the emphasis? Does she look into his eyes as she says this? Is she smiling? If so, is the smile genuine? If the intonation is flat or she doesn't look into his eyes, or has a scowl on her face, he may respond coldly, "So you say." The words carry a different implication if she looks into his eyes and smiles as she speaks. The accompanying gestures (scowl or smile), and not only the words, produce a response in the husband; they qualify the message conveyed by the words.

Many have commented on two major forms of communication, but have used different terms: report/command (Ruesch & Bateson, 1951), symbolic/spontaneous (Buck, 1984), symbolic/gestural (Mead, 1934), linguistic/kinesic (Scheflen, 1974), digital/analogic or content/relationship (Watzlawick et al., 1967). There is overlap in these dichotomies as described by different authors; every communication has a topic or *content* (what is communicated) and *manner* (the "how" of communication).

Words are arbitrary. They are culturally learned, indispensable for the manipulation of objects and the transmission of culture. Without words human society would be impossible. They allow people to talk about the past and future, and to use information to plan and negotiate in the present. Although symbolic language has a highly complex and powerful syntax (structure), it lacks adequate semantics (meaning) to describe most aspects of *relationships* (Watzlawick et al., 1967). A gesture readily refers to the thing it stands for; it is represented in the present, and cannot refer to past or future. There are many aspects of experience (e.g., what goes on in a quarrel) that are extremely difficult to describe in words; certain feelings are conveyed largely by facial expression or manner. What we say is only a part of the communication process. How we communicate is at least as important as what we say, and sometimes more important. Understanding gestures is important for understanding conflict, because they are unique in gaining immediate responsiveness (Blumer, 1936). Gestures (manner) influence how the communication is taken; they define the relationship (Jackson, 1965a; Ruesch & Bateson, 1951; Watzlawick et al., 1967). The importance of understanding gestures is evident, but, because of the usual emphasis on symbolic communication, manner is often ignored. Words alone are just a part of the communicative process, and they are very limited in communicating relationship processes, particularly during conflict.

The ambiguity of communication helps to explain why "talking things out" does not always lead to a resolution of a problem and why heated arguments can arise over trivial things. A couple can have a heated argument over whether to eat at McDonald's or Wendy's. Conflict can rapidly escalate (even to homicide) over who pays the bills. But manner reveals emotions and gestures behind even seemingly trivial topics. Topics may be trivial, but manner is not, since it can convey disgust or contempt.

If manner is offensive, even the most trivial topic can lead to escalation. If manner is managed effectively, readjustment or change can follow, no matter how weighty the topic. Focusing only on the topic of argument is fruitless; the manner in which disputed issues are managed or settled needs to be accounted for. Studies of marriages suggest that spouses show less consideration (respect) and tact toward each other than they show in their routine exchanges with others (Birchler, Weiss, & Vincent,

1975; Stuart & Braver, 1973). It is essential to take a closer look at the tactics of communication used in disputes. The manner of communication has profound implications for the state of the bond.

MARITAL CONFLICT

Most relationships involve a certain amount of conflict, though a few have little or appear to have little. In some relationships conflict is frequent and intense, escalating into serious struggles (even at the slightest provocation) and ending in verbal, psychological abuse, physical violence, or separation. Kelley et al. (1983) view relationships as conflictful to the extent conflict occurs frequently, intensely, and/or for long periods of time.

Frequent, intense quarrels over long periods of time are not uncommon in marriages. Simmel (1955) asserts that conflict among intimates is more intense than that among strangers and can have tragic consequences: "The deepest hatred grows out of *broken love*. We cover our secret awareness of our own responsibility for it by hatred which makes it easy to pass all responsibility on to the other" (p. 46). There is evidence from many sources to support Simmel's claim, making marriage relationships a rich source for studying escalation. Several studies have suggested that the failure to deal with conflict is the single most powerful force in dampening marital satisfaction (Cuber & Harroff, 1965), if not the most prominent cause of marital failure (Mace, 1976).

Like other work on conflict, the earliest studies of marriage and family were sociological (Burgess & Cottrell, 1939; Locke, 1951; Terman, Buttenweiser, Ferguson, Johnson, & Wilson, 1938; Terman & Wallin, 1949). These studies showed correlations between satisfaction and stability, mate selection, the family life cycle, and demographic characteristics. Early studies emphasized the role of emotion in group and normal family processes (Bales, 1950; Parsons & Bales, 1955). Families characterized by positive emotion were said to foster high self-esteem and assertion; families characterized by negative emotion were thought to produce low self-esteem and withdrawal.

Theories of family conflict were originally developed to explain frequency of intrafamily conflict within a given sector of society (Gelles & Straus, 1979a; Sprey, 1979). On a micro level, several attempts have been made to help explain why conflict occurs more in some families than in others; that is, researchers have tried to isolate variables that differentiate marriages from each other (Bateson, 1972; Deutsch, 1969; Gelles & Straus, 1979b; Raush et al., 1974). While the macrotheories refer to characteristics of the family as an institution, the variables in microtheory help to explain differences among families. This book deals mainly with micro aspects of marital relationships and variables leading to conflict escalation, which depend on and reflect the nature of the larger social order.

As in traditional conflict theories, but independently, Olson (1986; Olson, Lavee, & Cubbin, 1988) has shown that the relationship between external stress and a family's ability to function constructively is related to the level of cohesion in the family, which implies the importance of secure bonds. If a family is either too isolated or too engulfed (isolation is akin to counterdependency, while engulfment involves overdependency), it is more vulnerable to external stressors than are securely bonded families.

Recently, there has also been a renewed interest in classifying marriages in terms of communication patterns (e.g., Duck, 1988; Fitzpatrick, 1988; Roloff & Miller, 1987). Using videotapes of couples interacting, Fitzpatrick (1988) has developed a typology of marriages based, in part, on how couples deal with conflict. Fitzpatrick integrates several dimensions: power/affect (relationship between autonomy and interdependence) and access/target, which gets at the interplay between social forces and relationship issues. Depending on the type of marriage, couples deal with conflict differently, in part because of the different tolerance each has for emotional discomfort and in part because of the social-emotional distance between them.

There have also been studies conducted concerning family therapy (Bateson, 1972; Bateson et al., 1956; Bowen, 1978;

Gottman, 1979; Gottman, Markman, & Notarius, 1977; Kerr & Bowen, 1988; Mishler & Waxler, 1968; Olson & Rider, 1970; Raush et al., 1974; Ruesch & Bateson, 1951; Scheflen, 1973; Watzlawick et al., 1967) and social learning theory (Birchler et al., 1975; Jacobson, 1977; Patterson, 1982; Reiss, 1981). Each tradition has contributed to the understanding of marriages in some fundamental way; each has focused on communication—interaction, reciprocation, or exchange. Few have focused directly on conflict escalation or have attempted to develop a theory of conflict.

Following the early studies of marriages, family therapists and learning theorists have dealt with distinguishing satisfied or functional marriages from dissatisfied or dysfunctional ones. Consistent patterns have been found in research on marital interaction. The most consistent pattern has been that dissatisfied couples express more negative emotion than satisfied ones, with a greater reciprocity of negative emotion (Gottman, 1979; Jacobson, 1977; Margolin & Wampold, 1981; Markman, 1981; Noller, 1984; Notarius & Markman, 1981; Patterson, 1982; Sillars & Weisberg, 1987). Sequential analysis has indicated that when one spouse expresses negative emotion, the other reciprocates in kind more often in dissatisfied marriages than in satisfied ones (Gottman, 1979). While most studies have dealt with general categories of negative and positive emotion, Gottman and Levenson (1986) have coded specific emotions. They classified as negative emotions such as "anger, contempt, sadness, fear and their blends" (p. 42).

While observing specific emotions can be revealing, there have been several problems with this approach. The most obvious is the confusion between emotion and behavior. Behavior can indicate that a certain emotion is occurring (see Chapter 3), but *behavior* and *emotion* are not synonymous. For example, in their analysis, Gottman and Levenson (1986) included "whining" as a "negative affect" along with anger, contempt, sadness, and fear. While the latter four are emotions, whining is a behavior. Labov and Fanshel (1977) have suggested that this behavior is a cue for an underlying emotion that they call "helpless anger." Although aggression is associated with anger, the two are not equivalent. Aggression is a behavior; anger is an emotion. Anger sometimes leads to aggression, but often it does not. A second serious but less obvious problem with marital interaction studies involves the use of a simple dichotomy, positive and negative. Dichotomization of emotion imposes a value judgment that neglects the usefulness of such emotions as anger, fear, and grief, which are labeled negative. These studies imply that for a couple to have a good relationship they should reduce "negative" emotions and increase "positive" ones. Why is it that anger, grief, and fear are considered negative or dysfunctional? Grief, for instance, is a response to loss—of a loved one or of some other important element in an individual's life. It has been shown that grieving is a necessary process for healing, for making it possible to get on with one's life after loss (Lazare, 1979). The value of anger as negative (and smiling as positive) is culturally determined; anger is not inherently negative. Little has been mentioned about the *function* of anger in marital conflict; it is often simply assumed to be intrinsically dysfunctional.

Freud (1926/1959) has proposed that anxiety is a crisis response; it has a signal function, an internal warning that something is wrong. Bowlby (1973) views anger in much the same way, noting that it can be functional or dysfunctional, depending on the use or outcome. If anger serves to strengthen the bond it is functional; dysfunctional anger destroys the bond.

According to Mead (1964), gesture is an expression of emotion; its primary purpose is social communication. Only recently have researchers begun to focus on communicative and regulative functions of emotion (Campos & Stenberg, 1981; Klinnert, Campos, Sorse, Emde, & Svejda, 1982; Sorse, Emde, Campos, & Klinnert, 1985). Sorse et al. (1985) have shown a signal function of fear: When approaching a visual cliff, infants stopped short when their mothers displayed fear, but continued over the (imaginary) edge when their mothers smiled.

If emotions serve a survival function, surely they cannot be entirely negative. Perhaps without these emotions the human race would have died out. How then are they negative? Behavior can have very detrimental consequences, but anger in itself can be harmless. It may not be the anger in itself that leads to acting out, but the rigidity of the system (as suggested by Coser) that prevents adequate expression.

Placing value judgments on specific emotions may be more of a hindrance than a help in understanding the role of emotions. According to Coser (1956), for instance, there is a tendency to suppress grievances in intimate relationships, where anger is inevitable yet deemed inappropriate toward a loved one (i.e., it is seen as a negative emotion). If anger is viewed as negative, the signal will be suppressed or ignored, and the system may become rigid in order to prevent its expression.

Holtzworth-Munroe and Jacobson (1985) found that unhappy couples are less willing to take responsibility for control over negative behaviors and to question their own behavior and feelings; consequently, they blame their partners. The denial of responsibility is rampant in conflictful relationships (Bowen, 1978; Holtzworth-Munroe & Jacobson, 1985; Horowitz, 1981; Jacobson, McDonald, Follette, & Berley, 1985; Lansky, 1980): One spouse denies his or her part and projects responsibility and blame onto the other.

When responsibility is denied it is difficult to resolve disputes. When couples are unable to resolve conflicts, the same patterns of dispute occur repeatedly; no new ways of dealing with problems emerge. A conflict about a seemingly simple issue can escalate to threaten the entire relationship, resulting in bitter quarrels, emotional withdrawal, lack of affection, and/or violence.

Escalation or repetitive cycling of conflict is usually conjoint. Defensiveness of one partner is likely to result in communication that causes the other to become defensive (Sillars, Jones, & Murphy, 1982). An argument seldom escalates because of one person alone; both parties usually contribute. Conflict is not attributable to a particular partner; rather, it is an outgrowth of a *conjoint system* involving continued successive feedback (Raush et al., 1974). Both partners play a part in escalation. Construction or destruction of a relationship is a joint process.

An important concept for understanding reciprocity, change, and stability in family systems is *homeostasis* (Jackson, 1957). All members of a system help to maintain that system;

the family's patterns of communication reveal the process of maintaining the status quo. "To observe homeostasis in a system one need only witness the immediate and frequently violent reaction to the recovery of an 'ill' patient, to be convinced that there are powerful family mechanisms for maintaining norms" (Jackson, 1965b, p. 14).

Characteristic of destructive family systems is oscillation that can go on seemingly *ad infinitum*, accompanied by charges of "badness or madness" (e.g., husband and wife argue over who is right and who is wrong). Watzlawick et al. (1967) call this spiral an "infinite oscillating series" (p. 58). They illustrate their conception of reciprocation using a spiral with an arbitrary beginning point as to who started the quarrel—H: "I withdraw because you nag." W: "I nag because you withdraw" (p. 57).

Raush et al. (1974) also point out the irrelevance of blame— arguments are seldom one-sided: The "intermeshing of individual styles in a conjoint approach to the management of conflict makes the attribution of individual causality within the ongoing interaction arbitrary. Who does what to whom is part of a continuing feedback process in which both participate" (p. 202). What affects one member of a marriage affects the other member and the whole family.

Some conflicts are *overt*, with blame, threats, and nagging, as already mentioned. Conflict can also be *covert*, for instance, when such avoidance tactics as withdrawal, distraction, computing, and placating are used (Satir, 1972). Although on the surface it may appear as if the relationship is harmonious, it can be marked by coldness, indifference, or lack of affection. The conflict has gone underground, except for covert hostility. A silent impasse exists, as in a cold war (Scheff, 1987). In silent disputes there is a static quality to sequences of interaction; nothing new occurs, the quarrel is circular (Raush et al., 1974).

Quarrels are maintained, in part, through reciprocation between interactants. Reciprocity refers to those exchanges that are rigidly responsive to each other: tit for tat, quid pro quo. Each partner reacts to the other's characteristic way of responding. Partners collude with one another on issues. They form a system—that is, the husband's externalization and denial are often supported by parallel externalization and denial by the wife, and vice versa. The husband's style of responsiveness is also likely to be repeated or opposed by the wife's. According to Raush et al. most communication is symmetrically reciprocal in nature, a form that helps maintain the status quo.

Kelley et al.'s (1983) model of meshed intrachain sequences (MIS) (Figure 1.1) portrays sequences evoked *within and between* participants, on both verbal and nonverbal levels. It is broader than other perspectives in that it subsumes both inter- and intrapersonal sequences during all types of interaction. The action of one person evokes emotions in the other that lead to thoughts and feelings in both parties, which then lead to action, and so on within and between persons.

The relationship between husband and wife is defined by the messages the two agree to be acceptable between them. In the Kelley et al. model, conflict can be viewed as a collusive process in that it involves what is going on within and between parties at a given time—it takes two to quarrel; both parties contribute to ongoing and escalating conflict. If person P insults person O, O feels humiliated (affect) and may think P does not love her. O then withdraws (action), which causes P to think O is not attentive, P becomes angry (affect) and scolds (action) O, and so on.

In line with earlier work, recent studies specify factors leading to conflict:

(1) criticism, disparagement, or other acts perceived as demeaning, which lead to feelings of injury or injustice
(2) coercion, demands, or requests perceived as unfair
(3) rebuff or feelings of being devalued
(4) attribution of blame to one's partner (Holtzworth-Munroe & Jacobson, 1985; Jacobson et al., 1985)
(5) challenges, threats, or deception
(6) issue expansion (use of such words as *always, never, all,* or *none*)
(7) "crucializing" ("If you really loved me you would/wouldn't ...")
(8) denial and double-binding messages (Coser, 1956; Deutsch, 1969; Holtzworth-Munroe & Jacobson, 1985; Jacobson et al., 1985; Kelley et al., 1983; Raush et al., 1974)
(9) the cumulation of all these factors (identified through analysis of events precipitating conflict; Peterson, 1979)

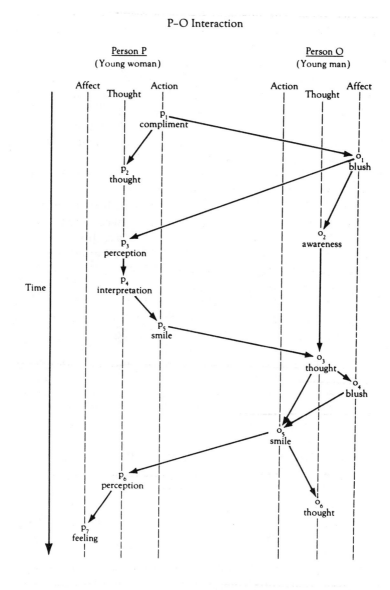

Figure 1.1. Meshed Intrachain Sequences

SOURCE: From *Close Relationships*. Edited by Harold H. Kelley et al. Copyright © 1983 by
W. H. Freeman and Company. Reprinted by permission.

 Each of these tactics implies a *threat to the bond.*
Each of the theorists mentioned above touches on important aspects of escalation, but none is sufficiently specific or comprehensive. What are the dynamics and boundaries of the system? How do threats and/or blame by one partner elicit threats and/or blame by the other? It is necessary to infer not only what is going on *between* partners, but, simultaneously, what is going on *within* each.

CONCLUSION

Integration of several disciplines suggests a dynamic model of conflict. A review of the previous work on conflict has made it clear that alienation has an important place in sociological theories of conflict. Conflict theorists have also shown the role of *face-saving* in escalating conflict. Family and communication theorists have dealt with characteristic behaviors such as increased threat, demeaning criticism, contempt, disgust, blame, perceived injustice, rebuff, and feelings of being devalued—all terms that have strong *emotional* connotations.

Conflict, Kreisberg (1973) suggests, involves social relationships: "This means that at every stage of conflict the parties socially interact; each party affects the way the other acts, not only as each responds to the other but as each side may anticipate the responses of the other" (p. 20). Implied in this statement is the importance of the social bond, which involves communication and emotion.

Patterns found in the sociological tradition have a common theme—the *social bond.* Conflict can be a means of restoring solidarity and a catalyst for social change. Many have viewed conflict as inherently functional, in that it leads to change. Not all change is desirable, however, and some conflict can be destructive. Simmel (1955) describes an integrative process when he notes underlying hatred generated by rejection, which leads to denial and attribution of the cause onto the other person (blame).

I draw upon these conflict studies for concepts of alienation and the social bond. Studies of marital conflict suggest the centrality of emotion. Work on communication has been particularly useful in increasing my understanding of conflict escalation processes, showing how nonverbal process can be important in understanding interpersonal relationships. How is it that emotion is communicated, and what role does it play in the bonding system? The quality of the bond is not readily visible, but through emotion cues it may be possible to infer the state of the bond.

Studies of marital conflict have contributed methods of observing couples through videotape as well as useful concepts such as reciprocation, homeostasis, emotion, and communication processes. Fitzpatrick (1988), for instance, has helped to explain the "what" and "how" of marriages, with methods that are descriptive as well as predictive. Her methods do not answer the "why" of conflict in relationships, however—the discovery of emotions and complexity in interaction during conflict. An intensive, rather than extensive, analysis is needed to get at some of the subtler dynamics of conflict, meanings in context and the complexity of disputes. As Sillars and Weisberg (1987) point out, conflict does not follow a logical order, but appears irrational and disorderly—often involving core relationship issues. Sense needs to be made of "irrational" behavior in terms of emotional interaction, revealing hidden agendas and core issues. This book looks at the logic of emotion and how it is communicated during conflict.

If the basic function of emotion is to maintain social bonds, then both individual arousal and communicative aspects of emotional states need to be studied in interaction. Chapter 2 is a restatement and focus of variables found in the work on conflict: the social bond, the role of emotions, escalated anger, and emotional systems.

Most of us have been led by the prevailing perspective to believe that experiencing emotions is a trivial event. However, human science should recognize emotion as playing a central role in behavior. By emphasizing the communicative aspects of emotion, I attempt to understand conflict escalation in terms of bonding systems, alienation, and emotional process. This book deals with the most intimate and intense conflict: that between husband and wife.

2 Toward a Theory of Conflict

> Always and everywhere men seek
> honor and dread ridicule. (Cooley,
> 1909/1962, p. 28)

The idea of the social bond is developed further in this chapter, because of its importance for understanding conflict. The state of the bond may explain escalation, as well as why some relationships are more prone to destructive conflict than others. The bond in itself is largely invisible, but the kinds of emotions operating in its maintenance are visible; they reveal the state of the bond at any given moment. In a biosocial framework, the primary motive of human behavior is to secure important bonds. Emotions play a central role—intact bonds are flexible, accompanied by pride, joy, and happiness; damaged or threatened bonds are marked by insecurity, sadness, anger, and shame (for a discussion of pride and shame, see Scheff, 1990).

Foundations for the bond include at least three dynamic and interacting components: the social self, level of differentiation (regulation of separateness and togetherness), and the emotional system. These components can help explain the intricate wiring of conflict.

HUMAN NATURE AND THE SOCIAL BOND

Many theorists have taken the perspective that human beings are social by nature (Bowlby, 1969; Cooley, 1902/1964; Gaylin & Person, 1988; James, 1910; Lewis, 1976; Marx, 1844/1964; McDougall, 1908; Mead, 1934). Mead has stated: "A self which is so evidently a social individual that it can exist only in a group of individuals is as much a result of the process of evolution as other biological forms" (in Strauss, 1965, p. 40). By this, he means that human beings are social by reason of their biological and cultural inheritance. Human beings are, and always have been, organized into groups governed by moral law (Gaylin & Person, 1988; Lewis, 1983). Society, according to this view, is the unique means by which human beings have adapted to their physical and human environment.

Solutions to the problem of survival have been shaped by social regulation of exchanges. Social regulation is evidenced by the species-specific configuration of the adaptive features of mother-infant dyad, food sharing, tool use, division of labor, male-female reciprocity, symbolic communication, and rule giving (Tronick, 1980). We need other human beings as much as we need food and oxygen for survival (Gaylin & Person, 1988; Lewis, 1976; Marx, 1844/1964). Within this framework "intimate emotional bonds are seen as neither subordinate to nor derivative from food and sex" (Bowlby, 1988, p. 121).

Studies of social isolation and confinement support conjectures about the importance of human sociability (see, e.g., Bowlby, 1973; Harlow, 1962; Spitz, 1946). The maintenance of bonds is a primary motive of human conduct. Before all else, human beings are social creatures. Sociability is a human universal (Brown, 1991); emotions, with their communicative functions, are an important mechanism of bonding.

That the human being is social has been the basis for many theories, both sociological and social psychological. Marx, for instance, takes this view in discussing species needs; he says that "the individual *is* the social being" and "the need of the greatest wealth [is] the other human being" (in Tucker, 1978, pp. 85, 91). William James (1910) also has written of human beings as gregarious animals with an "innate propensity to get ourselves noticed, and noticed favorably, by our kind" (p. 179). Cooley's (1902/1964) conception of human interaction is organic; in his view, the human being is an innately social entity: "I take it that the child has by heredity a generous capacity and need for social feeling" (p. 86).

A biosocial view of human nature is not new; what is new are the systematic, microscopic analyses that have recently emerged based on complex interaction between neonate and caregiver. There is a rapidly growing body of evidence that shows that from the day of birth infants are organized to respond socially (Adamson & Bakeman, 1982; Ainsworth, Bell, & Stayton, 1974; Bowlby, 1969; Brazelton, 1982; Brazelton, Koslowski, & Main, 1974; DeCasper & Fifer, 1981; Field, Woodson, & Cohen, 1982; Rheingold, 1969; Sorse et al., 1985; Stern, 1981; Tronick, 1980; Tronick, Ricks, & Cohn, 1982). Bowlby particularly stresses a biologically given "system of attachment" between human caretaker and infant, similar to the "affectional system" that Harlow (1962) demonstrated in primates. The first mechanism for survival in the human infant is not fight or flight, but clutching and clinging.

Recent work suggests the importance and power of the social bond not only in infancy but over the life span. The desire for strong bonds is a basic component of human behavior, present from the beginning to the end of life. P. Shaver (1987) shows the similarities between adult romantic love relationships and attachment behavior in infants, following Bowlby (1969). Human adult behavior is oriented toward social interaction as a means of maintaining the bond.

Bonding is not a single response to a single stimuli, but a complex sequence of behaviors, a social-emotional system. The infant-caretaker dyad is an emotional regulatory unit. The idea here is that attachment is mutual; both parties are involved in a system of the matching and sharing of communicative acts involved in the regulation of interaction. In this way sociability and affectionateness (with its clutching and clinging) occur prior to conflict and aggression (fight and flight).

The nature of the bond is complex, but understanding it is crucial for understanding conflict. In Darwinian psychology, matters relating to human survival have the likelihood of engaging emotions. The emotional system is essential to this process because it functions to preserve the group. Emotional gestures are the product of evolutionary adaptiveness, which serves the function of maintaining bonds in adulthood as well as in infancy; they have communicative value and serve a signal function. In Mead's (1934) view, the gesture is primarily an expression of emotion—the external manifestation of a physiological experience. From this perspective the purpose of gesture is social communication.

One function of emotion seems to be survival. Sorse et al. (1985) have demonstrated the social signal function of fear: When approaching a visual cliff, infants stopped short when their mothers displayed expressions of fear, but continued over the (imaginary) edge when their mothers presented smiles. Unable to communicate symbolically, infants employ the emotional system as a primary means for monitoring themselves and modulating their behavior in relation to others. In adulthood emotions are not replaced by symbolic communication (spoken language), but the two forms combine to create a complex means of communication. The bonding system continues to be based in gestures. A basic unit of the bonding system is the self.

THE SOCIAL SELF

Most theorists of self postulate both social and biological components. Self is neither a physiological phenomenon nor a cultural one, but a complex process involving the simultaneous interaction of society and biology, on intra- and interpersonal levels (Allport, 1937; Cooley, 1902/1964; Dewey, 1922; James, 1910; Lewis, 1958; Lynd, 1958; Mahler & McDivitt, 1982; Mead, 1934). Although the structure of the self reflects the behavioral patterns of the group (Mead, 1934), these patterns should not be confused with the self. Structural definitions of self appear to focus on social/cognitive constructs, ignoring biological and emotional processes. Biological components are common to all humanity, while cultural elements are variable. The social self subsumes the bond, and is at the same time the basic building block of relationships.

In "The Looking-Glass Self," Cooley (1902/1964) views the self as innately social, with three principal elements: "the *imagination* of our appearance to the other person; the imagination of his *judgment* to that appearance, and some sort of self feeling, such as *pride* or *mortification*" (i.e., shame) (p. 184). Mead also views the self as a cybernetic system of regulation between the biological and the social, with his concept of the "I" and the "me." Self involves both biological impulses (the "I") and social symbolic experience (the "me"). Through the balancing of the "I" and the "me," each person develops a self able to differentiate itself to a greater or lesser degree from others. Both "I" and "me" are essential for full expression of the self; peak functioning depends on the way in which these two components are regulated.

If contact is lost with the "I," that is, if "me" overfunctions, there will be overconformity, excessive concern about what others think. Certain parts of one's self may become unacceptable. Feelings, impulses, and needs may be denied, if unacceptable to the other. One's self is likely to be overly dependent on the relatedness of the other, forming itself around the feelings, needs, and wishes of others—loosing contact with one's own unique feelings and needs. One may become unable to distinguish one's own emotions from the other or unable to feel at all. A fragile self develops that is overly dependent—engulfment occurs.

A person with a fragile sense of self—that is, one imbalanced between "I" and "me" (overfunctioning "me" component)—is one who requires relationships with other people to hold him or herself together. In other words, such a person has little self-cohesion; he or she depends on others to a large extent for sense of identity. The feeling might be that without the other he or she would be nothing, fall apart, or shrivel up and die.

When "I" overfunctions, a person may be unable to bond with others; he or she may lack impulse control and may be unable to monitor self in social settings. Such a person is necessarily isolated from others and may lack social skills. For example, a person whose "I" outweighs his or her "me" may engage in sociopathic behavior.

Possible responses to the inability to differentiate include remaining in a state of extreme dependency or cutting off emotionally. Durkheim's (1851/1966) observations on the causes of suicide (altruism or anomie) on a societal level correspond with these states. Both states involve alienation—fragile bonds with others. Although it might appear that engulfment is a secure bond, no secure bond can exist without complete functioning of self.

The self system works as a control system that helps sustain a person's relationship to important others between certain limits of distance and accessibility. Bowlby (1973) has termed this process "environmental homeostasis." The interrelationship between the individual and relationship process is complex, involving closeness and distance, approach and withdrawal, attraction and repulsion. The communication between the "I" and the "me" involves the self system, which helps regulate the social distance of togetherness and separateness (and vice versa).

REGULATING SOCIAL DISTANCE

Tension between togetherness and separateness appears to be a fundamental dilemma in all human relationships (Bowen, 1978; Bowlby, 1988; Fitzpatrick, 1988; Hess & Handel, 1959; Laing, 1965; Olson, 1986; Raush et al., 1974). The idea of togetherness/separateness appears under various rubrics: communion/agency (Bakan, 1966), connection/autonomy (Baxter, 1988), approach/withdrawal (Bowlby, 1963), altruism-fatalism/egoism-anomie (Durkheim, 1851/1966), intimacy/isolation (Erikson, 1963), interdependence/autonomy (Fitzpatrick, 1988), solidarity/alienation (Marx, 1844/1964), enmeshment/separateness (Olson, 1986), fusion/individuation (Rank, 1936/1968), and approach/avoidance (L. Rubin, 1983). The idea of togetherness/separateness is subsumed under the rubric of differentiation of self (Bowen, 1978) and differentiation out of the affectional matrix (Lewis, 1976).

The regulation of togetherness and separateness is a life force—an existential fact of life. Each person is a biological being separate from others, with impulses, sensations, and desires; but each person is also a social being, needing to be connected with others. In itself separateness/togetherness does not present a problem. Each person needs to individuate from others as well as be connected. The way a couple handles conflict may, in large part, be dependent on how they handle this dimension of a relationship (Fitzpatrick, 1988). Fitzpatrick's typology of marriages is based on this idea: "Traditional" couples favor connection, whereas "Separates" and "Independents" favor autonomy. Some mixtures may be ripe for conflict, such as a match between a Traditional man and a Separate woman.

The ability or inability to regulate the distance between these two forces is formed very early in life. Many studies in infant-caretaker interaction note distance regulation in the form of eye contact. In the first few months of life, visual-motor behavior is the only system in which the infant has substantial voluntary control—it is the only on/off system (Robson, 1967). Control of eyes cannot be separated from the role of regulation of the physiological state (Stechler & Carpenter, 1967; Stechler & Latz, 1966; Walters & Parke, 1965). Gaze is used to initiate, maintain, and avoid social interaction with caregivers. While turning toward and looking makes contact, looking away breaks contact. This early behavior reflects the need for both closeness and distance. The violation of the bounds can lead to strong emotion (Tronick, Als, Adamson, Wise, & Brazelton, 1978).

In the early stages of development, the infant is completely dependent on others for survival; he or she is helpless without the caregivers. With maturation the infant individuates from the caregivers, developing his or her own identity. In the process, people do not become isolated human beings—islands in themselves. Each is an entity at the same time that each is connected with others. Although each is social, needing a secure base, each also has "the urge to explore the environment" (Bowlby, 1988, p. 163). When secure, an infant explores away from the attachment figure; when threatened, the infant moves toward that figure. Exploration can take place only from a secure base.

Following Bowen (1978), I refer to the ability to regulate distance as *differentiation*, which incorporates the social self into relationships with others. A relationship with a high level of differentiation is marked by persons with solid self; they are able to move freely between togetherness and separateness, with little or no discomfort or emotional reactivity. There is a tolerance for feelings and emotions. Communication is direct, clear, and specific. The system is elastic and flexible—an open system.

Low-level differentiation is marked by persons with a sense that each person is incomplete without the other—that each is an appendage of the other. Each believes that self can be complete only in engulfment with another, or else one feels isolated. Each is unable to move freely in either direction without disrupting the relationship; that is, closeness can feel like engulfment and distance like isolation. The comfort zone of distance is very narrow. There is intolerance of emotion because one person's emotion leads to emotional reactivity in the other; therefore communication is indirect, unclear, and nonspecific. Blaming, distracting, avoiding, and the like are rampant. The system is narrow, rigid, and inflexible.

Figure 2.1 represents a secure bonding system in three phases: the basic level of differentiation, both together, and the two separate. Persons are differentiated, able to form secure bonds; they have a tolerance for aroused emotion in both self and other and are able to move between being close and distant without reacting emotionally; the relationship is flexible.

Figure 2.2 represents a threatened or insecure bonding system. Each person has a low level of differentiation; sense of self is dependent on the other. Each has little tolerance for emotion—his or her own or the other's (each may deal with emotion differently; for instance, one may become ultrarational, while the other becomes hysterical). The relationship is rigid, and there is little room for movement between togetherness and separateness; closeness is engulfing, separateness feels like abandonment. Each extreme position is alienating, and is experienced as disrespect by the other person.

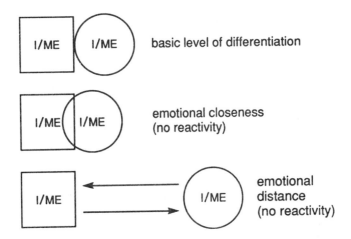

Figure 2.1. High Level of Differentiation: A Flexible Bonding System
SOURCE: By permission of *The Psychoanalytic Review* published by the National Psychological Association for Psychoanalysis, Inc. Volume 58, page 434.

In engulfed relationships spouses may be so concerned with fitting together that they are unable to see each other as separate people; there is a kind of "pseudomutuality" (Fitzpatrick, 1988). Marriages that are chronically engulfed have strong influence on the partners, pressing for togetherness; any form of uniqueness (e.g., individual thoughts and feelings) is experienced as betrayal or disloyalty—abandonment. Members have consensus in thought, behavior, and feeling (and may feel prevented from having their own thoughts and feelings). Each person functions in emotional reactivity to the other. In families or marriages where one partner is chronically engulfed, complaints might take the form of "I'm being suffocated by the relationship," "Give me some breathing space," or "He doesn't pay enough attention to me" (Raush et al., 1974; Rubin, 1983).

Figure 2.3 represents a continuum between engulfment and isolation; both extremes represent inadequate bonds, are rigid systems, and may be marked by high levels of overt or covert conflict. Most families fall somewhere between the extremes.

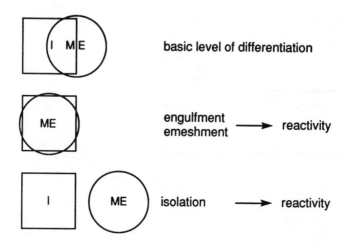

Figure 2.2. Low Level of Differentiation: A Rigid Bonding System
SOURCE: By permission of *The Psychoanalytic Review* published by the National Psychological Association for Psychoanalysis, Inc. Volume 58, page 435.

When persons in families are insufficiently differentiated, there also may be "cutoff," in which an individual isolates self from members in an attempt to escape the engulfing forces. Isolation is the other extreme on the spectrum. When spouses are extremely alienated from each other, they may use "pseudohostility" to hide their need for intimacy (Fitzpatrick, 1988, p. 67). As Figure 2.3 indicates, the extremes can occur between persons in families, organizations, and nations (Scheff & Retzinger, 1991).

In his family typology, Olson (1986; Olson et al., 1988) demonstrates the emotional difficulties generated by extreme types. Olson and his colleagues wanted to find out "what makes families crisis prone"; they found that families who were prone to crisis were rated either low cohesion (isolated) or high cohesion (engulfed). Even when external stressors were similar, connected families had a much higher level of well-being than alienated families. Families with either type of alienation—emotional isolation or engulfment—had problems

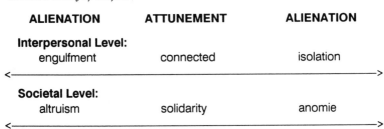

Figure 2.3. A Continuum of Relatedness Between Togetherness and Separateness

of emotional reactivity (anxiety, anger, and guilt). To cope with these feelings persons may deny the need for either togetherness or separateness, and this denial further alienates them from others.

Olson's emotionally isolated families had "forced emotional distance," artificial barriers between members' goals and needs (i.e., engulfed families had emotional fusion and confusion of self with others). Not being able to distinguish between self and other or setting up artificial barriers as defense are both states of alienation. Chronically alienated families were found to have a high level of problems with their children.

Differentiated families were securely connected, communicated effectively, and were thoughtful of the goals and needs of others. Persons in these families owned up to their emotions and took responsibility for self, while still considering the other. Persons function in relationships to the degree in which the self is formed in reaction to the needs of others and to the degree in which the individuals can think, feel, and act for self rather than react against other. The family's functioning is dependent on the degree to which each member's emotional self is distinct from other, acting with thought as well as feeling (rather than in emotional reactivity or emotional cutoff).

Like families, larger social systems wax and wane in their levels of functioning. The move from rural settings to urban centers and dense population may precipitate alienation; effective distance from others is difficult to accomplish, and emotional separation may be one result. At the level of society, bonds are likely to be based on roles—behavior and abstract duties; in communities, bonds occur between identified persons. Community bonds are less abstract than societal bonds. In an alienated society it is not surprising that regulation between togetherness and separateness is difficult.

In *The Division of Labor in Society*, Durkheim (1893/1964) takes the view that as communal bonds disappeared they were simply replaced by "organic" solidarity, which was tougher and more advanced than the bonds of mechanical solidarity. Solidarity between persons was replaced by solidarity between roles. In his analysis of Durkheim's notion of solidarity, Scheff (1990) points out that organic solidarity may be based on false consciousness, giving only an illusion of solidarity; a deeper look may reveal a form of alienation between persons.

In alienated relationships bonds are insecure, damaged, broken, or rigid. Chronic enmeshment and struggle can be seen as an attempt to repair damaged bonds; if uniqueness is denied there can be an illusion of community. In this case community is based on rigid conformity in thought and feeling rather than emotional attunement and understanding—on false cohesiveness (Longley & Pruitt, 1980), similar to Durkheim's (1851/1966) altruism. In anomic societies people develop a fetish for individualism, with the belief that each person is an island unto him- or herself. They deny the necessity of social bonds. Both "altruism" and anomie are states of bondlessness—alienation.

It is interesting to note that the regulation between separation and connection is not unlike the two forms of communication: symbolic and gestural. It may be that these forms of communication help regulate the distance between the social states. Symbolic communication represents the cognitive or separate component; gestures, the emotional or together component. Just as each person needs to master the two forms of communication, each needs to be connected with others, as well as to be an autonomous being.

EMOTIONS AND THE SOCIAL BOND

At every moment the bond between people is being built,
maintained, damaged, or repaired (Neuhauser, 1988). If a relationship is not being built, maintained, or repaired, it is being damaged by default. As previously indicated, the state of the bond is difficult to detect directly, but manner and emotions continuously reveal it.

Social emotions, particularly pride and shame, play a crucial role; shame signals a threat to the bond—either too much or too little distance. An inadequate level of differentiation is maintained, in part, when emotional signals are ignored. The emotional system helps maintain a person's relationship to important others, pushing toward restoring the bond (Bowlby, 1988; Lewis, 1985). Building and maintenance of bonds is signaled by pride; reparation is signaled by complex patterns, and can involve constructive conflict.

Emotions are not only culturally shaped, as suggested by constructionist theories, they are also biological givens. No newborn baby has to learn to smile or cry. As already discussed, emotions are one of the earliest signaling devices in human beings. Neither "positive" nor "negative" emotions are irrational or frivolous components of human behavior; they are both necessary. From an evolutionary perspective, emotions serve a biosocial function, operating in the service of species survival and well-being; they serve as signals of the state of the bond from the earliest moments (Berscheid, 1983; Darwin, 1872/1965; Gaylin, 1984; Kerr & Bowen, 1988; Lewis, 1976).

Initially, the primary means of communication between infant and caregivers is gesture. Although gestural communication is later incorporated with language, "emotionally mediated communication nonetheless persists as a principal feature of intimate relationships throughout life" (Bowlby, 1988, p. 121). Goffman (1967) suggests:

> Emotions function as moves, and fit so precisely into the logic of the ritual game that it would seem difficult to understand them without

it. In fact, spontaneously expressed emotions are likely to fit into the formal pattern of the ritual interchange more elegantly than consciously designed ones. (p. 23)

Emotions are part of the self-governing system innate in each person; they operate as homeostatic mechanisms that help regulate the distances between people. Anger, for instance, prepares the organism to fight and at the same time serves a communicative function (because of its accompanying facial and bodily gestures) to warn others, so readjustments can be made on both sides. Shame signals threat or damage—telling us we are too close to or too distant from the other for comfort and well-being of self. Emotions can help preserve the status quo (Scheff, 1988), as well as serve as catalysts for social change. Emotions serve the social order by restoring balance.

"Families" of Emotions

Common roots can be found among various forms of emotions that make up discrete families. For example, although the various forms of anger (resentment, rage, annoyance, irritation) arise in different circumstances and have varying intensities, their common characteristics (that they are active, forward moving, and involve specific facial expressions, voice tones, and physiological changes) place them all in a family called anger (Barrett & Campos, 1987; Gaylin, 1984). This is the case with each major emotion: anger, fear, grief, shame, joy, and pride.

Shame appears to be the most social of all human emotions. It has been said to be the emotion second to none in its importance in human relationships (McDougall, 1908). Although the process is virtually invisible, all human beings live in the minds of others (Cooley, 1902/1964). Unlike other families of emotion, a major characteristic of shame is the self in its relationship to other persons; it is a self-other process, the only emotion with this characteristic.

The Social Emotions

The human animal, unlike any other creature, has a very long period of dependency on its caregivers. It is unable to flee or to fight early in life. If early relationships were dependent on fight or flight, the infant mortality rate might be very high, perhaps moving toward species extinction. Rage and fear are oriented to the survival of the organism (with fight and flight preparedness). The human infant is primarily organized to clutch and cling; another group of emotions have developed to ensure social (group) survival. Social emotions are distinguished by the fact that they are about survival of *relationships*. The social emotions are oriented to survival through preservation of the relationship. Shame is not concerned with the organism as an isolated entity, but with relationships between persons, the regard of others—preservation of solidarity. Shame guards the boundaries of privacy and intimacy (Schneider, 1977; Wurmser, 1981). Although we may be afraid in the presence of animals, such as snakes, shame always occurs in response to other human beings, if only in the imagination. Shame concerns the functioning of relationships.

As already mentioned, an individualistic notion of human behavior (with its categorization of emotions into positive and negative) impedes the advancement of knowledge of conflict and relationships. The myth of individualism denies an inherent bond with others, as well as an emotional system that helps to preserve the bond. This myth also denies the importance of shame.

One difficulty in the study of shame has been the reaction people have to the word *shame*. It is often considered something that only children and primitives in traditional societies experience, not mature adults, and certainly not properly functioning members of modern society. Shame has been deemed unimportant in this day and age; the focus, instead, has been on guilt. This is regrettable, since shame—however well disguised—may be ubiquitous in all social interaction (Cooley, 1902/1964; Goffman, 1967; Scheff, 1990). Once the dynamics of shame are understood and identified, it becomes clear that it is not an alien or childish phenomenon.

Shame is a powerful human mechanism, a normal and necessary part of a well-functioning society. Goffman (1967) has pointed out that embarrassment (shame) is not a "regrettable deviation from a normal state. . . . it is not an irrational impulse breaking through socially prescribed behavior but a part of this orderly behavior itself" (pp. 97, 110). Shame is an essential part of the ritual order. Each human being is acutely aware of self in relation to others; shame is a human mechanism used to monitor the self in social context. We usually avoid behavior that causes self or others shame, and attempt to repair interactions that have become threatened or damaged (Goffman, 1967). "Always and everywhere men seek honor and dread ridicule" (Cooley, 1909/1962, p. 28).

Shame Versus Guilt

Shame and guilt have been contrasted extensively by several authors (Gaylin, 1979; Lazare, 1987; Lewis, 1971a; Lindsay-Hartz, 1984; Piers & Singer, 1953; Wurmser, 1981); I will deal with the differences only briefly here. Gaylin (1979) contrasts shame and guilt by comparing their use in the Old and New Testaments:

> The theology of the New Testament, with its emphasis on individual salvation, is dominated by guilt; but the Old Testament in its preoccupation with duty and responsibility, with its need to serve as a guide for survival for a community, elevates shame to the highest position. . . . Guilt is the mediator of individual conscience, as shame is the primary mediator of community-oriented conscience. (pp. 60-61)

Writers of the Old Testament were members of a traditional society in which shame was the major emotion of social control. The writers of the New Testament were members of a society in transition to a new form, where social control involved guilt. Several researchers have made a distinction between "shame cultures" and "guilt cultures" (Benedict, 1946; Dodds, 1951;

Piers & Singer, 1953), but the distinction is misleading, because it assumes that shame states are infrequent in adults in modern societies.

It is possible that the role of shame in modern societies has not decreased but has gone underground. In traditional cul- ✗ tures shame is spoken of openly. References to shame still appear in modern society, but in more disguised forms. The denial of shame appears where there is a breakdown in community—alienation in relationships and societies. Whereas guilt is internalized, implying individualism (a characteristic of modern societies), shame binds us to those who are needed for our survival, and serves in the most direct way to preserve community.

Shame and guilt are often confused, because they frequently occur together. They serve similar purposes in that they facilitate socially acceptable behavior required for group living (shame and guilt are often called the "moral" emotions). While guilt is an internalized and individual emotion, shame incorporates the other directly into the feeling. Shame is a force for group identity (Scheff, 1988).

Shame concerns *the whole self*. It involves sudden exposure of deficiency in one's own eyes as well as in the eyes of the other. In shame the self feels helpless, not in control; the reaction in a shame experience is to *hide*. In contrast, guilt is about things done or not done. In the guilt experience the self feels in control, intact; the reaction is to do or undo something—to make restitution. The other is less prominent in guilt ideation than in shame. In shame the bond with other cannot be denied; both self and other are involved in shame imagery. In guilt each person can be (or feels like) an island. In an alienated society where individualism is the norm, guilt is more visible than shame. One can be proud of the capacity to feel guilt. Guilt is prestigious; feeling it makes one a moral person. Shame feels disreputable.

The importance of the bond is denied by giving anxiety and guilt preeminent roles. Since Freud, anxiety and guilt have been seen as elemental emotions; although pride and shame have been mentioned, they have been played down until quite recently. Excessive shame, not guilt, has been found to

be prominent in depression (Lewis, 1981a), narcissistic vulnerability (Lansky, 1985), schizophrenia (N. Morrison, 1987;
Retzinger, 1989), anorexia (Scheff, 1989), protracted conflict
and violence (Johnston, Campbell, & Tall, 1984; Katz, 1988;
Lansky, 1987; Retzinger, 1989; Scheff, 1987), dysfunctional families (Fossum & Mason, 1986), and even medical encounters
(Lazare, 1987).

One product of alienation in the modern world is the valuing
of individualism and material things over relationships among
persons. If no secure bonds can be made, one defense is to deny
the importance of the bond; with the denial of the bond comes
the denial of shame. The view that emotions are negative and
maladaptive—and the denial of emotions this leads to—is a
product of alienated social systems.

Nature of Shame

To grasp the shame construct in it broadest sense is to view
shame as a dynamic *social* process as it occurs in interaction
within as well as between persons: as a unique human phenomenon with functional value (Lewis, 1971a, 1983; Lynd, 1958;
Schneider, 1977). It is important to extend the concept of shame
beyond the feeling of *being ashamed*, as we think of it from
childhood experiences. One can be in a *state of shame* without
being ashamed; having a *sense of shame* is different from being
ashamed or being in a state of shame.

Having a sense of shame is to be a moral person; to be
shameless is to be immoral. "The person who can witness
another's humiliation and unfeelingly retain a cool counte-
nance himself is said in our society to be 'heartless,' just as he
who can participate in his own defacement is thought to be
'shameless' " (Goffman, 1967, p. 11). Having a sense of shame
is crucial in the ability to regulate social distance.

The difference between feeling ashamed and a shame state
is characterized by the terms *overt shame* and *bypassed shame*
(Lewis, 1971a). In her ground-breaking work, Lewis has identified shame that had been virtually invisible to earlier researchers. She identifies two shame states, one she calls "overt,

undifferentiated," and the other "bypassed" (covert shame). Overt shame is the familiar type, marked by bodily arousal (blushing, sweating, rapid heartbeat, and so on) and feelings of discomfort—this is the type of shame that *feels* ashamed. Bypassed shame is a low-visibility state that is more difficult to detect; it is covert. Bypassed shame cannot be detected in bodily arousal, but in thought processes and ideation of the self in relation to others; sometimes it is confused with guilt. The concept of bypassed shame is very important; it is virtually invisible, but it has a dramatic effect on relationships. Characteristics for identifying overt and covert shame states include variants, vocabulary, stimulus or source, position of self in the field, conscious content, experience, appearance, and defenses against shame.

The word *shame* refers to a family of emotions with certain characteristics. This genus includes many variations, from social discomfort and mild embarrassment to intense forms such as humiliation or mortification. Variations belonging to the shame family are embarrassment, dishonor, disgrace, humiliation, chagrin, and mortification. The nature of shame is such that it always involves the self in its relationship to another, even if only in the imagination (imagining ourselves being viewed negatively). This characteristic gives a clue to its vast prevalence—we live in the minds of others.

There are hundreds of ways of disguising the shame experience. Lewis (1971a) has noted that certain words continually reoccur in contexts of shame and are accompanied by the use of certain gestures. Some of the vernacular terms include feeling *uncomfortable, insecure, uneasy, tense, blank, confused, small, worthless, inadequate, stupid, foolish, silly, weird, helpless, unable, weak, curious, funny, idiotic, restless, stunned, alone, disconnected, alienated, split, impotent,* and *low self-esteem* (Gottschalk, Winget, & Gleser, 1969). Each of these words (as well as numerous other everyday words) belongs to an experience with common characteristics, mainly the self in its relation to another, with at least the imagination of *how we look in others' eyes.* If the vocabulary for shame states is compared with the much smaller vernacular

language used to describe anger, guilt, fear, or grief, the vast-
ness of shame vocabulary becomes evident. Words describing
shame are far more numerous than can be found for any other
emotional experience. This is another clue to the prevalence of
shame.

Stimulus situations that evoke shame may be either overt or
covert, real or imagined. These include an other-to-self message
that is perceived as involving an injury to self (imagination of
or possibility of injury): Self is the object of disappointment,
defeat, rejection or fear of rejection, betrayal, devaluation, discrimination, judgmental comparison, loss of face, exposure,
reproach, rebuff, inattentiveness, unrequited love, disappointment, failure, defeat, errors or mistakes, disrespect, deficiency,
scorn, ridicule, contempt, and so on. Stimuli can take very
subtle forms, involving only slight gestures (e.g., nose wrinkling, speech cadence slightly off) or blatant, overt forms. The
other in these situations is perceived in some way as alienated.
The other is viewed, perhaps, as caring less about the relationship than the self (abandoning) and/or is experienced as the
source of injury. The other is focal in awareness and may appear
to be laughing, ridiculing, powerful, active, in control, unjust,
hostile, unresponsive, and so on; the other's self appears intact.

On the overt side, a person in a state of shame may feel
paralyzed, helpless, passive, childish, out of control of the
situation. She or he may blush, weep, or have other unpleasant
bodily arousal. Overt shame is the easiest to detect.

Bypassed shame, more difficult to detect, is seen mainly in
conscious content, which includes many varieties of thoughts
about the deficiency of self; the self remains focal in awareness.
Thoughts may take the form of what *should* have been said, or
might have been said, or may include playing earlier scenes over
and over in mind; it could be manifest in rapid speech as well
as thought. Comparisons between self and other are frequent;
the self comes out as appearing inferior in some way—less
beautiful, intelligent, strong, or whatever—or the self may simply wonder if it is sufficient. Persons in a covert state of shame
might simply function poorly as agents or perceivers; thought,
speech, or perception is obsessive. Thoughts might be divided
between imaging the self and imaging the other. Imaging the

TABLE 2.1 Summary of Working Concept for shame

Stimulus	(1)	Disappointment, defeat or moral transgression
	(2)	Deficiency of self
	(3)	Involuntary, self unable
	(4)	Encounter with other
Conscious content	(1)	Painful emotion
	(2)	Autonomic reactions
	(3)	Connections with past feelings
	(4)	Many variants of shame feelings
	(5)	Fewer variations of cognitive content (the self)
	(6)	Identity thoughts
Position of self in field	(1)	Self passive
(see Table 2.2)	(2)	Self focal in awareness
	(3)	Multiple functions of self at the same time
	(4)	Vicarious experience of other's view of self
Nature and discharge	(1)	Humiliated fury
of hostility	(2)	Discharge blocked by guilt and/or love of other
		Discharge on self/other
Characteristic defenses	(1)	Denial
	(2)	Repression of ideas
	(3)	Affirmation of the self
	(4)	Affect disorder: depression
	(5)	Negation of other
	(6)	Conflict and violence[a]

SOURCE: Adapted from Lewis (1971b). By permission of the *Psychoanalytic Review*, published by the National Psychological Association for Psychoanalysis, Inc., volume 58, p. 435.
a. My addition.

self involves thoughts about self-identity and whether self has been discredited.

The position of the self in relationship to the other is what is important in distinguishing the shame experience from other experiences; in this way shame comments on the state of the bond. Self-other involvement suggests the ubiquity of shame. Table 2.1 is a summary of Lewis's working concept used for identifying shame. It includes the characteristics of shame: stimulus (context), conscious experience of a shame state, the relationship between self and other, reactions, and defenses.

Table 2.2 summarizes the perceived relationship between self and other during shame. Note the position of self in relation to other; the self is always perceived to be in the inferior position.

TABLE 2.2 Self/Other Relationship in Shame

Self (unable)	Other
(1) *Object* of scorn, contempt; ridicule; reduced, little	(1) The *source* of scorn, contempt, ridicule
(2) Paralyzed; helpless; passive	(2) Laughing, ridiculing; powerful; active
(3) Assailed by noxious stimuli; rage; tears; blushing	(3) Appears intact
(4) Childish	(4) Adult; going away; abandoning
(5) Focal in awareness	(5) Also focal in awareness
(6) Functioning poorly as an agent or perceiver; divided between imaging self and the other; boundaries permeable; vicarious experience of self and other.	(6) Appears intact

SOURCE: Adapted from Lewis (1971b). By permission of the *Psychoanalytic Review*, published by the National Psychological Association for Psychoanalysis, Inc., volume 58, p. 434.

Shame is about the entire self (Lynd, 1958); it symbolizes mutual social involvement and reminds us of alienation. Shame tells us that we are both separate and social beings. For shame to occur we must care, in some way, about the other. To refuse to acknowledge damaged or threatened bonds leaves relationships open to destruction.

Events that elicit shame often appear trivial to the outer world, but because of the importance the experience has to the self, the feelings often refuse to subside. A characteristic defense against shame is that persons want to turn away from the experience in some way in order not to feel the pain of rejection. The turning away makes shame difficult to recognize or communicate (Lynd, 1958), and it often remains unacknowledged. When shame remains unacknowledged it can play havoc in relationships.

RELATIONSHIP BETWEEN SHAME AND ANGER

It is common knowledge that conflict involves some amount of anger, but the presence of anger itself does not explain why anger sometimes escalates and sometimes does not. As already suggested, anger serves a signal function, but most of the research on anger debates the consequences of expressing anger (or refers to it simply as a negative emotion—needing to be extinguished or controlled).

One position concludes that the expression of anger is likely to lead to further anger (Averill, 1982; Berkowitz, 1983; Feshbach, 1956; Hall, 1899; Kahn, 1966; Kaplin, 1975; Quanty, 1976; Sipes, 1973; Straus, Gelles, & Steinmetz, 1980; Tavris, 1982). This position takes the perspective that anger in itself breeds anger and leads to conflict escalation.

The other side of the argument holds that the expression of anger results in well-being for the self and the relationship (Bach & Wydens, 1968; Funkenstein, King, & Drolette, 1957; Jackins, 1965; Janov, 1970; Nichols & Zax, 1977; Perls, 1947/1969; T. I. Rubin, 1970). This argument implies that "holding anger in" leads to outbursts and escalation. Persons are encouraged to express their anger, assert themselves, and, by some of the proponents, even to act aggressively.

I have argued that perhaps *both* the expression and the withholding of anger can lead to escalation (Retzinger, 1987). Since neither of these views can adequately explain escalation, an alternative view is necessary. To understand consequences (i.e., escalation) of expressing or withholding anger, it is essential to pay attention to the *manner* in which anger is communicated and the context in which it occurs; this takes into account other emotions that may be present along with anger.

Most of the research on anger has neglected the influence of other emotions, which may account for some of the contradictory findings. Although it was not their central point of focus, several theorists have observed in passing that anger rarely exists alone (Cooley, 1902/1964; Freud & Breuer, 1896/1961; McDougall, 1908; Nietzsche, 1887/1967). Cooley (1902/1964) observes:

> The commonest forms of . . . hostility are grounded on social self-feeling, and come under the head of resentment. *We impute to the other person an injurious thought regarding something which we cherish as a part of our self*, and this awakens anger . . . [that] rests upon a feeling

that *the other person harbors ideas injurious to us*, so that *the thought of him is an attack upon our self.* (pp. 269-270; emphasis added)

Cooley's statement is rampant with the ideation of evaluation of the self in relation to the other, as well as how anger arises. Recently many researchers and theorists have observed the co-occurrence of anger with other emotions such as shame, guilt, fear, or anxiety (Beck, 1976; Deutsch, 1969; Ekman & Friesen, 1975; Goffman, 1967; Groen, 1975; Horowitz, 1981; Izard, 1971; Kohut, 1971; Lansky, 1987; Lewis, 1971a, 1981a, 1983; Retzinger, 1985, 1987, 1991b; Scheff, 1983, 1987; Tomkins, 1963; Wallace, 1963). Shame seems to play a particularly important role in anger and hostility.

> To avoid [loss of face], some classic moves are open to them. For instance, they can resort to tactless, violent retaliation, destroying either themselves or the person who had refused to heed their warning. Or they can withdraw . . . in a visible huff—righteously indignant, outraged, but confident in ultimate vindication. (Goffman, 1967, p. 23)

Using hundreds of transcribed psychotherapy interviews, Helen Lewis (1971a) observed actual sequences from humiliation to anger. She traced sequences of evoked emotion backward from the moment anger first appeared, and found that shame, caused by real or perceived rejection, invariably had preceded anger. She hypothesized that if shame is evoked but not acknowledged, anger or withdrawal is likely to follow. When shame is evoked *but not acknowledged*, anger is aroused by indications that the other does not value the self or imputes injurious thoughts toward the self.

Shame is often experienced as an attack coming from the other (which may or may not be the case). The self in shame feels like the target of the other's hostility:

> So long as shame is experienced, it is the "other" who is experienced as the source of hostility. Hostility against the rejecting "other" is almost always simultaneously evoked. But it is humiliated fury, or shame-rage. (Lewis, 1976, p. 193)

The special quality of emotional communication in shame-rage is a "self-to-other message about how rageful the self feels at its inferior place 'in the eyes of' the other" (Lewis, 1981a, p. 190). When shame is not acknowledged, the other is almost always seen as the source of hostility. This creates a type of entrapment that can easily lead to escalation.

Those with low self-esteem might perceive another person's behavior as degrading even when it is not. Since the shame-rage experience is usually regarded as an inappropriate state, it is most difficult to stop the cycle: "Its characteristic defense is turning away from the stimulus situation. Denial is . . . a characteristic defense against shame" (Lewis, 1971a, p. 89).

It is unusual to find protracted anger without the presence of shame and vice versa, but only a few studies have made explicit the prominence of shame and its role in both conflict and physical violence. Lansky (1987) has shown that in spousal abuse, the perpetrator usually feels shamed by the victim's manner, however subtle; the violence he or she engages in can be seen as a form of self-defense against a perceived or imagined attack on the self, which is overly dependent. Katz (1988) has shown humiliation underlying homicide; the quarrel is seldom about the topic discussed but about the moral implications behind the topic. Scheff (1987) has shown the prominence of shame process as it occurs in a quarrel between a therapist and client over a slight by the therapist.

In my own earlier studies of resentment, I observed that whenever a person described a situation that caused him or her to feel angry, shame was also prominent (Retzinger, 1985, 1987). I recorded rapidly alternating sequences from shame to rage, using videotapes and printed photographs. The six photographs in Figure 2.4 illustrate sequences going from shame to anger, back to shame, and so on, in a *5-second time span*. The number in the lower right of each photograph shows minute, second, and frame in the sequence (e.g., 00:20:04:21 represents the twentieth minute, fourth second, and twenty-first frame; 30 frames = 1 second).

The sequence shown in Figure 2.4 begins with an expression of shame masked by a "false smile" (S-R1), followed by a further shame cue (gaze aversion, S-R2) less than a second later.

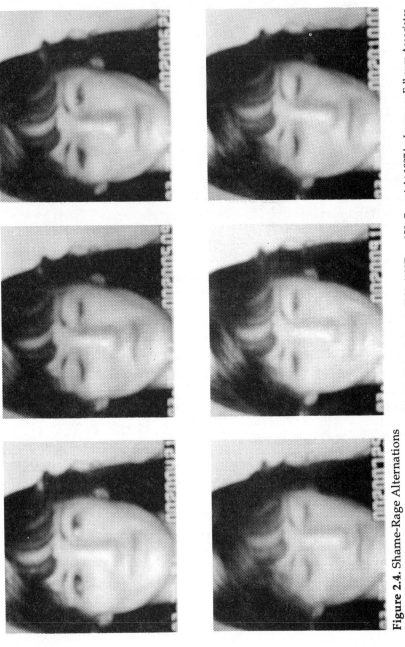

Figure 2.4. Shame-Rage Alternations
SOURCE: From *The Role of Shame in Symptom Formation*, by Helen B. Lewis (Ed.), (1987), p. 159. Copyright 1987 by Lawrence Erlbaum Associates, Inc. Reprinted by permission.

Photograph S-R3, an anger expression, occurs 1.5 seconds later. Less than a second after the anger expression (S-R3), a further shame cue (gaze aversion, S-R4) occurs. This is followed by another anger expression (S-R5), 23 frames later. The final expression in this sequence of events is a shame cue (gaze aversion, S-R6) 13 frames later. These expressions (shame and rage) flow into each other, without any neutral expression between events.

Moreover, when shame is prominent, anger subsides very slowly, asymptotically, leaving a residue of anger. Figure 2.5 graphically represents the asymptotic occurrence of anger. The first two profiles of the duration of emotion are theoretical, showing onset, apex (the level of highest intensity), and offset of emotional expression. The second set of profiles—actual anger expressions (first and third)—did not have any clear-cut offset, but subsided only gradually. They were asymptotic; they could be seen in the facial muscles for some time. Each anger expression built upon the previous one was shown to be of greater intensity and duration.

This particular study involved the relationship between resentment (shame + anger) and laughter (Retzinger, 1987). In all the interviews of this and another study (Retzinger, 1985), many of the anger expressions had long durations (between 3 and 10 seconds) preceding laughter. I hypothesized that resentment would be reduced following laughter, as observed in facial expressions. Following laughter, no asymptotic expressions of anger were found (second actual emotion profile in Figure 2.5).

The lamination of one anger expression upon another may be one of the mechanisms of an angry mood. In such a mood not only will there be a greater frequency of anger expressions, but the magnitude and duration of the expressions is likely to be greater. One anger episode built on another may increase the probability of the occurrence of a new anger outburst.

Unacknowledged shame acts as both an inhibitor and a generator of anger, rendering the person impotent to express anger toward the other (withholding behavior), while simultaneously generating further anger, which may eventually emerge as demeaning or hostile criticism, blame, insult, withdrawal, or

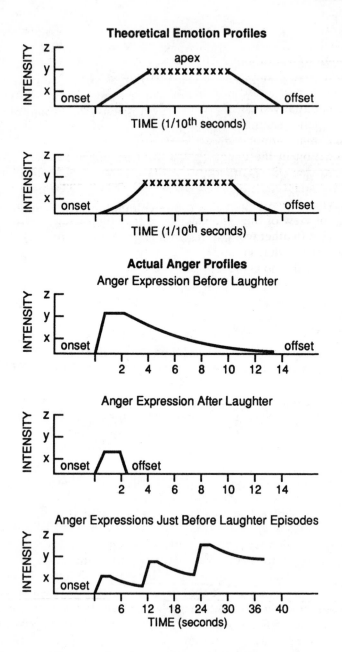

Figure 2.5. Theoretical and Actual Emotion Profiles

SOURCE: From *The Role of Shame in Symptom Formation*, by Helen B. Lewis (Ed.), (1987), p. 161. Copyright 1987 by Lawrence Erlbaum Associates, Inc. Reprinted by permission.

worse. Shame-rage sequences may explain Peterson's (1979, pp. 381-382) finding that in satisfied couples anger is fought through to resolution; a cycle of aggression followed by withdrawal is common in maladjusted couples.

The shamer and the shamed have common roots. A person who habitually shames others may be using a weapon to ward off personal shame. Max Scheler (1961) has written that "a hatred that cannot content itself with revenge . . . seeks its satisfaction in the deeper injury of making the enemy blush with shame" (p. 71). Shaming another person can be a potent form of social control (Braithwaite, 1988; Scheff, 1988). Shaming behaviors toward another are observed and described from the point of view of the shamer and not the target of the shaming behavior. In other words, actual shaming of others can be a form of hostility—that is, anger. The starting point of who is the shamer and who is the shamed is arbitrary.

A THEORY OF ESCALATION:
ALIENATION, SHAME, AND CONFLICT

> The emotional system governs the dance of life in all living things. (Bowen, 1978, p. 305)

Bowlby (1988) and others suggest that when the social bond is intact, effective functioning results; a lapse in the bond generates emotions that serve a function:

> Not only do threats of abandonment create intense anxiety but they also arouse anger, often also of intense degree. . . . This anger, the function of which is to dissuade the attachment figure from carrying out the threat, can easily become dysfunctional. (p. 30)

Angry protest, in Bowlby's sense, functions to preserve social relationships by signaling the need to repair lost bonds or lost face.

Social theorists have pointed out the innate propensity for sociability in human beings and what happens when this system is disrupted (Cooley, 1902/1964; James, 1910; Marx,

1844/1964; McDougall, 1908; Mead, 1934). For instance, Marx argues that "alienation" occurs not only from the mode of production but from others and self; the results of alienation are feelings of "impotence" (shame) and "indignation" (anger) (Tucker, 1978, pp. 133-134).

According to James (1910):

> No more fiendish punishment could be devised . . . than that one should be turned loose in society and remain *absolutely unnoticed* by all the members thereof . . . as if we were non-existing things, a kind of **rage** and *impotent* despair would ere long well up in us. (p. 179)

Cooley observed the reaction to separation in the behavior of his 4-month-old infant: the ways she behaved to get herself noticed, and the rage she expressed *when she was ignored.*

Like Marx, James, and Cooley, McDougall (1908) has observed:

> [One] finds in the praise of his fellows evidence that his emotions are shared by them, and their *blame* or *disapproval* makes him experience the pain of *isolation. . . .* this sense of *isolation, of being cut off* from the habitual fellowship of feeling and emotion, is, no doubt, *the source of the severest pain of punishment; . . . moral disapproval,* even though not formally expressed, soon begins to give them this painful sense of *isolation;* while approval . . . makes them feel at one with their fellows. (p. 173)

The common thread here is the primacy of connectedness with others and the feelings that result from alienation, the excruciating pain of being cut off or isolated from other people.

Many infant-caretaker studies have reported the effects of separation and isolation on caregiver and infant (Adamson, Als, Tronick, & Brazelton, 1977; Brazelton et al., 1974; Hansburg, 1972; Massie, 1982; Stern, 1971; Tronick, 1980). In one study, Hansburg (1972) showed that abusing mothers were extremely sensitive to any type of separation and responded with high levels of anger. Tronick (1980) has demonstrated the possibility of conflict very early in life. He speculated that the infant attempts to reinstate interaction when it has been

Sense I am being
ignored – clown,

disrupted. In his study, when the mother was instructed to sit still-faced (keep their faces in a neutral mask) and unresponsive in front of the infant, the infant made attempts to elicit contact and to engage the mother in interaction; after attempting several times, with repeated failure, the infant withdrew by turning away, became "fussy," cried, or became otherwise agitated. This behavior seems parallel to adult conflict (e.g., husband is not being responsive to wife, she withdraws or becomes angry and nags in an attempt to reinstate interaction).

Stern (1984) has also demonstrated the importance of responsiveness. He found that caregivers responded to the gestures of the infant, either verbally or gesturally, matching the baby's feeling states—that is, the infant and caregivers were emotionally attuned. Attunement is a state of emotional connectedness between persons. When caretaker and infant feeling states are matched, babies play harmoniously. When caretakers are instructed to mismatch their infants' feeling states, the babies stop what they are doing and turn attention to the caretakers. Emotion helps regulate the behavior of one person in relation to the other.

Threat or damage to social bonds (e.g., unrequited love, loss of face, rebuke, unworthiness in the eyes of others) is the primary context for shame; shame follows directly from separation, which then often leads to angry conflict or silent impasse. The infant studies seem to support Simmel's (1955) premise that conflict arises from separation rather than the other way around. There is a parallel between shame dynamics and conflict dynamics. Those who have attempted to understand conflict escalation have characterized it by threat to the bond: demeaning criticism, contempt, disgust, blame, perceived injustice, rebuff, and feelings of being devalued—all of which elicit shame in the recipient.

When shame, the emotional signal of an impaired bond, is not acknowledged, escalation is likely. If intense shame is evoked but unacknowledged, rage is quick to follow. Shame-rage seems to be self-perpetuating. Each emotion serves as a stimulus for the other. When unacknowledged shame is present, one partner is likely to project the problem onto the other, rather then acknowledge his or her own shame, which would bring into consciousness the damaged state of the bond. The direction often taken is to perceive the self as a victim and the partner as the problem, rather than acknowledging feelings, joint involvement in the problem, and the need for love, care, and connection.

Studies involving the attribution of blame are illustrative (Holtzworth-Munroe & Jacobson, 1985; Horowitz, 1981; Jacobson et al., 1985; K. Shaver, 1985). Shame experience is followed by denial (hiding) of vulnerable feelings or one's own responsibility, followed by projection of responsibility (blame) onto the other. Shame helps explain why it is so easy to blame or criticize the other, and how it is that some quarrels never end. Because of the virtual invisibility of shame, and its painfulness, it is easy to deny one's own feelings, to claim that the other is at fault (tit for tat).

Summary

The main ingredients in protracted conflict are as follows:

(1) The social bond, with its component parts (attachment system and ability to differentiate self from other emotionally), is threatened; this threat often involves disrespect.
(2) Shame signals disruption in the bonding system.
(3) Shame is denied (not acknowledged); the self feels alienated and experiences the other as the source of attack.
(4) Anger follows, further signaling threat to self and bond, and may be a protest against the threat. When the bond is ignored, anger serves as a mechanism for saving one's own face.

This formula should not be taken lightly; people kill for social reasons, "lost affection, lost 'honor' or other highly 'moral' reasons" (Lewis, 1976, p. 3).

Figure 2.6 depicts the course of action in marital relationships with secure and threatened bonds. The first triad illustrates a secure bond. When words and manner are perceived as responsive, the attachment system is secure, each feels pride. The parties are connected; this is a conflict-free situation.

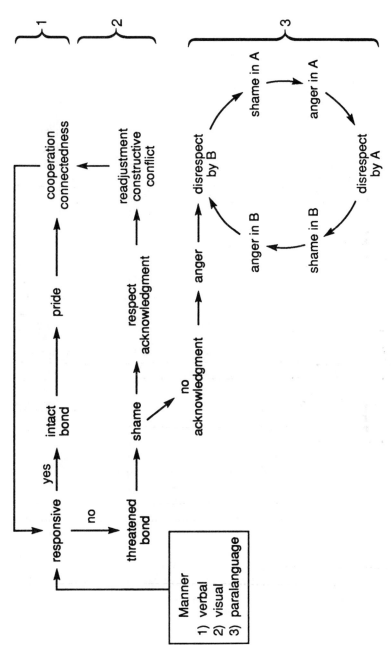

Figure 2.6. Toward a Theory of Conflict

Another course of action between spouses is that the manner of one party is perceived as unresponsive (the weaker the bond, the more sensitive the persons are to the possibility of disrespectful behavior). The other feels disconnected, enters a shame state (second triad in Figure 2.6). At this point some form of acknowledgment is crucial—of shame, hurt, or the state of the bond (acknowledgment can take place through apology, statement of feeling, taking responsibility for one's own part in the quarrel, or the like; see Chapter 8 for a discussion in greater detail). Even though anger is likely, when there is no further shaming (manner is respectful), readjustment occurs. Conflict in this form leads to repair of the bond and feelings of being understood (attunement). This is functional conflict, which can lead to cohesion and change.

The ability to engage in constructive conflict marks differentiation and flexibility of bonding systems in the face of external stressors and changing relationships and roles. The more differentiated the participants, the less emotionally reactive, and the more likely they are to acknowledge emotions and damage to the bond.

Escalation takes place when the bond is threatened and shame is elicited, persons are alienated, shame is not acknowledged, and manner is perceived as disrespectful (the third triad of Figure 2.6). The more emotionally reactive and undifferentiated the parties, the more likely they are to engage in dysfunctional conflict. The behavior of one spouse is experienced as an attack by the other, who in turn shows like behavior toward the other (blame, disgust, contempt, withdrawal, and so on). Each feels injured by the other, but each is also unaware of his or her own injury of the other; each person's behavior is perceived as unjust by the other.

Since each sees only the part played by the other, each reciprocates with more vehement assault. The loop continues, with each party placing responsibility on the other rather than acknowledging his or her own part. The idea of functional and dysfunctional conflict is very similar to Bowlby's (1973) analysis of functional and dysfunctional anger. The first restores social bonds; the second erodes them further.

Escalation can vary in frequency, intensity, and duration. Examples of high-intensity escalation include physical or emotional violence (name-calling, put-downs, and so on), depending on proneness to shame, the amount of dependency (and denial of the dependency), and the ability or inability to acknowledge feelings. Conflict can also continue indefinitely at a low-intensity but chronic level (interminable quarrel). Conflict can submerge but continue without the couple's awareness; this can take the form of loss of feelings of connectedness or affection, or withdrawal (silent impasse).

CONCLUSION

Connection with others is a primary motive in human behavior. The maintenance of bonds is reciprocally related to and involves emotions: Emotions are means of cohesion (Lewis, 1981a, 1983). The emotional system is a primary means of regulating joint interpersonal exchange. Emotions function to help direct behavior within and between persons so that they can move smoothly within (and help maintain) social relationships (Goffman, 1967).

Within a framework of human sociability, a new view of conflict emerges. If humans are inherently social, an important source of conflict and aggression is how people react to lapses in important bonds. Threatened or damaged bonds create an environment for conflict. The purpose of conflict is to signal the need for readjustment or change when the system is no longer functional.

The inability to acknowledge shame and bondlessness go hand in hand. Shame-bound conflict characterizes rigid relationships; instead of acknowledging shame, one holds fast to a relationship or abruptly severs it. All relationships are subject to the tests of external pressures. Couples engaged in conflict not bound by shame adapt more easily to external pressures when they arise.

Conflict behavior appears to be centered on the maintenance of the bonding system. Emotion plays an important role in governing this system. Emotion has a signal function that helps regulate social bonds. The emotional system is a troubleshooting device, allowing individuals to monitor self in relation to others, even before language. Mutual states of pride, delight, and security signal intact bonds; mutual feelings of anxiety, shame, anger, or grief signal threat or damage to bonds. Both positive and negative emotional states can be adaptive.

Angry conflict can be viewed as a reaction against a real or perceived injury, and as a means by which people attempt (though often not effectively) to save face. Anger is a protective measure utilized to protect self from vulnerability, that is, shame. When shame and anger function properly (that is, when feelings are acknowledged), readjustment occurs; the bond is reinstated.

Unacknowledged shame and the rage that may follow seem to be crucial factors in the inability to resolve conflict. When the self-monitoring system fails to serve its function (shame is denied), persons continue to feel alienated; inability to communicate their feelings effectively further separates them from each other.

Dysfunctional conflict may be the result of a multigenerational family process of insecure bonding systems. Communication styles are learned that distract from relationship issues and feelings. Participants are unable to separate themselves emotionally from others; they become emotionally reactive (the more emotionally reactive, the more dysfunctional the conflict).

Although many conflicts may appear to be interest based—the result of clashes over scarce resources rather than of lapses in the bond—a close investigation may reveal hidden bonding issues. I suggest that if the bond is intact between parties with scarce resources, and there is no hidden shame, the parties can work out a solution that benefits all involved, or the least destructive outcome will be found. It is when the bond between parties is not adequate that destructive forms of conflict over scarcity develop, with little awareness of the consequences for the other party, or even for self.

I argue that specifying the presence or absence of concrete emotions such as shame, contempt, or disgust may untangle the knot of protracted conflict. Both internal arousal and the communicative aspects of emotional states need to be assessed as they occur in interaction. As yet, there have been few moment-by-moment investigations of specific emotions as they occur in sequence.

It is not possible to eliminate conflict or shame; to do so might be undesirable even if possible. A more productive direction is to find sources of destructive conflict and ways of managing them. Observing the state of the bond and the role shame plays in damaged and threatened bonds, and how alienation is related to angry conflict, may lead to new possibilities. Some conflict may serve a restorative function, allowing for change in the system. Other conflict is solely destructive, leading to escalation and perpetuating the very problem it attempts to solve. When the state of the bond is not commented on, conflict escalates. Shame involves the search for identity; its acknowledgment can lead to greater awareness of both self and the social world (Lynd, 1958).

In Part II of this volume I pinpoint sequences leading to conflict escalation by describing emotions that are being exchanged between husbands and wives. The case studies presented illustrate how specific emotional states, particularly shame and shaming behaviors, precede increase in conflict. Escalation occurs with increasing damage to bonds, whereas resolution occurs when bonds are repaired. Chapter 3 provides a method for identifying emotion and the state of the bond at any given moment.

3 Investigating the Bonding System

A Working Concept

> The strange thing about life is that though the nature of it must have been apparent to every one for hundreds of years, no one has left an adequate account of it. The streets of London have their map; but our passions are uncharted. (Virginia Woolf, *Jacob's Room*)

The state of the bond at any given moment can be determined through observation of both symbolic and gestural communication. Conflict can be either constructive or destructive, depending on whether it repairs or damages bonds. The theory presented in Chapters 1 and 2 maps a way in which outer behavior (communication tactics and level of respect) and inner feelings (shame and anger) interact to reveal the state of the bond and determine behavior.

This book differs from past work on conflict, marital interaction, and emotions in several ways. First, the goal is to illustrate a theory of protracted conflict; second, sequential rather than aggregate data are used (verbatim transcripts); third, specific emotions are identified in context, and <u>emotions are not viewed</u> ⚔ <u>as positive or negative, but functional</u>; and fourth, recurring patterns preceding escalation are shown, rather than differences between satisfied and dissatisfied couples.

Only four cases are used, but they are rich in information—verbal and nonverbal discourse. This type of analysis is intensive rather than extensive. Specific emotion sequences are observed as they occur during quarrels between husbands and wives; no judgments are made about the "goodness" or "badness" of emotion.

While there are strengths and weaknesses to any method, intensive case studies have been neglected in contemporary human science. From the rich information provided by case studies, a gap can be filled with information relevant to many aspects of marital conflict, leading to more adequate concepts and hypotheses. The price we pay for this method is that it is tedious, time-consuming, and expensive. Observation of case studies can add further insight into the dynamics of escalation.

In the last 50 years it has become customary to use large samples and aggregate data in studying social phenomena. Findings from large-scale studies can lead to important generalizations, but at the expense of richness and understanding. Studies using aggregate data have not specified moment-by-moment sequences. With the complexity of human behavior involved in conflict, and the slow progress in this area, more intense analyses may prove valuable. Case studies, such as Piaget's and Cooley's with children, and Freud's case histories, can provide major contributions.

Many types of discourse analysis have been developed (e.g., Heritage, 1985; Labov & Fanshel, 1977; Mishler, 1986; Sillars et al., 1982). My analysis utilizes many of the procedures and insights of the established methods, but combined in a new way. I do not use established discourse or conversation analysis, but combine several approaches that deal with more than one channel of communication (verbal, facial, paralinguistic).

Many coding systems for interaction have been developed over the past decade; they are too numerous to include here. There are almost as many objectives for observation as there are coding systems for marital and family interaction (for reviews, see Gottman, 1979; Markman & Notarius, 1987; Noller, 1984; Olson & Rider, 1970; Patterson, 1982; Sillars et al., 1982). I deal primarily with the identification of emotion as it is expressed in interaction.

New methods may be useful in exploring unknown territory. Often emotions are hidden because they are deeply *embedded* in the moment-by-moment context. Standard methods of aggregating cases strip away contextual and sequential cues. To uncover and map hidden emotions, one needs a method that is exquisitely sensitive to both context and sequence. My method discloses the hidden emotions that other methods have not been designed to uncover.

METHODOLOGY: SUBJECTS AND PROCEDURES

Married couples were found through ads in newspapers, flyers posted in marriage and family counseling centers, and word of mouth. One of the four tapes comes from an earlier study (Gottman & Levenson, 1986); Randy and Karin's interaction was kindly lent to me by Robert Levenson.

Each member of each couple was asked to come to the session separately, after the couple had been apart for several hours. Couples were given questionnaires to complete in separate rooms, including a demographic information form and Spanier's (1976) Dyadic Adjustment Scale (DAS). The DAS, a short scale for assessing the quality of marriage, contains several components designed to measure consensus, satisfaction, cohesion, and emotional expression. The validity of this scale is not crucial for the success of my study; it is used as an adjunct.

Two cameras were used in order to get frontal faces of each spouse in interaction. Each person was asked to sign a release giving permission for taping. The Gottman technique (R. Levenson, personal communication, 1986) was used: In the first 15 minutes, the couple discussed events in their day; in the second 15 minutes, they discussed a topic of argument; in the last 15 minutes, they engaged in pleasurable time. They were signaled at the end of each 15-minute interval. Debriefing involved asking couples about their experience of being taped, and further discussion of specific pleasurable times spent together as a couple.

This ordering first provides a neutral situation of interaction between husband and wife, to allow them to relax in front of the cameras. The second stage has proved to be an effective way to elicit conflict in a studio setting (R. Levenson, personal communication, 1986). The purpose of the positive exchange following the argument is to allow the couple to "cool down."

The Gottman method of engaging couples in quarrel was reported to me by his collaborator, Robert Levenson, who stated that they never studied a couple who did not actually quarrel. Using this technique, I also found this to be true. Some couples have told me that the quarrel I have witnessed was not as intense as they would have had at home, while other couples have reported that their quarrel in the laboratory was more intense than they might have had elsewhere. The quarrels were not feigned, as the intensity of emotions and the couples' inability to stop quarreling when time was up illustrate.

Fitzpatrick (1988) points out that "neophytes to marital communication research often wonder how researchers induce conflict between spouses," and if all quarrels in a laboratory setting are feigned. The quarrels presented here are not just simulated, as in the work of Raush et al. (1974), Brockner and Rubin (1985), or Pruitt and Rubin (1986)—they are actual quarrels. When couples are asked to list topics of frequent argument, they *inevitably* quarrel, with all the accompanying emotions. Although these quarrels took place in a laboratory setting, they were often quite heated.

Since gestures often occur outside conscious awareness, people have little control over this aspect of communication. "What is at stake is not the issue under discussion but the structure of the relationship" (Fitzpatrick, 1988, pp. 142-143). The structure and process of a relationship are mostly invisible to interactants; in these terms they have little control over what they present to the camera, even if they consciously subdue the quarrel.

Couples were invited to return to view their tapes several days later, at which point they could decide whether they would allow the tape to be used for teaching and publication of photographs.

During the recording, the tapes are encoded with the minute, second, and frame number (00:00:00) on each frame (30 frames = 1 second) so that events (behaviors specified below) could be recorded for frequency and duration (such as the location and timing of pauses). The transcribed interviews were then prepared with a method similar to that used by Gottschalk et al. (1969), in which all utterances and pauses are recorded. Table 3.1 lists the conventions used in transcription, many of which are derived from Heritage (1985). They are used to mark changes in utterances and to indicate paralinguistic cues, as well as code words.

Extensive segments of transcripts are included for each couple, divided into excerpts. Each excerpt is broken into components of words, cues, feelings, and exchanges. The cues are all ordered according to onset. Levels of analysis involve verbal and nonverbal data—words, gestures, and paralanguage—used in interpreting the emotions present.

ANALYSIS OF DISCOURSE

The categories of discourse used for coding emotion involved both verbal behavior and gestures. _Verbal behavior_ included words and symbolic representation. Gottschalk et al.'s (1969) content analysis scale and Lewis's (1971a, 1979) analyses were used as models in this study—detecting emotion through spoken words, code words that indicate particular emotions. Also used were Labov and Fanshel's (1977) linguistic analysis and Sillars et al.'s (1982) communicative acts scale.

Gestures included both paralinguistic cues (vocal behavior that is not symbolic, such as tone, pitch, loudness, and speed) (Labov & Fanshel, 1977; Pittenger, Hockett, & Danehy, 1960) and visual cues (facial and bodily behavior) (derived

TABLE 3.1 Conventions of Transcription

Boldface	=	anger
Italics	=	shame
Bold underlined	=	shame-rage
[ ]	=	interruptions
- between words	=	rapid, condensed speech
(inaud)	=	inaudible
< >	=	words laughed
CAPITAL LETTERS	=	heavy emphasis
( )	=	untimed pause (less than 1 second)
(0:00)	=	timed pause (seconds and frames 1/100 of second)
::	=	previous syllable drawn out
/	=	rising intonation at end of previous syllable
00:00.00	=	a time code stamped on each frame of videotape; represents the minute, second, and frame number; used for identification of events
*	=	marks *counterfactual* alternatives: what was not said but was implied, or what could have been said but was not

NOTE: These conventions have been adapted from conversation analysis (Heritage, 1985) and linguistics (Steiner, 1981).

from Darwin, 1872/1965; Edelmann, Asendorf, Contarello, Zammuner, et al., 1989; Ekman & Friesen, 1978, 1982; Izard, 1977; Scheff & Retzinger, 1991; Tomkins, 1963).

Evidence for emotion comes from both symbolic and gestural cues. The *message stack* (Scheff, 1990) of words, gestures, and implication (implication is inferred from words and gestures— what was not said but implied) is analyzed to determine emotions. Direct and indirect indications of anger, shame, and respect/disrespect are described in a sequential time frame. These items, and the context in which they occur, give clues to the state of the bond.

IDENTIFYING SHAME AND ANGER

Verbal References

Verbal references include direct use of words that indicate shame. They also include references to oneself in relation to another in which a negative evaluation is placed on the self, as well as references to alienation from significant others, that is, loss of support or love. Negative ideation about one's appearance in relation to another and obsessive ideation of what one might have said or done are also included.

Code Words Used to Describe Shame

Hundreds of words refer to shame without calling it by name. Table 3.2 lists some of the main categories for identifying shame in words and phrases. This list is not intended to be complete; it is meant only to provide a starting point for identifying shame. These words have been found to occur frequently in the shame context (Lewis, 1971a). In their Shame-Anxiety Scale, Gottschalk et al. (1969) include words or phrases that reveal both contexts and feelings for shame. Any reference to self in relation to other in which self is negatively evaluated is likely to involve feelings of shame.

Each event mentioned in Table 3.2 concerns others' perception and influence on the self, that is, how the self is affected by others. Behavior that is aimed at the other, that shames another, is coded as anger because it is hostile (whether conscious or outside awareness). The behavior of the person displaying the cues is used to code that person's behavior. For example, if person A is putting down person B, person A's behavior is coded for anger. Person B, we might assume, is feeling some humiliation, but B must exhibit shame cues before we can infer that B is in a shame state.

Code Words Used to Describe Anger

Gottschalk et al. (1969) also provide lists of verbal behaviors for anger. Identifying anger in verbal behavior involves words

TABLE 3.2 Code Words/Phrases Representing Shame and Its Context

(1) *Direct indication:* embarrassed, humiliated, chagrined, ashamed, mortified, and so on

(2) *Abandonment, separation, isolation:* statements that indicate feelings of not belonging, or otherwise separated from significant others (examples: alienated, alone, deserted, detached, disconnected, distant, divorced, dumped, estranged, ostracized, rebuffed, rejected, split, withdrawn)

(3) *Ridicule:* words or phrases about being hurt (emotionally) or threatened by another person, put down, or made to look foolish or different (examples: absurd, asinine, bizarre, defeated, dejected, foolish, freak, funny, hurt, idiotic, injured, intimidated, offended, ruined, strange, upset, weird, wounded)

(4) *Inadequate:* statements that reveal one feels one does not measure up to own or another's ideal image (examples: defenseless, deficient, exposed, failure, helpless, impotent, inept, inferior, insecure, oppressed, powerless, shy, stupid, unable, uncertain, unfit, unsure, worthless)

(5) *Discomfort:* references to social setting; social-emotional discomfiture as referred to by Goffman (1967) (examples: antsy, fidgety, hyperactive, jittery, jumpy, nervous, restless, tense, uneasy)

(6) *Confused/indifferent:* statements that indicate muddled thought processes or absence of fluster in an emotionally arousing situation; momentary forgetting (Lewis, 1971a) (examples: aloof, blank, dazed, empty, hollow, spaced, stunned)

---

or phrases that refer to mild anger, such as being annoyed, to extreme forms, like being enraged. Table 3.3 provides code words that represent anger and anger contexts; this list is not exhaustive. Some of the references to anger can also imply shame states (shame and anger often occur together). Hostility directed inward on self (putting down or criticizing self) would be coded as shame, or shame-anger.

Words such as *resentful, bitter, spiteful,* or *holding a grudge* usually involve shame-rage compounds. When these words occur, it is particularly important to look for nonverbal shame cues.

Verbal Behavior

Labov and Fanshel (1977) and Sillars et al. (1982) provide further methods for identifying emotion in verbal behavior.

TABLE 3.3 Code Words/Phrases Representing Anger and Its Context

---

(1) *Direct indications:* aggravated, angry, annoyed, bothered, cross, enraged, fuming, furious, incensed, indignant, irate, irritable, mad, pissed, teed-off, and so on.

(2) *Hostility:* includes references of anger toward self, others, animals, and objects, on overt and covert levels (examples: abandoning, blaming, causing suffering, criticizing, cruelty, cursing, deprecating, destroying, dislike, dying, fighting, harming, hating, injuring, killing, mutilation, threatening, violence)

Although Sillars et al. look at communicative acts rather than emotion, it is important to note their categories of acts for looking at conflict in relationships: avoidance acts, distributive acts, and integrative acts. The descriptions of these categories are very much like my own. *Avoidance* is similar to hiding behavior involved in shame states, *distribution* is similar to the hostile challenge that gives cues for anger, and *integration* is similar to my concept of connection or community (see Chapter 8). Rather than categorizing according to communicative acts, I use the emotion categories of shame and anger, or combinations of emotions.

Shame

Table 3.4 includes categories that imply shame through verbal hiding behaviors. That is, an important issue or feeling is hidden behind words and behaviors; these often occur in combination and precede code words for shame (Harrington, 1990).

Harrington (1990) has shown projection to be associated with code words for shame. It has two functions: It disassociates the feeling from the self, and it serves as a kind of collective defense, which includes others into the emotional experience. It may be an attempt to affirm the bond. Harrington has also shown that fillers serve a similar function as projection; they attempt to affirm the bond and include the other in one's experience, or to deny one's experience.

TABLE 3.4 Verbal Hiding Behaviors

(1) *Mitigation:* word or phrase that makes something appear less severe or painful; downgrading an event so it no longer appears to need attention (Labov & Fanshel, 1977)

(2) *Abstraction:* talk about to oblique, general, or suppressed reference, such as "they" or "it," rather than referring to specific events or people

(3) *Denial:* direct or implicit statement that explicitly denies a feeling or provides a rationale for the feeling (Sillars et al., 1982, p. 85)

(4) *Defensive:* a statement that either denies or includes challenging or critical statements; occurs in reaction to a challenge from the other
    (a) *Indifference:* acting "cool" in an emotionally arousing context, such as asking someone for a date for the first time (somewhat like Satir's, 1972, computer type; can be defensive as well as hostile)

(5) *Verbal withdrawal:* change in verbal behavior from talking in sentence form to talking in word form; also minimal response and long silences

(6) *Distraction:* can include a number of behaviors, from topic change to joking to triangling; involves words or phrases that shift the discussion away from key relationship issues that involve feeling
    (a) *Projection:* disclaims the experience as one's own, placing it onto another person or group of people (examples: "Sometimes *you* get *embarrassed*"; "*no one* likes to be *rejected*") (Harrington, 1990)

(7) *Fillers:* phrases such as "you know" or "I don't know" interjected in a conversation

Anger

Each of the behaviors in Table 3.5 gives clues to the presence of anger; each challenges the other person. "A challenge is any reference [direct or indirect] to a situation, which . . . would lower the status of the other person" (Labov & Fanshel, 1977, p. 64). All of these behaviors involve a kind of acting out of hostility rather than speaking directly about feelings.

Shame-Rage

Often shame and anger co-occur; some verbal behavior implies involvement of both emotions. The main cues are temporal expansion and triangulation; both involve hiding behaviors, as well as hostility toward the other.

Temporal expansion includes phrases such as "you always." (Temporal condensation or contraction includes "you never.")

TABLE 3.5 Challenging Behaviors

---

(1) *Interruption:* the act of cutting another off before he or she ends his or her turn

(2) *Sarcasm:* statements that say one thing in words and another in gesture, and that put other down or make other look foolish

(3) *Blame:* statements that place responsibility or fault on the other

(4) *Criticism:* negative evaluation of another

(5) *Questioning:* repeating the same question over and over; a form of interrogation

(6) *Presumptive attribution:* "statements that attribute thoughts, feelings, intentions, or motives" to the other (Sillars et al., 1982, p. 86)

(7) *Prescription:* statements that seek to change the other's behavior in a specific way; request, demand (Sillars et al., 1982, p. 86)

(8) *Threaten:* give the other an "either/or" alternative, or imply abandonment

---

Temporal expansion/condensation is implicitly hostile because it attempts to overwhelm the other person; rather than a specific complaint being stated, the entire universe is included or excluded.

Triangulation is the bringing up of an irrelevant third party or object (Bowen, 1978). Triangles involve third parties (as well as things) drawn into a conversation to distract from the main point.

Paralinguistic Gestures

Emotions can be detected in nonsymbolic verbal gestures as well as in words. Labov and Fanshel (1977) and Pittenger et al. (1960) provide paralinguistic cues. Table 3.6 indicates ways of identifying shame through paralinguistic cues; these include vocal withdrawal/hiding behaviors and disorganization of thought. Table 3.7 lists paralinguistic cues for anger; they are marked primarily by harsh voice qualifiers.

Visual Gestures

Gestural data involve facial and body behavior (Ekman & Friesen, 1978; Izard, 1971) as well as paralanguage. Although we are able to hear our own auditory messages, we cannot see

TABLE 3.6 Paralinguistic Cues for Shame

Hiding behavior

   (1) *Oversoft:* drop in volume so that the utterance becomes almost inaudible; often occurs at the end of a sentence or when discussing a shameful or taboo subject, such as sex
     (a) Lax articulation, incoherence, breathiness
   (2) *Hesitation:* stalling before getting into a sensitive area or topic
   (3) *Self-interruption:* stopping an utterance in midsentence to change or censor a topic
   (4) *Pause:* includes long pauses or silences; often occurs before code words or taboo topics (normal pause is less than a second; longer pauses become problematic)
   (5) *Rapid speech:* hides what is being said by condensing words so as to be almost incomprehensible
   (6) *Laughed words:* often occurs with overt embarrassment or as a mask for anger or shame; tense laughter

Disorganization of thought

   (7) *Irregular rhythm:* jerky speech associated with frequent pausing
   (8) *Filled pauses:* frequent use of filler sounds such as "uh" to fill lapses in speech
   (9) *Stammer:* uncertain and incoherent speech; repeated sounds
   (10) *Fragmented speech:* speech marked by rapid change in topic, so that it become incoherent

our own facial changes. Many of these changes occur outside awareness, and are usually good indicators of emotional states. Nonverbal analysis involves observing facial and body movements in conjunction with verbal and paralinguistic data. Table 3.8 shows the visual cues that represent shame through bodily manifestations (Darwin, 1872/1965; Edelmann et al., 1989; Izard, 1977; Lewis, 1981b; Retzinger, 1987; Scheff & Retzinger, 1991; Tomkins, 1963).

Cues for shame can occur alone or in any combination. Often they occur in sequences of events, such as biting the lip → false smiling → cover face with hand. Sometimes one event follows another, but events may occur simultaneously. In an independent study, Edelmann et al. (1989) found these behaviors to be associated with embarrassment across cultures.

TABLE 3.7 Paralinguistic Cues for Anger

(1) *Loud:* volume of the voice increases
(2) *Heavy stress:* volume and emphasis increase on certain words
(3) *Staccato:* distinct breaks between successive tones.
(4) *Singsong:* repeated pattern of pitch and stress
(5) *Whine:* nasally spoken utterance

TABLE 3.8 Visual Cues for Shame

Hiding behavior
   (1) hand covering all or parts of the face
   (2) gaze aversion, eyes lowed or averted
Blushing
Control

   (1) turning in, biting, or licking the lips; biting the tongue
   (2) forehead wrinkled vertically or transversely
   (3) false smiling (Ekman & Friesen, 1982) or other masking behaviors
   (4) fidgeting

Table 3.9 illustrates the bodily manifestations of anger as discussed by Ekman and Friesen (1978) and Izard (1971). Many of the expressions for anger are facial, though anger is also manifest in bodily movements.

Cues are context related; that is, their relevance to shame depends on the relationship between self and other. The more categories (e.g., visual, verbal, paralinguistic) involved, and the greater the number of cues from each category, the stronger the evidence for the particular emotion. For instance, if a person is talking about feeling small or helpless while averting his or her gaze and speaking oversoftly, in a fragmented and hesitant manner, the evidence that shame is occurring is stronger than if the person had only averted his or her eyes. For evidence of any particular emotion to be considered strong, the cues need to occur in combination. Based on constellations of cues, in this study I have inferred emotions being expressed and exchanged between husbands and wives.

TABLE 3.9 Visual Cues for Anger

(1) Brows lowered and drawn together, vertical lines appear between them.
(2) Eyelids narrowed and tense in a hard, fixed stare; eyes may have a bulging appearance.
(3) Mouth closed with lips pressed together, corners straight or down, or mouth open but tense and square. Closed mouth position may occur in an attempt to control shouting or hostility. Open-mouth anger occurs during speech (Ekman & Friesen, 1975, 1978; Izard, 1971).
(4) Hard, direct glaring.
(5) Leaning forward toward other in challenging stance.
(6) Clenched fists, waving fists, hitting motions.

DISRESPECT AND IMPLICATION

Disrespect can be seen in the manner of communication, in how one person addresses or responds to another. Combinations of words and gestures can reveal emotions through implication (Labov & Fanshel, 1977). Disrespect can be detected in combinations of words and gestures that imply hostility. Words and/or gestures can imply what is not stated directly; behind implicit messages there are often intense emotions expressed and exchanged. For example, if your partner tells you "I love you" (words), but does not look up from behind the newspaper (gesture), we can guess as to what is implied by the words. The words are clear—they say "I care"—but if we give weight to the gesture, the meaning changes: *"Not that again, don't bother me" (the attached asterisk indicates a counterfactual; see Table 3.1).

Each indication of shame or anger may imply the presence of the other emotion, as well as disrespect. If there are visual signs of anger but it is verbally being denied rather than expressed directly, shame is likely to be present. Often when anger takes overt form, shame is covert. When shame is overt, we are likely to find anger absent or covert.

CONCLUSION

A qualitative sequential analysis provides a holistic picture of the interactive process between the spouses, charting emotional communicative processes. The major variables are the state of the bond (degree of alienation), shame, anger, and disrespect. Emotions provide cues that specify the state of the bond; at any given moment it is being built, maintained, repaired, or damaged.

This is an exploratory study. The quest is to develop a testable theory and hypotheses. I used this method to observe particular cues and to infer sequences second by second, because the method does not strip away context, but instead explicitly relies on contextual understanding. A definitive answer as to the reliability of this method can come only with further use and testing. Chapters 4-7 present an application of the theory and method discussed thus far.

The case analyses that follow are rather detailed at times. It is exceedingly difficult to translate all the nuances that occur in interaction between persons from visual and paralinguistic media to verbal ones. This translation process is a matter of changing analogic information into digital information, and there is some resulting loss of richness. The detailed analyses of these cases are intended as an attempt to refine this translation process and to provide as much of the analogic information as possible so that we can better understand how escalation works.

PART TWO

Case Analyses

4 Rosie and James

Silent Impasse

So that "words may again be the word" and the living truth said, a new language must be created. (Steiner, 1981, p. 185)

Rosie and James (pseudonyms) are a white middle-class couple, ages 32 and 35, respectively. They have been married 11 years. James works for the forestry service and has a $50,000 annual income. Rosie has recently completed a bachelor's degree in social science; she was unemployed at the time of the taping. Neither have had previous marriages; they do not have children.

This is a couple who do not discuss feelings, and who avoid conflict. They distance themselves from each other emotionally; they are isolated. They seem to be uncomfortable with quarrels, avoiding them at all costs; instead of discussing issues directly, they withdraw, placate, or compute. Although James says he almost always confides in Rosie, she confides less often in James. They are frequently in disagreement over financial matters, philosophy of life, goals, and amount of time they spend together, but they rarely quarrel. Rosie comments on their style of arguing:

> We usually avoid [arguments]. This is a very covert family. There's no overt, there's no fighting. I would say there's, there's little blow-ups, there's a little bristle, then the other one backs down, and both of us do that, but there's no argument.

Their relationship lacks closeness and affection. Although they both said they would like their relationship to succeed, they were considering divorce at the time of the interview. Rosie and James had been living apart for the past year. While Rosie attended college in one town, James's job was in another. On a scale of 1-10 (10 most happy, 1 least) concerning the degree of happiness with their relationship, Rosie rated 5, James 4. Rosie further comments:

> I'm not sure this relationship is going to last. I would like it to but there needs to be some major changes. We are seeing each other 1 [day] a week.

James also comments:

> Very difficult to maintain a relationship when each partner is living (primarily) in separate locations.

The topic Rosie and James chose to discuss involved an airplane that they own, a topic on which they are "diametrically opposed." James says the plane is his "pride and joy" and a "big part" of his life, as he has been involved with planes since he was a teenager. Although she also has a pilot's license, Rosie says the plane is a "financial burden" and she "hates" it.

This particular quarrel is unusual for Rosie and James in that Rosie refers to specific feelings of anger, resentment, and loathing about the plane. This was not her usual manner. She said that because the interviewer was in the other room she felt safe enough to talk openly; if anything happened she thought the interviewer would help her.

The segment that follows from Rosie and James's quarrel is divided into seven excerpts. Only the first three (34 seconds) will be broken down into emotion cues to illustrate the covert nature of Rosie and James's quarrel: threats to the bond, shame, the emergence of anger, and how quickly resentment can arise. The first 34 seconds illustrate how the bond is maintained through collusive action and damaged through threat, and how attempts are made to repair the damage. The other four excerpts will be discussed to illustrate several points about the way in which Rosie and James deal with emotions (the entire transcript, written in ordinary English, can be found in the Appendix). After agreeing on the topic they would discuss, Rosie begins:

Excerpt 1

```
22:23.25  a  R:  so what-aspect of the plane do you wanna talk about?
          b  J:  oh jis airplanes in general it doesn't have to be (   )
          c  R:                                              [oh]
          d  J:  specifically the one we have now (laugh)
   30.09  e  R:                              <no:: I wanna
                 NARROW it RIGHT down TU that one>
```

WORDS: Rosie 1a

CUES:
lick lips false smile tight lips evasive hesitant tentative passive question rather than statement

FEELINGS: Rosie's
shame

EXCHANGE:
relinquishes power; passive; maintains distance

Rosie begins preparing for the exchange by licking her lips. She requests information, referring to a particular plane ("the plane"), but is hesitant and evasive. Her manner is childlike, as though asking permission from a parent. She projects a self that is unable and passive. She displays a false smile as she mentions "aspect of" the plane. Besides visual and paralinguistic hiding behaviors, there is a focal awareness of self in relation to other. She also says "the plane" rather than "our plane," separating herself from involvement.

Rather than making a statement, *"Let's talk about such and such aspect of the plane," or making a direct statement as to how the situation affects her, or negotiating possible solutions, she formulates a question, giving James the responsibility for the direction they will take. When "expanded" (Labov & Fanshel, 1977), this excerpt says *"I don't want responsibility; it's your plane so it's your problem." This illustrates her discomfort with the topic, as well as the part she plays in their relationship. She claims to want to be strong and independent, but turns the power of decision making over to James, "taking a backseat"; she plays a *passive* rather than active role. Her sentence ends with tightened lips.

While Rosie speaks, James looks at her, displaying a false smile, which fades at the end of her utterance. James's verbal response at first glance appears to be direct, in control, but tense; there are many cues, both visual and paralinguistic:

WORDS: James 1b-d
  b J: oh *jis airplanes in general it doesn't have to be ( )*
  c R: [oh]
  d J: *specifically the one we have now (laugh)*

CUES:
  (1b) *false smile   mitigation   generalization   pause*
  (1d) *vagueness   avoidance   tense laughter*

FEELINGS: James
  shame

EXCHANGE:
  colludes in avoidance; passive; maintains surface level

The cues involve mainly hiding behaviors; there is no evidence for anger at this point. Both Rosie and James avoid dealing directly with the topic and collude in the avoidance; neither is willing to level about his or her own feelings. By saying we can talk in general, he avoids the tension of talking about the particular airplane they own. Together they work at maintaining their relationship at a certain distance—they are alienated. Neither discusses feelings directly: she avoids by using a question and relinquishing her power, he avoids by being general and ambiguous. Each denies responsibility.

Although James makes a decision, he also takes a passive role, and implicitly makes a request that they remain vague. It may appear that he rescues the interaction by saving face for both of them, but as it turns out this is not the case. Rosie continues:

WORDS: Rosie 1e
      <no:: I wanna **NARROW** it **RIGHT** down **TU** that one>

CUES:
emphasis on "no" challenge *head tilted away* **very soft** *"I wanna"*
tight eyes/mouth looks through corner of her eye heavy emphasis
raised voice increased tempo *laughs phrase indirect*

FEELINGS: Rosie's
embarrassment
anger

EXCHANGE:
ambiguous

The interaction in line 1e is ambiguous. Rosie makes no direct reference to what she is feeling, the cues are visual and paralinguistic. She begins Excerpt 1 in a passive mode, but appears to challenge James when he does not give the right answer to her first question.

Hiding behaviors are still present, seen in tense laughter (22:30.09), but another set of cues begins to emerge: interruption, challenge, emphasis on certain words, raising of her voice, and a facial expression of anger (2.22) on "narrow it . . . ." Disrespect begins to become evident, first seen in her interruption of James. As Rosie speaks, James makes several of his own attempts to interrupt with an explanation ("because"), reciprocating the disrespect. James exhibits a tight smile, and laughs nervously at each attempt. Their emotions are covert.

Excerpt 1 illustrates collusive attempts to maintain the bond at a certain distance; the collusion helps maintain the status quo of the relationship. At first glance it appears to be a normal conversation, but there are many cues for emotion that increase as the conversation progresses. Both parties appear tense and controlled. Shame is prominent, but not acknowledged.

In Excerpt 2 the emotions escalate quickly. The bond is damaged as Rosie and James subtly threaten each other; language of separation and shame cues are evident. The interaction takes a sharp turn as James explains why its all right to discuss airplanes in general:

Excerpt 2

22:34.15	a	J:	[<be]cause> I don't **plan** on it being
	b		the <u>las-the</u> end of the line *ha*
37.07	c	R:	**NO::** *well* I don't either ( ) **not for YOU::** ( )
	d	J:	**Oh good** <soft)

WORDS: James 2a-b

CUES:
   (2a) **interrupts Rosie** *laughs words tense smile*
   (2b) **challenge** *self-interruption mitigation laughs as he finishes his assertion indirect statement*

FEELINGS: James's
anger-shame alternation

EXCHANGE:
  challenge

By expanding James's utterance in 2a-b, his statement implies: *"It doesn't matter which plane we discuss because this is a major part of my life and I'll always own a plane, no matter what you want." Emotion cues rapidly appear.

James interrupts and subtly challenges Rosie with the idea that airplanes are here to stay, with little forewarning. Again he smiles and laughs uncomfortably. James might have prepared Rosie for this assertion, had he acknowledged his anger and his feelings about causing her "so much grief" (34:20.16); or he could have discussed the issue in terms of the bond. They maintain their secret emotional world. Excerpt 2 illustrates ideation of separation; James's threat damages the bond seen by Rosie's strong emotional reaction and use of "you," that is, language of separation.

Although there are cues for anger, James is unaware of it; the anger is covert, formulated as an assertion about the plane and interruption. It is accompanied by many cues for shame: self-interruption—changing "last" to "end of the line," mitigating the severity of his intent—and his tense chuckle at the end of the sentence. As James speaks Rosie looks at him with a false, fixed smile. Instead of anger being stated directly and explicitly, it emerges disrespectfully through James's dropping a line on Rosie without adequate preparation, just after he *appears* to be supportive. Interruptions also show disrespect. A response to disrespect is some form of embarrassment, often appearing as an angry attack.

This particular exchange is important in understanding Rosie's "little blowup." Rosie does not comment on the effect that James's statement has on her, but responds with an attack of her own, with greater force:

WORDS: Rosie 2c
  NO:: *well I don't either* ( ) **not for YOU::** ( )

CUES:
looks away (up/right) **shakes head no   heavy emphasis** *mitigation*
tentative   false smile   pause/hesitation   **narrow eyes/tight mouth**
heavy emphasis   facial expression of anger   sarcasm   criticism
pause **glare** *indirect*

FEELINGS: Rosie's
shame-rage alternation

EXCHANGE:
attack; hostile implication

At first Rosie seems to agree with James's disguised aggression, but she adds a little twist. She pauses and adds "not for you," which has a tone of <u>contempt</u>. "<u>You</u>" is emphasized and dragged out, sounding like two syllables with a rise and fall of intonation; it seems to carry the implication that James is a hopeless case. Expanding Rosie's statement: *"I don't think it will be the last plane you own either, but it is for me; you are a hopeless case."

The interaction at this point shows considerable disrespect, hidden beneath false smiles. Emotion cues multiply dramatically in Excerpt 2c. Rosie is indirect with her anger and attacks James. Facial expression of anger and a sarcastic tone mark her rising anger, which is covered by a soft, "sweet" voice tone. All the while Rosie is firing at James, he keeps a tense, false smile on his face. He responds with a double message:

WORDS: James 2d
  Oh good <soft)

CUES:
  false smile   overly soft   minimal response   **<u>withdrawal</u>   cutoff**

FEELINGS: James's
  shame and covert anger

EXCHANGE:
withdrawal

Rosie's attack cuts deeply. James's words are affirmative, but his manner reveals another message. By saying "oh good," he may be responding to the first part of Rosie's sentence (2c: "no, well, I don't either") as if she is really agreeing with him, while his manner responds to the second part of her message ("not for you"). His words and manner are dissonant: His words say "good," but his manner says "not good." James's manner exposes his feelings, while his words cover them.

Whereas James had been speaking in sentences, his response is now minimal and oversoft (compared with previous and following responses). Withdrawal suggests intense feelings—hiding from engagement, as well as from attack. Cutting off from the other represents a break in the bond. He disengages from social contact rather than clarifying or stating feelings; separation increases.

James could have asked for clarification: *"What do you mean?" He could have expressed his feelings: *"It hurt my feelings when you said that." Their relationship seems to be characterized by withdrawal and absence of direct communication. They seem to have no language to communicate about feelings and relationships.

Rosie looks at James during his utterance (line 2d), displays an expression of anger, and shakes her head no. On her turn to speak she quickly proceeds with a stronger attack:

Excerpt 3

```
22:40.28 a R:  no-I wouldn't take yer toy from you
         b J:  alright <oversoft)
   42.14 c R:  I-I sacrificed a LOT for you to have toys (1.79)
(both laugh tightly)
   49:00 d R:  but you-didn't-ask-for-it-an-I-resent-later-an-
         e     an-we're-still-going-over-it (  ) ok
         f J:  Ya (  ) ut it (3)
```

WORDS: Rosie 3a

CUES:
   shakes head no narrowing of eyes *false smile* *soft, sweet voice*
   derogatory sarcastic condescending *indirect*

FEELINGS: Rosie's
  shame-rage alternation

EXCHANGE:
demeaning criticism; nonleveling

The interaction becomes increasingly hostile and disrespectful; Rosie attacks James's adulthood by implying that he is a
child who plays with toys. "Toy" carries the connotation of
being frivolous and unimportant. The message seems to be *"I
can't change you, so I'll diminish you." She trivializes the
importance of James's airplane. James has a fixed false smile
throughout her attack. The quarrel has escalated rapidly in 7
seconds.

Rosie's tone is condescending and contemptuous, with increasing anger, expressed as sarcasm. Rosie's statement (3a)
shows indirect anger and a marked disrespect; she derogates
James rather than being point-blank about her own feelings.
Rosie appears to have taken James's previous response ("I don't
plan on it being the last") as an attack. She feels rejected, so
rejects him in return, tit for tat. Neither Rosie nor James levels
about feelings; instead, each focuses on topics.

It should be noted also that Rosie gave away her power of
control at the start of this argument (1a), subjugating herself
to James. However, she now implies that she can control him,
and has the power to take his plane away if she wants to.
"Deliberately shaming someone is used for the establishment
and maintenance of power" (Gross & Stone, 1964). At this
point Rosie might have taken control and dealt with the situation differently. Had she responded with her own feelings
about James's statement ("end of the line") very directly and
respectfully, she could have saved her own as well as James's

face—the argument may have never escalated. James responds with further implosion:

WORDS: James 3b
 alright <oversoft)

CUES:
 false smile fades rapidly <u>*oversoft (almost inaudible)*</u> *head tilts slightly downward minimal response* **withdrawal** **cut off**

FEELINGS: James's
 shame/covert anger

EXCHANGE:
 further withdrawal

James's voice is barely audible in 3b; his verbal response is again minimal. He appears to be "hurt" in the visual recording: his smile (although false) rapidly fades, he shrinks down in his seat. He becomes sullen; he looks and sounds withdrawn. Rosie listens with her eyes narrowed and a tense, false smile.

Again, he does not comment on the manner of communication, nor does he acknowledge his feelings, which are presumably "hurt." He might have said, *"I don't like the way this conversation is going, it's too hurtful." He hides through withdrawal. (He said at the viewing that what prevents him from expressing his anger is that he feels like his "legitimacy wanes . . . in her eyes" when he expresses anger; that is, he becomes ashamed.)

James's utterance is another double message: The words say one thing, but the manner says another. The implications of James's utterance may be several: *"All right, already, shut up, I've had enough," or *"All right! If you want to be that way about it I'm withdrawing." Either way, James disengages, giving a minimal response both in words and loudness of the utterance. Visually James appears to implode as Rosie continues to attack:

WORDS: Rosie 3c
I-I sacrificed a LOT for you to have toys ( )
(both laugh tightly)

CUES:
eyes widen *stammers* *tight smile* *vertical wrinkling in forehead*
heavy emphasis anger expression *smile fades* *long pause*
complaint condescending *tight laughter (at end)*

FEELINGS:
shame-rage alternation

EXCHANGE:
complaining attack; blame

Rosie complains and puts James down, stammering as she does. Cues for anger are many—words, paralanguage, and visuals—intermingled with shame cues. She has a tight smile throughout her utterance. Rosie is talking to James as a parent to a child; her shaming behavior toward him shows hostile anger. As Rosie speaks, James has no smile for the first time; his head is slightly tilted downward, and he displays a false smile as Rosie finishes her utterance. They both laugh nervously, indicating their discomfort (shame).

Rosie must have noticed how her manner affected James, because she attempts to repair the damage. Her next sentence is marked by a greatly increased tempo; she speaks very quickly and so softly toward the end of her sentence that her words are almost inaudible. She appears to be in a state of shame about what she has said, and perhaps remorse:

WORDS: Rosie 3d-e
R: *but you-didn't-ask-for-it-an-***I-resent***-later-an-an-
   we're-still-going-over-it ( ) ok*

CUES:
(d) *looks away oversoft/inaudible fragment* **anger word**
(e) *bite tongue/lick lips rapid/condensed speech repair*

FEELINGS:
  shame in fore
  remorse

EXCHANGE:
attempts repair

Her use of other inclusion, "we're," occurs for the first time, including both of them in the experience. Use of "we" may be a means of repairing the damage, and perhaps of including James in her experience. She speaks rapidly and almost inaudibly, hiding behavior increases. The implication is that Rosie is still angry, but that her anger (or at least the manner in which it emerged) was hurtful or otherwise wrong; she attempts to take back what she previously said. As she ends her sentence she bites her tongue, then her lips, in rapid succession.

James displays a tense, fixed smile as Rosie tries to make amends; he appears to be at a loss for what to say; he stammers and mumbles:

WORDS: James 3f
J: *Ya (   ) ut it (3)*

CUES:
  oversoft pause fragmentation stammer lax articulation mumble
  long pause

FEELINGS:
  shame

EXCHANGE:
confusion; withdrawal

The quarrel submerges just as quickly as it escalated. It is manifest exactly as Rosie described their way of quarreling: "there's little blowups, there's a little bristle, then the other one

backs down." They both backed down. On first view of the tape
it almost appears that there is no quarrel.

After this "blowup" Rosie and James go back to talking
vaguely and abstractly about advantages and disadvantages of
owning an airplane. It appears that the quarrel has stopped, but
it has merely gone underground, only to reemerge sporadically
throughout the rest of the interview. Eight minutes later, the
conversation moves on to the topic of their house not being
maintained properly. The quarrel has now expanded to include
the house; expansion marks continued presence of feelings.
Intense feeling reemerges as Rosie attempts to explain what
motivated her to change her place of residence:

Excerpt 4

```
31:30.10  J:  uh what do you mean opted out
   32.00  R:  well tu go tu school and to be away from like the
               house an everything an-an-uh working towards (1.34)
   38.20      the relationship an the house an everything (2.44)
               yu-know I'm not really in-I can't do much there (  )
   53.28      I'm here (2.75) so (3.56) (laugh) isn't it great I
               get totally blank
          J:  (laugh)
          R:  (laugh) repression's a MARvelous defense
               mechanism
          J:  (laugh)
          R:  it saved me more than once O::K um
32:05.20  J:  anyway we got off the airplane=
```

Excerpt 4 illustrates the reemergence of unexpressed emotions. Rosie avoids direct discussion of the relationship, sand-
wiching it in between repeat mention of the "house and
everything." Although she mentions the relationship, it is surrounded by a constellation of hiding behaviors. This is the first
time she mentions the relationship in the interview; she goes
blank as she does. The entire excerpt is marked by many cues
for shame: mitigation, temporal expansion, fragmented speech,
many long pauses, filler words, tense laughter, fragmented and
repetitious speech, nervous laughter, going blank, and ideation
of self being unable.

Instead of discussing what is occurring in the relationship in the present, James attempts to save the situation by getting back on the topic of the airplane. Again they collude in avoiding feelings and the real issues in their relationship. Rosie agrees to get back on the topic of the plane, but goes about it from a new angle:

Excerpt 5

```
32:08 20  R: . . . ya it hhh <forceful exhale) (1.75) you know I resent it
              I::=
   16.25  J:  =ya I know
   32.04  R: you know (  ) I feel like I've had tu bail it out
              a couple-u times an bailed out the first
              airplane I feel like I bailed out this one
              financially when it needed a thousand dollars
              fer its taxes an (  ) I resent it cause I really
              try li-live very (1.06) cheaply (  ) and not
              spend money (1) and then to see mm you know
              (  ) money go for THAT (  ) which is something I
   48.26     resent, hate, despise, loathe, (2.28) jist hee
              really negative emotions towards (1) i-i-it
              it really (  ) causes me a lot of pain (1) I'm
              feeling like I'm scrimping on myself tu save
              money but then if the airplane needs it then
              i-it's gone to the airplane (2.22) an that's real
33:01.20     painful (3.22)
Both laugh tensely
33:08.20  J:  (laugh)
          R:  (laugh)
   10:05  J:  ya we-well I feel (1.91) feel you know different
              from that
          R:  umhm=
```

She brings herself out of the blank mental state by talking about her feelings of anger, which she had been avoiding, but is still in a state of shame-rage. The anger is focused toward the plane rather than James or the relationship; she uses general suppressed references, "it" and "they," indicating the presence of shame. Excerpt 5, which occurs 10 minutes into the quarrel, is the first time in the interview that either party acknowledges any strong feelings. (During the postviewing interview, I learned that this couple never directly expressed intense feelings during quarrels. Rosie said she "felt safe" to talk about her anger because the interviewer was nearby; she said she thought that if anything terrible happened the interviewer would "save" her.)

Excerpt 6 illustrates James's discomfort with feelings; he has difficulty in giving a proper name to Rosie's anger:

Excerpt 6

```
34:04.10  R:                                                       =but to
                you it's not (  ) it's:: it's:: means something to you
      08.01  J:  ya (1.13) it makes it it makes it for me it makes
                it real difficult (1.78) it's not (2.10) you know
                it's not (  ) not PLEASANT owning it (3.25) in that
      20.16     respect (  ) in that you know that it does (1.53)
                <ha cause you so much grief> (Laugh)
```

Excerpt 6 is marked by many cues as James struggles to talk about his feelings: repetition, frequent pausing, fragmented speech, hesitation, mitigation, and nervous laughter. James makes 13 references to "it" in one sentence—a masterpiece of vagueness and ambiguity indicating suppressed shame. James is not comfortable with feelings, as can be seen in the disguised way in which he expresses emotions and in his difficulty commenting on Rosie's feelings. Rosie goes on to describe what is occurring with her emotionally:

Excerpt 7

```
34:29.10  R:  (laugh) ya no I-I resent it (  ) I honestly don't
                like it I resent it I hate it (1.34) I have a lotta
      38.25     negative emotions attached to it I-I think I(  ) taken
                maybe a lotta what with our relationship an:: life
                in general an put it HHH jis done a great projection
                job on the old airplane an=
      49.20  J:                               =ya=
          R:                                        =cause it's safe tu
                get mad at the airplane an=
```

```
         J:                              =ya=
53.15  R:  won't get rejected or anything (2.59) an an that's
           part of me an there's another part of me that
           understands that you know that's a dream of yours
35:01.10   an we're all entitled to drea::ms
```

Rosie's last utterance, as well as her first in Excerpt 7 ("ya no"), is an example of the havoc that shame-rage plays internally. She is angry "about the plane," but feels she has no right to be angry, because after all, she believes, James has a right to his dreams. Rosie also remains vague, using the reference to "it" six times in her first sentence. The split between her understanding self and her angry self is an indication of a bypassed state of shame; the self is divided. Her anger feels unjustified, and emerges in a covert way. She projects her anger onto the plane, but she knows how important the plane is for James. They maintain their distance from each other by avoiding feelings and getting angry at airplanes.

After the 15-minute period of argument, Rosie's feelings refused to subside. She was still emotionally "aroused" as they begin the 15-minute period for "positive interaction"; she commented, "I'm still <u>flying.</u>"

Summary

Rosie and James's relationship is almost always a silent impasse, signaling separation between them. The overt part of their dispute is so brief (34 seconds) as to be almost invisible. There appear to be some conventions about feelings between Rosie and James that remain unspoken. One rule is that feelings are not directly addressed. The little arguing they do centers on topics, avoiding acknowledging feelings or discussion of the relationship; they do not comment on the manner in which they present the issue. Denial of feelings and passive resentment reinforce each other, pervading the dialogue.

Rosie and James's dispute is very cognitive, lofty, and "rational." Both cut off from their feelings, putting further distance between them. Emotions rise in a brief burst and quickly disappear. As the quarrel submerges, the topic becomes vague, skirts around the edges, and evolves into a "rational" conversation.

Their relationship is marked by lack of closeness and warmth. A gap of unspoken feeling separates these two; their bond is insecure, and the tactics they use damage the bond further. The 34-second quarrel is marked by collusive maintenance of closed communication, damage through indirect hostility emerging as disrespect, and an attempt at repair by cutting off feelings. This "intellectual" discussion does not go far before feelings begin to reemerge.

A silent impasse can be likened to a cold war. The escalation of this quarrel began with shame in both parties, rather than anger; neither person acknowledged these feelings. Each partner shows disrespect toward the other in subtle innuendo and emotional withdrawal. The two seldom interrupt each other, nor do they call each other derogatory names or blame each other; instead, they withhold affection and withdraw. Anger emerged in quick, subtle jabs throughout the segment. They attack each other through mixed messages: Their words claim that everything is fine, but their manner reveals their unhappiness with the relationship. They collude.

This particular couple display emotion primarily through paralanguage, although Rosie also shows emotion visually; neither of them is sufficiently verbal in expression of feelings. There are higher amounts of shame displayed compared with the amount of anger displayed.

Both partners are uncomfortable with feelings, as reflected in their cognitive style of discussing issues and the constellation of hiding behaviors surrounding the mention of emotion words. James displays discomfort with feelings by tense laughter whenever a feeling is mentioned, and by misnaming feelings. This is a couple who express little overt anger; their perspective, which they share, is that anger will damage the other in some irreparable way. Avoidance of feelings does not seem to be helpful in reducing conflict; their relationship is cool and distant. Avoidance, in this case, has been unsuccessful in resolving the marital conflict. The lack of emotional expression has led to considerable strain in the marriage.

Although Rosie and James had been planning divorce and had been separated at the time of the taping, they are back together at the present time. They returned to the lab to view their tape and reported that watching themselves on videotape had helped them to improve their relationship. Three years later this couple is back together; the airplane is no longer an issue. James is building a new plane and Rosie has just received a master's degree (see Chapter 8 for events during their viewing of the tape).

This couple has difficulty in regulating distance between togetherness and separateness. Their relationship is marked particularly by isolation; their style is more of isolation than of engulfment, as opposed to the other couples, although both occur. The manner in which they communicate helps keep them isolated: use of vague, suppressed references and language of separation. Their communication tactics damage the bond, eliciting shame and rage in each person, with rage being suppressed in silent impasse. Although they make attempts to maintain the bond, both Rosie and James's emotional states are permeated with shame as they quarrel covertly. Not all couples suppress their anger as do Rosie and James; David and Colleen, whose case study is presented in Chapter 5, display their anger vividly, but this is no more productive in leading to social regulation and connectedness than is Rosie and James's suppression of anger.

5 David and Colleen

Interminable Quarrel

> All understanding is at the same time
> misunderstanding, all agreement in
> thought and feeling is also a parting of
> the ways. (Steiner, 1981, p. 173)

David, 38, and Colleen, 35 (pseudonyms), are a white middle-class couple; they have been married for 15 years, the first marriage for both. David is a salesperson for mobile homes and a real estate developer, Colleen is a dancer/fitness instructor, currently unemployed. David has been the primary financial provider in this relationship; his annual income is $30,000. He has three years of college; she has a B.A. in liberal studies. They have no children.

The problems in David and Colleen's marriage have been left unresolved. The two claim to share the same philosophy of life in one sense: They both are products of the 1960s and share a love of nature. However, they do not share beliefs about relationships. Colleen is traditional in that she believes in togetherness and is offended by differences between them; her sense of self is dependent on agreement from David. David, on the other hand, wants more independence and free thinking in the relationship; he is disturbed by Colleen's inability to stand on her own in thoughts and feelings. The couple are untraditional in that it is David who does the feeling work in this relationship; that is, he takes the initiative to discuss feelings and problems that arise between them. Colleen has difficulty expressing feelings, particularly "negative" ones, which she avoids. In order to compensate for Colleen's avoidance, David does much of the work in this area; because he does the work Colleen does little (the starting point is arbitrary). At the time of the taping they were on a trial separation for three months, planning divorce. They were in individual psychotherapy as well as couple counseling at the time of the interview.

David and Colleen disagree on many topics: financial matters, career decisions, spending leisure time; they are unable to work together on joint projects. When asked to rate their overall satisfaction with the relationship on a 1-10 scale (10 the most happy, 1 the least), David rated 4 and Colleen rated 2. Commenting on their present relationship, David wrote:

> In one respect our relationship is very good in that we as individuals are growing enormously hence creating the groundwork for more successful relationships in our futures. On the other it appears painfully hopeless to resolve at this time.

Colleen also commented on their relationship:

> Friendly but strained. I'm impatient, resentful, gruff. This time apart is helpful for our own individual process of growth. I don't know what the future brings but we are getting stronger as individuals. If we get back together it will be different with more knowledge about who we are and what we need.

David and Colleen chose to discuss the remodeling of their house. They begin with the topic of remodeling, but digress onto a series of tangents: complaints about Colleen's mementos, whether or not Colleen is being responsive to David, whether David has been speaking up, complaints about how Colleen finishes particular projects, David's criticism, whether or not Colleen can do a better job; each topic reminds them of another. They overwhelm each other with constant topic changes, each trying to outdo the other.

Remodeling their house has been difficult: David feels like he has the entire burden of the remodeling; Colleen cannot seem to get involved. As well as being dissatisfied with her inability to get involved, David expresses dissatisfaction with Colleen's collection of "mementos," which he considers superfluous. She says she has decorated with what she has collected, to "make do" with the money they have. Their quarrel has been going on for several years, but they have not been able to reach agreement. Although the quarrel became heated, when asked about its intensity David and Colleen said that at home their quarrels are "more animated." Colleen said it was "more polite because I was conscious of the camera." David described the intensity of feeling when he asked, "What can we tear apart in here?"

During the first five and a half minutes of the quarrel David questions Colleen about her preferences in decoration, and whether she has been satisfied with the outcome: "Are you comfortable with whatever's there?" "What would you really like to decorate with?" "Do you know what you want? "If you know what you want, why haven't you implemented it?" "Why didn't you do something . . . to decorate the way you wanted?" "And that's satisfactory?" The questioning is like testing, since David seems to know the answers already. He's checking to see if Colleen knows the "right" answers. Instead of being direct about his own feelings, he projects onto Colleen by questioning—a form of interrogation. Much of the dialogue consists of this type of questioning, with Colleen trying to answer correctly.

Colleen is drawn into each question, as if it were the first, and tries dutifully to answer each one; of course she answers "incorrectly." She has a fragile sense of self that seems to be dependent on what David thinks; she has difficulty in maintaining her identity separate from him. David seems to push toward separateness, isolating himself from Colleen. Each is unable to step out of frame and comment on the dynamics between them.

The quarrel begins with a comment from Colleen about how hard she has taken David's "criticism and happiness"; she ends her turn with a description of their alienation: "What I'm comfortable with is not what you're comfortable with." Her initial comment is marked by frequent pausing, hesitation, self-correction, and inaudibility.

The lengthy question/answer period lasts 4 minutes, 57 seconds, after which their quarrel begins to escalate. The moment-by-moment analysis below begins at 29 minutes, 58 seconds, and 12 frames, just before the first escalation. This particular segment lasts 2 minutes, 35 seconds. It is divided into four excerpts; the first three are broken down into cues (for dialogue in ordinary language, see the Appendix). In Excerpt 1 Colleen justifies her collection and the way she has decorated:

Excerpt 1

29:58.12	a	C:	... to me ( ) the way that I decorate ( ) is not
	b		*I'm gonna go out I'm gonna (2) you know throw*
	c		*all my (1.2) um (1.9) history away*
	d	D:	umhm=
	e	C:	=things that are **meaningful to me** ( ) *and*
	f		*just start ( ) new (4.4) um*
30:15.20	g	D:	**has it been satisfactory to you ( ) all this**
	h		**time ( ) to:: decorate with your history** ( )
	i		**instead of ( ) MAKING your history** (1.70)
24.19	j	C:	**I'm making my history all the time** ( ) I
	k		*decorate with new things as they come in (4.31)*
	l		**its ONLY JUS::T** beginning (1.35) to=
30:34.21	m	D:	=do you know what I'm ( )
	n		saying do you understand what I'm saying=
	o	C:	=ya/
	p		(2.77) that-you-wanna start ( ) new

WORDS: Colleen 1a-c, e, f

CUES:

(1a) *head tilted away* **looks directly** *pause pause*

(1b) *fragmentation   pause   mitigation   long pause   hesitation*
  long pause   wrinkle forehead

(1c) *controlled face/manner*   **expansion**   *pause   ideation of separation*

(1e) **hostile implication**   *pause*

(1f) *mitigation   pause   long pause*   sweeping hand gesture
  averts gaze   indirect

FEELINGS:
shame; some anger

EXCHANGE:
distract; triangulate; no leveling

Excerpt 1a-f shows ideation of separation by implication: The couple use the language of separation ("me" and "you"). Colleen believes that the things she values are not meaningful to David and have no value to him. Both self and other are in Colleen's focal awareness. Colleen speaks in a calm, almost monotone, voice that is very controlled. Her utterance is marked by a constellation of cues: frequent pauses, hesitation, mitigation, vertical wrinkling of forehead, and so on, suggesting the presence of shame.

The implication of Colleen's utterance also suggests a hint of anger: She implies that David would want her to throw her "history" away (one of his complaints is that there is too much "junk"), and that David is unreasonable. She is not direct about her feelings and does not level; instead she triangles onto the topic of "history," distracting from both her feelings and the relationship between her and David. They are alienated.

While Colleen speaks, David *appears* to be listening. He picks up on her reference to history and uses this idea to add to his repertoire of questions about Colleen's satisfaction with the decor.

His next question is more forceful than the previous, as he repeats it with the added component of history (1g-i). It may seem that David is merely requesting information from Colleen, but his utterance shows disrespect in several ways. David asks, for the third time (28:07.00, 28:13.10) in 2 minutes, if it has been satisfactory for Colleen to decorate the way she has.

Repeating the same question is challenging and shows disrespect (Labov & Fanshel, 1977)—a form of interrogation. One implication might be that Colleen has difficulty in understanding; another could be that David is looking for a certain response (and therefore knows the correct answer). It may be a form of harassment. The cues reveal that David has strong feelings:

WORDS: David 1g-i

CUES:
   (1g) *Gaze aversion   fixed face   question/statement   pause*   **expansion**
   (1h) *pause*   **staccato   singsong**   *pause*
   (1i) **derogatory implication   condescending**   *pause*
      heavy emphasis   critical   *pause   indirect*

FEELINGS:
alternating anger and shame

EXCHANGE:
complaint, distract, triangle, no leveling

Many cues for anger are present, but David does not discuss his feelings directly; he disguises them by questioning Colleen. His question baits a trap: If she says "yes," his reply will be "it hasn't been for me," as he said previously (28:18 and 28:21); if she says "no," he will say "then why don't you do something about it?" as he also said earlier (27:58).

There is further evidence for David's anger; it is expressed in the form of a derogatory remark. He disparages Colleen in utterance 1h-i: "**decorate with your history ( ) instead of ( ) MAKING your history.**" One implication is that Colleen lives in a fantasy world of the past, and that he is above this, as he lives in the "here and now." They grew up in the 1960s and developed values from that era: It is philosophically correct to live in the "here and now." His manner is condescending and his tone contemptuous: 2g-i is said in a staccato manner with an increase in tempo after the last pause; David emphasizes

"MAKING," showing both disrespect and anger. The tone is that of a parent scolding a child. His communication tactics increase the gap between them.

As well as disrespect and anger, lines 2g-i say more about David's feelings. He is not direct, but hides behind a question. Verbal hiding behavior takes form in distraction and denial of his own feelings, attempting to pass responsibility onto Colleen. Aside from verbal cues, there are visual and paralinguistic ones: David averts his gaze and pauses frequently.

How is it possible for Colleen to answer a question that is really a statement, and for which the other person already has a response? It is very difficult for her to respond unless she is able to step out of the frame and comment on it from a distance. When this is not possible, a message disguised as a question is confusing, and is likely to arouse emotion. While David is asking his question Colleen has deep vertical wrinkles in her forehead and averts her gaze as he nears the end of his utterance. David's words have a strong impact on Colleen—the quarrel begins to escalate rapidly:

WORDS: Colleen 1j-l

CUES:
   (1j) *averts gaze* **leans forward** *oversoft* **increased tempo**
         rapid, condensed words *controlled manner* **glare** *pause*
   (1k) *long pause* *averts gaze*
   (1l) **increase volume** **heavy emphasis** *long pause* **tight lips**

FEELINGS:
alternating shame and anger

EXCHANGE:
triangles, no leveling; defensive, alienation

Colleen's response addresses *what* he said (the words), rather than the *manner* or *implication* behind them. She immediately appears defensive, her voice becomes oversoft and her pace quickens: **"I'm making my history all the time."** The language suggests separation: "I" and "you" are used rather than "we," "us," or "our." Neither feelings nor the relationship is discussed.

Colleen's anger can been observed visually: As she speaks softly but in a controlled manner, she leans slightly forward toward David in a challenging stance; her head is tilted downward but her eyes look directly at him from under her brow. There is a very long pause (4.31). She appears powerless to make a strong, direct comment on the insult she just received. From here Colleen's voice picks up volume (**its ONLY JUS::T**), giving a hint of rising anger.

Colleen's manner in turn affects David. As Colleen says: "*I decorate with new things as they come in ( )*," David averts his eyes downward until the end of her utterance (7 seconds), disengaging; perhaps this expresses disrespect toward the speaker as well as hiding behavior. He turns his head away and tightens his lips. Instead of stating their feelings explicitly, they use tactics that insult each other. Neither expresses anger directly by leveling. David interrupts with another question (1m-n).

Again at first glance it may appear that David is asking for clarification, but his impatient and condescending tone, as well as the interruption and repetition of his question, shows disrespect. The cues reflect the feelings:

WORDS: 1m-p

CUES:
David

    (1m) **interruption** *question/statement pause*
    (1n) *still controlled face question/statement* **condescending**
Colleen
    (1o) **tight lips rise and fall of pitch on "ya"**
    (1p) *long pause rapid/condensed words pause ideation of separation*

FEELINGS:
shame-anger alternation

EXCHANGE:
challenging, defensive, disrespectful, alienation

David characteristically disguises his anger in the form of questions for which he already has answers. This could be used as a form of dominance—reducing the other to a child's position. This type of questioning, when not commented on, leaves the other person in a state of confusion (Labov & Fanshel, 1977).

But again Colleen falls into the trap by not commenting on David's manner, instead responding to the ostensible question with her answer, which will inevitably be wrong. "Ya" is said in an angry yet matter-of-fact way; the pitch rises at the end of "ya" then quickly falls, so it sounds like a mixture of a statement and a question. It is followed by a long pause.

Her final statement in Excerpt 1 again implies that her things and herself are not important to him—she thinks he wants to get rid of both. This is her perception of his perception of her things (ideation of how self appears to the other in a negative way). There is a great gap of unspoken feeling that separates them. As before, Colleen's answer to David's question is wrong:

Excerpt 2

	a	D:	**NO!** ( ) *I'm suggesting* ( ) *I'm-I'm (2.71) one-u*
30:50.17	b		*-the uh: (1.95)***bones-u-contention has been** ( )
50.25	c		*for me anyway (1) between us (1.12) from my*
	d		*point-u-view* has been ( ) that **there's just**
	e		**CHACHKAS EVERYwhere** all around the house ( )
31:01.00	f		there's hardly a surface tu put anything down
	g		an **there's no place where the eye can REST**
	h		(3.06) an um (4.87) **not-only that but every**
15.01	i		**little cubbyhole has been** ( ) **jis** ( )
	j		**STUFFED with stuff** *from uh*
	k	C:	**[you think its because ( ) that stuff]**
19.25	l	D:	**HOARDED with stuff of YER history**
	m	C:	**uhhu**
21.25	n	D:	the **stuff from yer past that you've HAU::LED**

    o   **all over the different places we've been ( )**
    p C: *umhm*

Excerpt 2 begins with David's anger: a righteous "NO!" forceful and loud, implying *"Wrong again!" "NO!" is followed by "fluster" patterns: fragmented speech and perhaps disorganized thought. David averts his eyes downward (9 seconds) as he states his "NO!" and "bones-u-contention"; he does not look at Colleen until 30:50.25. Emotion cues expand rapidly:

WORDS: David 2a-h

CUES:
- (2a) **loud** *pause pause fragmentation long pause*
- (2b) *self-interruption filler long pause* **anger code word** *pause*
- (2c) *filler pause self and other focal in awareness long pause*
- (2d) *pause mitigation avert eyes wrinkle forehead* **sequence** *cover face with hand*
- (2e) **emphasis demeaning words** <u>temporal expansion</u> *pause*
- (2f) *gaze aversion*
- (2g) **complaint emphasis**
- (2h) *long pause filler long pause* **extended complaint** <u>expansion</u>
- (2i) *pause mitigation pause*
- (2j) **emphasis derogatory term demeaning criticism** *filler*

FEELINGS:
alternation of shame and anger, with increasing intensity of anger

EXCHANGE:
demeaning complaint, blame, critical, no leveling

The quarrel continues to escalate, and anger words are now being used: "bones-u-contention" ("having a bone to pick" with someone is a slang expression for having cause for a quarrel; *contention* is also about dispute). *Alternation* between shame and anger is suggested by the constellation of cues. David's ideation of perceiving Colleen perceiving him, self-interruption, frequent pause, and diminuendo of his tone as he explains "for me anyway . . . point-u-view" suggests shame. Visual cues include wrinkling of the forehead as he says "for me," hand covering his face and looking down almost simultaneously.

This sequence quickly alternates into further anger, indicated by the derogatory term—calling her things "chachkas" (petty things), trivializing them (David characterizes Colleen's possessions as "junk"). He continues to draw a verbal picture of their living space filled with "stuff." Even if the picture he draws is true, there could be a respectful way of discussing the issue.

While David speaks Colleen's face is unusually still. She leans back in her chair with a faint sneer. As David continues his complaint about every cubbyhole stuffed with stuff, Colleen looks away and tries to interrupt David in midsentence. David's anger continues to increase, while Colleen displays hiding behavior:

WORDS: Coleen & David 2k-p

CUES:
Colleen
  (2k) **interrupt** *indirect statement* *pause* *indifference*
David l, n, & o
  (2l) **heavy emphasis derogatory words** *ideation of separation*
      blame
  (2n) **derogation** *separation* **heavy emphasis**
  (2o) <u>**temporal expansion**</u> **hand gesture for emphasis, sweeping**
      pause
Colleen m & p
  (2m) *indifference minimal response withdrawal* **cutoff**
  (2p) *indifference minimal response withdrawal* **cutoff**

FEELINGS:
triple shame-rage spiral; David—anger prominent; Colleen—shame prominent with hints of anger

EXCHANGE:
demeaning criticism, blame, name-calling, withdrawal

Colleen is affected by David's comment: she interrupts (2k), showing disrespect; she formulates a question of her own, rather than making a direct statement. A characteristic of anger is to assert; a characteristic of shame is to withdraw. Note that Colleen's response becomes minimal during David's attack. Withdrawing from a loved one can also be an attack by rejection. David pays no attention to Colleen's attempt to interrupt, and continues with his attack; he insults her by stating that it is "your" history—*"not ours together as a couple." This illustrates disrespect and anger, as well as separation.

Colleen is particularly quiet during David's long attack; her meager attempt to interrupt is followed by withdrawal. Neither party has acknowledged feelings or manner, nor does either comment on the state of the relationship. They are lost in the topic and seem to have no language to discuss the relationship. The quarrel continues to escalate as David trivializes Colleen's possessions:

Excerpt 3

```
31:25.23 a D: because its (  ) MEMENTOS that mean every little
         b    (1.69) GNA::T an (  ) butterfly (  ) an everything
         c    (inaud)
         d C: [right so there-not they have no meaning to
         e    you]
31:33.10 f D: its not that they don't have (  ) meaning to me,
         g    yes they have meaning to me=
   38.05 h C:                        =I-mean-thas-ok-if-
         i    they-do::n't (  ) if they're my history
         j D: ya=
   40.20 k C: =they don't have tu have any meaning to you
         l D:                                        [hhhh]
         m C: an I can see=
```

WORDS: David 3a-c

CUES:
(3a) *pause* **expansion** trivialize C's things

(3b) *long pause* **derogatory term** *averts gaze* **emphasis** *pause*
     trivializes *pause* <u>**temporal expansion**</u>
(3c) *inaudible   hand to face* **tight lips** *avert gaze*

FEELINGS:
shame-anger alternation, with anger prominent

EXCHANGE:
demeaning criticism, derogatory labels, triangle

Disrespect increases in both words and manner. The image David presents in Excerpt 3 is doubly small: "little" and "gnat." Disrespect is extended by including "everything" into the category; the tension, as well as the derogatory image, illustrates the intensity of David's rising anger. His last words become inaudible when Colleen interrupts in midsentence. As she interrupts (3d), David covers his face with his hand and looks away.

While David speaks Colleen's face is still and controlled. When Colleen interrupts David, her voice is oversoft ("right"), almost inaudible; her speech is rapid and she stumbles over her words:

WORDS: Colleen 3d-e

CUES:
(3d/e) **interruption increased tempo** *self-interruption   oversoft*
       disguised criticism

FEELINGS:
anger and shame

EXCHANGE:
defensive, triangles, alienation

Toward the end of her utterance, Colleen raises her voice but concludes the sentence like a question, with a rising intonation.

The rising volume in her speech hints at emerging anger, but rising intonation gives a hint of uncertainty, rather than a direct forceful statement. Uncertainty and passiveness in the face of a blatant attack exemplifies her powerlessness. This hidden attack also shows disrespect: she tells David *his* thoughts and feelings.

David in turn reacts to Colleen's defensive stance. He covers his face with his hand and averts his gaze, disengaging from Colleen as she speaks. David may have realized Colleen's "hurt feelings" in 3f-g and tries, unskillfully and unsuccessfully, to make amends. Perhaps he feels some remorse for the degrading way that he described her possessions, because he now says they do have meaning to him.

While he speaks, Colleen sits very still, with her lips tight. As David completes his utterance Colleen leans forward in a challenging stance and says, in words, that it doesn't matter; but Colleen is in an emotional frenzy. Her tempo speeds up, she runs her words together. Lines h-k show denial and alienation, similar to the sour-grape syndrome. Colleen verbally denies her feelings; the words say it's okay, that it doesn't bother her if they have no meaning to him, but her gestures (vocal and visual) contradict her words. They imply that her feelings have been hurt. Her sense of self is so dependent on agreement with David, she is ruined. The cues Colleen displays reveal many feelings:

WORDS: Colleen 3h-i

CUES:
> (3h) *attempts indifference*   **fast tempo**   *rapid-condensed words*
> **leans forward**   *mitigation*
> (3i) *denial pause mitigation acts controlled*

FEELINGS:
> shame-rage

EXCHANGE:
> mitigation, attempted indifference; defensive

Colleen could have stood up for herself under the face of this intense attack, but did not. Why does she try to say that it doesn't matter? I suggest that her feelings of shame are predominant over her feelings of anger, rendering her powerless to make a strong statement—the cues also suggest that shame predominates her mood. To protect herself she minimizes her feelings, mitigating the importance of David's caring, and pretends it doesn't hurt: cutoff.

David withdraws both visually and verbally after his attack on Colleen. His reply is minimal, a single "ya," which does not seem to indicate agreement with what she says; he averts his gaze. Colleen continues, repeating the former utterance, that her mementos don't have meaning to David; she denies both damage to the bond and underlying feelings. While her words say that it doesn't matter, her tone reveals a feeling of being hurt: she overtly denies, mitigates, and averts her gaze. The pitch gets higher and the tempo increases. She gives a double message.

David interrupts with a forceful outbreath ("hhhh"), as if he is exasperated or impatient. The communication lines are down; they are indirect, neither makes an attempt to level. Both deny hurt feelings verbally, although manner betrays them. No one comments on manner. Both deny their part in the problems. Their bond is being continually damaged by the *way* in which they discuss grievances—they are alienated. The quarrel continues to escalate in much the same manner, as David justifies himself:

Excerpt 4

```
31:40.20 a D:  =well the thing is I have tu take care of (1)
         b      an HAVE HAD to take care of proVIDING a storage
         c      facility (  ) for all this stuff an it happened
         d      to be (  ) in the environment
         e C:  [hee hee hee]
   50.18 f D:  where I ALSO (  ) abide (1.79) and that's VER::Y
         g      unsatisfactory tu me (1.53)(sniff) an since I'm
         h      having tu be the one that has gone out an had
         i      tu make the MONEY (  ) in order to BUY (1.81)
```

```
32:02.13  j     the material things PROVIDE the material things
          k     ( ) I would have THOUGHT ( ) that ( ) my
                PARTNER
          l     ( ) my mate ( ) would-of been SENsitive to ME::
          m     ( ) in what I:: would require ( ) to make a
          n     comfortable environment (1.82) would-u-been
          o     jist ( ) if I gave the money an bringing it
          p     (2.25) that I would think that you would be
          q     reSPONSive (1.37) to MY needs cause I'm trying
          r     to be responsive to yours
32:31.11  s  C: if you speak UP I would be
```

At this point David could have apologized to Colleen or addressed the manner in which they spoke to each other, or either could have addressed feelings directly before they got out of hand. Colleen could have simply stated that her feelings had been hurt. Instead, they continue to treat each other with disrespect.

David's anger increases as he continues: interruption, raised voice, heavy emphasis, derogatory term, long demeaning complaint. Cues for anger are scattered throughout with shame cues: many pauses, mitigation, self-interruption, ideation of victimization, and lip licking. David blames Colleen for not being responsive, yet does not acknowledge the part he plays. David views himself in relationship with Colleen with the ideation that he has come out with the short end of the stick. Colleen is perceived as a hostile other who will not meet his needs—he is the victim of her maltreatment. His complaint also illustrates his feelings of alienation, of having to go it alone.

As David spews his long complaint, Colleen's face is still and controlled. She displays a tense smile and breaks into a tight laugh when David mentions the storage facility. When Colleen finally speaks, she does not respond to what was said, but instead implies *"Well, it's your own damn fault; you didn't speak up," and that if he had, she would have responded appropriately. She is defensive and blames David in return, denying her part in the problem.

Each partner focuses on the other, wanting the other to change, without asking "What am *I* doing, and what can I do differently?" or "How can I express feelings in a respectful way, without blaming or criticizing the other?" Neither seems to have the skill to level about his or her own feeling or the state of the relationship between them. Neither seems to be sufficiently differentiated to step out of frame.

David and Colleen continue to argue in much the same way in the remainder of the 15-minute quarrel, changing topics several times. Although David's anger is more overt than Colleen's, and shame is more visible in Colleen, toward the end of the quarrel there is a reversal in the dominant emotion for each person. As Colleen's anger becomes forceful and overt (she shouts), David becomes flustered and unsure. The quarrel continues to escalate, ending with the two shouting at each other. Colleen actually threatens to walk out. Although no physical violence occurs, there is considerable emotional violence.

The diverse constellation of cues found in this couple's communication suggests the presence of both shame and anger. David and Colleen are in a *triple shame-rage spiral* (Scheff, 1987): Each is ashamed of being angry, both show disrespect that generates shame and anger in the other, and so on, ad infinitum. Both are equally caught up in the quarrel, both play equal parts in the escalation process. Shame-rage is being perpetuated by derogatory remarks and gestures. Their communication is not direct; neither understands the other.

Summary

David and Colleen are emotionally alienated. The tactics they use to communicate continually cause further damage—the quarrel escalates. Their quarrel is marked by blame, interruption of the other, demeaning criticism, and triangulation. Neither party takes responsibility for his or her own part in the quarrel; neither person levels. Although the quarrel begins with a particular issue chosen for discussion, the topic changes many times. The manner they use becomes increasingly disrespectful.

I characterize David and Colleen's interaction as an interminable quarrel. The quarrel is continuous and chronic, escalating five times in the course of 15 minutes, but marked particularly by the fact that it has been ongoing for at least three years, possibly longer.

Colleen is very uncomfortable with anger, asserting herself, or having a point of view of her own; she is unable to stand up for herself. At the viewing, when asked about asserting her position she commented, "I don't want to be like a man." David seems to be comfortable with anger, but was uncomfortable discussing things they enjoyed doing together. Although David gives the appearance of being sexist, he expressed several times that he would prefer Colleen to be independent, direct, and decisive. But his manner says the opposite; he sabotages this type of behavior when it does occur. The manner they use mutually helps maintains their style of communication.

The conflict is reciprocal; *they are mutually involved in its maintenance.* Their dispute tactics focus on *topics* and ignore the *manner* in which they discuss the topics. David's anger is expressed indirectly (e.g., by questioning and interrogating Colleen), and Colleen is insulted, hurt, and angry; she takes a childlike stance. Colleen's anger is expressed indirectly (e.g., by withdrawing and becoming indecisive), which drives David up the wall. He in turn uses further demeaning interrogation, which in turn leads her to withdraw further.

There is a seeming lack of reflective awareness of their emotional states; they only know they feel bad. This couple continues in the shame-rage spiral throughout the interview. The angry feelings continue into the "positive interaction" phase of the taping. Colleen says "switch" to change topics; David replies, "I'll have to change my entire body chemistry!"

The prevailing emotional dynamics are both shame and anger, each providing stimuli for emotional arousal, perpetuated by the disrespect toward the other and by lack of acknowledgment. While their quarrel began with ideation of isolation, and shame was not unacknowledged, disrespect and anger followed. Each moment of escalation followed the same pattern: alienation → shame → anger → disrespect → and so on. Although other emotions were expressed during the quarrel, shame and anger were predominant.

A follow-up phone call was made a year and a half after the original taping. Colleen and David are divorced, and each is living with a new partner. Colleen is with a man who has a foreign accent, perhaps Iranian. She seemed pleased to get my call and began talking about her new relationship. She sounded unhappy with the relationship, saying it was physically violent (her relationship with David did not involve physical violence). She began to whisper and said she could not talk; a man began shouting in the background, telling her to get off the phone. Colleen seems to have focused her life around another man, defining herself by the relationship. From the phone conversation, it was obvious that they had a clear-cut domination-submission pattern.

David revealed a different story. He said the divorce was difficult for him, that they were divorced in name but had not yet divided up the property they jointly own. He also disclosed that he and his new partner were both involved in a self-help counseling group. He thought it was important that each partner work on personal problems in order to keep up with the relationship, because relationships are so hard.

David and Colleen are unable to regulate distance between togetherness and separateness: David's style is separate, while Colleen needs engulfment to hold herself together. While David moves between isolation and engulfment, Colleen lacks the sense of self needed to maintain separateness; her style, therefore, is almost entirely one of engulfment.

Their relationship is marked by alienation: Each is in a state of shame-rage for almost the entire quarrel, except when they momentarily escape the quarrel, when they exhibit grief (see Chapter 8). The tactics they use perpetuate this emotional state, indicating continual damage to the bond. Although David expresses anger, it is not helpful in resolving the issues between them. In the next chapter, Roxanne and Brian provide a vivid display of emotion and are more direct then David and Colleen; Roxanne and Brian are also able to regulate social distance more productively than David and Colleen, as will be seen.

6 Roxanne and Brian

Quarrel/Impasse Pattern

> Thus they in mutual accusation spent
> The fruitless hours, but neither self-condemning:
> And of their vain contest appear'd no end. (John
> Milton, *Paradise Lost*)

Roxanne and Brian (pseudonyms) have been married for two years. They are a lower middle-class couple with an alternative life-style: They live in a canyon in a small community, where they built their own house, and they model some of their beliefs on those of American Indians. Brian's background is Anglo-Saxon Protestant; Roxanne comes from an Italian Catholic family. They are both high school graduates, and Brian has several years of college. He is self-employed much of the time as an inventor/musician; she is a full-time mother (she states that her occupation is mother/artist). Their income in 1984 was approximately $10,000.

Brian, age 35, has had two previous marriages, with one child (age 7) by the last marriage. Roxanne, age 33, has had a previous marriage, with one child (age 12) by that marriage. They also

117

have one child (age 1) from this marriage. Their relationship seems to centered on their children.

They are traditional in the sense that Brian is the primary breadwinner and Roxanne minds the children and takes care of the house. At the time of the taping she was not employed, although she had been before the baby was born (when the baby was 2 years old she returned to work as a waitress).

Roxanne and Brian have a tumultuous marriage. Roxanne is very emotional, Brian is ultrarational; they have difficulty understanding these traits in each other, each viewing his or her own style as correct. They fluctuate between feeling connected and being isolated; they have loud, tempestuous quarrels during which each feels like giving up on the relationship.

Roxanne and Brian say they quarrel often. The topics of their quarrels involve not showing enough love for each other, sexual relations (being too tired for sex), handling of finances, friends, stepchildren, and household tasks. Their quarrels are characterized by shouting and crying—intense emotion. Although Brian jokes with the interviewer ("Are you gonna stand there to keep us from hitting each other?"), there is no physical violence.

Both are fairly independent in thought and feeling, able to maintain their own thoughts and feelings even in the face of disagreement; they are not destroyed by differences. Roxanne and Brian have separate as well as together identities, although they oscillate between the two extremes. On the happiness scale from 1-10, each claims to be very happy with their relationship (9-10). There is a contradiction between their claimed level of happiness and their comments about their relationship, which are marked by ambivalent feelings. Roxanne comments on their relationship:

> We both feel a lack of respect/untrue. I love him dearly and know that we both have a lot of respect for each other. Before we had each other there was no one we could talk to.

Although Roxanne has a slight complaint about the relationship, she goes on to claim their love and describe how the relationship rescued them from alienation. Brian's tone is somewhat different:

More money, more sex otherwise I'm happy, kids are great!

The quarrel discussed in this chapter involves the division of household duties. Roxanne claims that she does "everything around the house," and complains that Brian leaves his "stuff" laying around all the time. He claims that this is the way the duties have been divided: She does the housework and he does the repairs and building. He claims that it is his right to "take his shoes off" where he "lands"; she complains that it makes more work for her. The following segment was taken from the beginning of the quarrel, where it has already become heated from the process of deciding what to discuss.

A close look at their interaction reveals the details of the emotional system between Roxanne and Brian. The quarrel is divided into five excerpts, four of which include cues (the transcript written in ordinary language is in the Appendix). Brian begins by complaining about Roxanne:

Excerpt 1

```
16:17.05  a  B:  It's the times when you feel like you're the
          b       only soldier on the field ( ) an you come ho-I
          c       come home and you're going OH MAN I've done
          d  R:  [hhh]            [hhh]
  26.20   e  B:  E::VERYthing today I've jis done e:verything
          f       I've dealt with this and that and this and that
          g  R:              [  laugh  ]
          h  B:  and now its YOUR-TURN tu DEAL with it ( ) an
          i  R:  [ah]              [cough]
          j  B:  here take Christopher ( ) an here change his
  36.05   k       diaper an let me eat an give me two
          l       minutes-uh-peace an I'm burned out (2.85)
```

Brian presents a potent image of being alone in battle (separated from the troops). Instead of stating his own feelings of separation in the beginning, he projects them (later in the interview [22:47.10], he says, "Sometimes I feel like I'm the only soldier going out there doing battle with the world"). This ideation of being the only soldier illustrates the extent of Brian's feelings of alienation. The image is about the self in relationship to other, with the self feeling abandoned.

Immediately following this ideation, Brian goes on to a long complaint about Roxanne's complaints that she has to do "everything." His complaint is a caricature of how he perceives Roxanne's behavior. His behavior illustrates how feelings are expressed and exchanged in this relationship—indirectly in terms of the other person's. The cues reveal Brian's emotions:

WORDS: Brian 1a-l

CUES:
- (1a) *indirect avoidance*
- (1b) *ideation of isolation pause self-interruption*
- (1c) **blame whiny, imitative voice heavy emphasis waves arms wildly distorts face**
- (1e) <u>**temporal expansion**</u> **heavy emphasis** *mitigation* <u>**temporal expansion**</u>
- (1f) **imitative criticism expansion**
- (1h) **heavy emphasis twists face** *pause*
- (1j) <u>**triangles in baby**</u> *pause* **demands**
- (1k) **further demands**
- (1l) **complaint** *ideation of victimization tilts head down wrinkles forehead* **leans forward**

FEELINGS:
isolation, to shame, to anger, to alternation between shame and anger

EXCHANGE:
blame, triangulation

Both words and manner show disrespect in Excerpt 1a-l. Brian is speaking for and "at" Roxanne, as well as criticizing and blaming her. He behaves as though the responsibility for the problem were hers: *"You feel like you're doing everything alone, which is not true and you complain as soon as I get home and want me to take over—what kind of a mother/homemaker are you anyway? If you would leave me alone we wouldn't have a problem." In a later exchange (30:30.17-52.22), Brian explains that *he* does not "rag on" anyone and does not deserve to be "ragged on" by Roxanne. He is seemingly unaware of his own "ragging."

They are already entrenched in the quarrel. The words, without the gestures, do not convey Brian's sarcastic, blaming tone. He waves his arms and twists his face in a grotesque manner, whines and emphasizes many of the words, as he imitates his perception of Roxanne's behavior. The words are intensified by the manner, which is disrespectful. His style, usually cool and rational, reveals intense emotion. There is ample evidence for both shame and anger, even though anger is more apparent.

Cues for shame emerge in ideation of isolation and victimization, in projective language, and in an indirect approach. Instead of leveling about his own feelings, Brian projects onto Roxanne, saying what she does and what she feels, rather than speaking in terms of his own feelings. (Perhaps projective language is an attempt to include Roxanne in his state of isolation; that is, he's not the only one who feels like an abandoned soldier.) Through disrespectful tactics he avoids dealing directly with his feelings. This kind of communication creates a gap between them: They are not attuned in thought or feeling; he focuses on her behavior while she focuses on his—they are alienated.

Roxanne has a sharp reaction to Brian's manner. She protests several times in utterances (1d, 1i): "hhh" and "ah." Much of her emotion, at this point, shows up in paralanguage and visual behavior rather than through verbal indicators. She smiles falsely and laughs tensely, exhibiting discomfort as Brian describes her behavior. Roxanne displays a large constellation of cues as Brian speaks:

WORDS: Roxanne 1d, g, i (as Brian speaks)

CUES:
  (1a-c) *false smile   tense laugh   averts gaze*
    (1d) **2 outbreaths** *tense laugh* **guttural noise**
    (1g) *tense laugh*

(1i-k) **deliberate cough   smile fades   tight lips**   *averts gaze*
   (1l) **looks directly   tight lips**   *tight smile*   **tight eyes**   *long pause*

FEELING:
shame-anger alternation

EXCHANGE:
avoid, placate, alienation

Roxanne's emotions rise rapidly. Although initially she displayed a false smile and laughed tightly, her smile fades and she tightens her lips and eyes; she turns her head deliberately and slowly toward Brian, looking directly at him with a long, sharp gaze. When Brian completes his description of Roxanne's behavior there is a 3-second pause during which he looks directly at her, raising his brows in the form of a probing question (*"You know I'm right, don't you?"). Its almost as if he is seeking reassurance about his perception of the situation.

Instead of separating herself from Brian's remark, stepping outside the frame and commenting on it, Roxanne is swept into the quarrel system. She picks up on the *topic*, bypassing comments about Brian's *manner* of presenting the topic. Roxanne displays many shame cues visually and with paralanguage as Brian complains, but reacts verbally with anger:

Excerpt 2

16:43.15 a R: **(2.85) OH I do that every day (2)**
       b B: **Mo::re:: often than not**
  48.05 c R: **Bull <u><shit> (1.75)</u>**
       d B: **More often than not <softer)**
       e R: **[uhuh]**

Immediately they're off on tit for tat, arguing as to whether or not Roxanne behaves as Brian claims. This continues for several exchanges, with intense emotions being expressed and exchanged. Emotion cues multiply:

WORDS: Roxanne 2a

CUES:
long pause (2.83) **exclamation emphasis raise voice**
half question/half statement false smile **temporal expansion**
incongruent words and gestures defensive

FEELINGS:
anger and shame; anger prominent

EXCHANGE:
indirect, sarcastic, no leveling, social disconnection

Roxanne cooperates with Brian in continuing the quarrel. Cues for anger rapidly emerge: raised voice, emphasis, expansion. Incongruence between the words and gestures marks sarcasm. She is not literally saying she does something every day, as it would sound if the emphasis were on "I." By emphasizing "do" and "every," her tone loud, abrupt, and preceded by an exclamation, she gives another meaning to the words: *"If you think I do that every day you're full of shit" (which she intimates in her next utterance).

What began with hiding behavior in Roxanne is followed by cues for anger. While Roxanne speaks, Brian looks away until he verbally responds. The conflict escalates in a tit-for-tat style, as Brian reasserts his position that the description of Roxanne's behavior is emblematic of her style. As he reasserts his position he *looks away,* has a *long pause, softens his voice,* and at the same time he **challenges** Roxanne again: "more often than not."

Roxanne again denies that she behaves as Brian says; she defends her position in an equally disrespectful way. "Bull shit" is accompanied by a *fixed false smile;* she *laughs* the words. Her use of slang carries the implication that what he says is garbage; he doesn't know what he talking about. Brian again reasserts his position that she complains the way he said she does, repeating "more often than not."

There are mutual accusations about who is right and who is wrong. Neither relinquishes his or her position. The tit-for-tat dialogue goes on for four exchanges; they get nowhere. They both believe they are right and the other is wrong. They seem to have forgotten, at least momentarily, the quarrel about who does what in the house, and instead argue about whether or not she behaves as Brian claims she does. They are alienated by their indirect style of communication.

Alternations between shame and rage occur rapidly; each insults the other and perceives the other to be unjust. Hostility is experienced as coming from the other (which it is); disrespect is reciprocated. Both act as though they are right and justified in their complaints: Brian feels he does not deserve to come home and be "ragged on," or to have to have responsibility for domestic duties; Roxanne feels justified because she feels over-worked, and Brian should not make more work for her.

Neither person levels; neither comments on the manner be-tween them. Neither person acknowledges the "hurt," but per-ceives the other as being unreasonable and in the wrong: She rags, he's a slob; if he weren't a slob she wouldn't rag; if she didn't rag, he wouldn't be a slob. Each is angry with the other for the inconsideration shown. Their mutual lack of communi-cation creates a gap between them. Their bond is being dam-aged by the disrespectful ways they treat each other; they appear to be unable to stop the fruitless recriminations.

Brian continues by attempting to justify why he is right, and continues telling Roxanne what she does and what she feels, while ignoring his own feelings and behavior:

Excerpt 3

16:52.05 a B: You're tired ( ) you don't wanna deal with it ( )
         b R: [ya/ I am tired]
         c B: you don't <u>wanna deal with</u>
         d   <u>Christopher ( ) You feel like ( ) YOU'VE</u>
         e R: [nah ( ) not all the time]
58.28   f B: had tu-do everything in the house an pick up
         g R: [hhhhhhh]
17:02.00 h B: everything an clean everything an you SAY::!

Again, Brian does not refer to his own feelings or thoughts, but refers only to Roxanne's feelings, thoughts, and behavior— six times. Brian tries to justify his position. He is speaking for Roxanne rather than for himself. This shows a blatant disrespect as well as denial of responsibility for his own feelings. Roxanne reciprocates disrespect with constant interruption in an attempt to defend and justify herself. Many cues reveal the feelings of each, increasing as the quarrel progresses:

WORDS: 3a-e

CUES:
Brian
   (3a) **blame** *pause* **blame** *pause* **blame** *denial*
Roxanne
   (3b) *false smile* **interruption rise/fall intonation**
Brian
   (3c-d) **blame** <u>**triangulation**</u> *pause* **blame** *pause*
      heavy emphasis *denial*
Roxanne
   (3e) **interruption** *diminuendo pause* *looks away mitigation*
      defensive **rolls eyes**

FEELINGS:
shame-rage alternation

EXCHANGE:
blame, placate, interrupt

Brian's complaint about not wanting to take care of her child went too far. Roxanne displays strong emotion: She mitigates his accusation and changes voice tone (soft and pleading); an outburst follows (Excerpt 4). Although her bond with Brian is being threatened, Roxanne is unable to tolerate threats to her role as mother.

In Excerpt 3a-e Brian's anger is in the fore, while Roxanne's shame is more apparent, although there are cues for each in both parties. Brian continues with his pounding blame; the sense one gets from listening to the tape is a "hammering": "you, you, you." Roxanne continues with attempted indifference, but becomes increasingly angry (forceful exhale—3g) as Brian continues his complaint. Cues for anger increase for Brian:

WORDS: 3f-h

CUES:
 Brian
  (3f) **blame temporal expansion exaggeration**
      denial of responsibility
 Roxanne
  (3g) **tight lips** *false smile* **exhale forcefully** *indirect*
 Brian
  (3h) **continuous complaint temporal expansion blame
      raise voice heavy emphasis draw out end of word** denial

FEELINGS:
 anger-shame alternation

EXCHANGE:
 blame, placate, passivity

Roxanne's attempt to deal with the complaint goes from agreeing that she is tired to mitigating his complaint. Brian persists. When Roxanne's attempts at mitigation fail, she lets out a forceful breath in exasperation. Approximately 3.5 seconds later she has an outburst, and resorts to shouting and name-calling. Her behavior changes to match Brian's, with extensive use of "you":

Excerpt 4

  a R: [YA I] GOTTA PICK up AFTER YOU
  b   ALL THE TIME you're such a SLOB you *jis* take

    c   **your clothes off in the** <*middle*> **of the floo::r**
05.22 d B: **[an ( ) you say that I] ( )   [don't]**
    e   **do any:thing**=

The quarrel begins to escalate; Roxanne's anger rapidly rises:

WORDS: Roxanne 4a-c

CUES:
  (4a) **interruption** *false smile* **raise voice—shouts**
       heavy emphasis   tight eyes/mouth
  (4b) **emphasis   temporal expansion   name-calling** *mitigation*
  (4c) **accusation** *tense laughter   emphasis   false smile*

FEELINGS:
  anger prominent

EXCHANGE:
  criticism, blame, name-calling

While Roxanne begins with mitigating, placating, and other
indirect tactics, she resorts to tactics similar to Brian's—blame,
projection, criticism, and the like—upping the ante with the
addition of name-calling. Roxanne interrupts and shouts over
Brian's last utterance. Her eyes and mouth are tensed as she
calls Brian a "slob." She justifies her behavior and tiredness by
saying it's because of him.

Again, neither person levels, acknowledges or comments on
the state of their bond or their feelings, or shows respect. Brian
does not respond to Roxanne's utterance, but goes on with his
complaint. He displays more discomfort:

WORDS: Brian 4d-e

CUES:
  (4d) *false smile* **interruption** *pause* **blame** *pause* *denial*
  (4e) **temporal expansion**

FEELINGS:
  shame-rage alternation

EXCHANGE:
  blame, criticize

Brian again points his finger at Roxanne (11 times in the first minute). He refers to himself once, in the context of saying Roxanne blames him. Roxanne refers to herself four times, to Brian five times. Roxanne spends much of her time defending herself, but launches into an attack when pushed too far:

Excerpt 5

09.09	R:	**you don't if I don't move** *(R & B slight laugh)*
		your shoes out of the middle of the living room,
		they just stay there, if I don't pick up your
		clothes in the middle of the floor they'll stay
17.06		**there. You'll walk all over them. You'll walk**
		over em when you get home from WORK. Your MESS
		in the CLOSET, its still there you don't put
		ANYTHING away. I fold your laundry and wash it
28.05		**and put it somewhere where you can put it away and**
		you don't put it away. *It's more work for me*
		(slight laugh)
38.08	B:	**I NEVER put it away.**
	R:	**WELL, before OUR parents come you usually tidy**
		up a little.
45.00	B:	**its not the only time ( )**
	R:	**and once in a blue moon, when you get the urge**
		to uh pick up

Roxanne's anger has increased dramatically, alternating periodically with cues for shame, particularly at the end of her utterance. As she explains "it's more work for me," she laughs tensely and displays a false smile; she is uncomfortable in making this assertion.

As Roxanne vehemently complains about Brian's behavior, he displays many cues for shame: He covers his mouth with his hand the first time during the quarrel. On first sight one may think he is just supporting his head with his hand, but in context this does not appear to be the case. First, this is behavior he had not displayed previously; second, it is coupled with tense laughter and smile, oversoft voice, and minimal response, as if he is trying to hide his feelings about Roxanne's attack by minimizing them.

What is interesting is that the couple's behaviors and responses are almost exactly reversed. When Roxanne begins complaining vehemently, Brian displays the same behaviors that Roxanne had when he was complaining. Their quarrel system continues in much the same manner throughout. It submerges at times, only to rise again with a further outburst. The 15-minute time limit ran out with this couple arguing about who does the yard work (see the Appendix).

The quarrel began not with anger, but with ideation of separation and unacknowledged shame; disrespect and anger were quick to follow. Unlike Rosie and James, this couple show disrespect in blatant and only partially disguised ways. Both blame the other; they interrupt each other (72 times in 15 minutes, each interrupting equally), call each other names, imply that the other is not a good parent, and so on. Neither one levels with the other or takes responsibility.

Summary

Of all the couples, Roxanne and Brian claim to be the most happy with their relationship, but have many ambivalent feelings. There is a sense of both connection and separateness in their relationship. Brian does not perceive them as being in it together; he views himself as calm and rational and Roxanne as emotional and irrational, a view Roxanne shares. When things are going well, they report being happy, but when a problem arises they use tactics (blame and expansion) that damage the bond rather than maintain, build, or repair it; they get nowhere in resolving the problem. She claims that she rags on him because he is a slob; he claims things would improve if she didn't rag. Nothing new is said, nothing new is heard, nothing changes. Each wants the other to change first and neither budges.

They share little that is positive about the relationship with each other. During the debriefing, Roxanne commented that the 15-minute segment of "positive" interaction was very nice, that it was something they rarely do together. She told the interviewer at a later date that she tried to get Brian to engage in appreciation of each other at home, claiming that he refused.

Their quarrel shifts from topic to topic: household duties, Roxanne's ragging, Brian's sloppiness, who takes care of the kids, yard work, who is right and who is wrong, who should change first, merit of Brian's sarcasm, and so on. Their style of conflict is characterized by quarrel/impasse: overt angry exchanges followed by impasse. Roxanne and Brian's quarrel appears fierce, in part, because emotion is displayed in all three areas: paralinguistic, verbal, and visual. Roxanne's facial expressions are particularly transparent and expressive; her style is marked by intense emotion display, placating, and name-calling. Brian displays more cues verbally and in paralanguage than he does visually; his tactics include projection, criticism, blame, and sarcasm. Both use expansion. Because of the fluid display of emotion in all three areas, this couple's quarrel appears very crude and vicious, although it was not the most destructive quarrel of those presented here.

Roxanne and Brian display a more equal proportion of cues for shame and anger at the start of their quarrel than do the other three couples. This couple does not seem to be uncomfortable with anger, but seem to be uncomfortable with vulnerable feelings, such as shame and expressions of affection. They appear to use anger and sarcasm to distance themselves from closeness, and from feeling vulnerable. Their comfort with anger does not help them to resolve issues. Expression of anger in itself does not solve problems any more than withholding anger does. Their anger serves to chip away at the bond rather than to create necessary changes in their relationship.

This quarrel illustrates most clearly the cyclic nature of shame-rage. What stands out in this quarrel is that as Brian displays anger, Roxanne manifests cues for shame; when Roxanne displays anger, Brian exudes shame cues. Each person's anger elicits the other's shame, which is experienced as an attack and generates further anger, disrespectfully. Neither person acknowledges his or her own feelings; although there is much overt anger, it is organized around the feelings and behavior of the other person, rather than the individual's own. Both have little awareness of their own manner.

Checking up on this couple a year and a half later, I found that the relationship had changed little. They are still "happy" in the relationship, and although they have the same complaints, Roxanne said Brian was "getting better about helping out." She also revealed that she was no more interested in sex than before, even though she had had a tubal ligation. Despite the many external stressors this couple face in their daily lives (low income, stepchildren, ex-spouses), they seem to be doing fairly well.

Roxanne and Brian have difficulty in regulating their bond. They use the language of disconnection often and view themselves as separate and often as opposing parties. The disrespect they show each other damages their bond and perpetuates the shame-rage spiral between them. Although they use destructive tactics, their selves are more clearly defined than those of the other couples and are not ruined by disagreement from the other person. They are able at times to step out of the frame and to comment on what is occurring and to avoid extensive escalation (see Chapter 8).

Randy and Karin, the couple discussed in the next chapter, are unable to step out of frame or to comment on what is occurring between them. They are swept into engulfment by each other's comments, use increasingly destructive tactics, and continue to escalate the quarrel until they are out of control.

7 Randy and Karin

Repeated Escalation

> Under stress . . . , great gaps open. . . .
> Abruptly the wires are down and
> the nervous pulse under the skin is
> laid bare in mutual incomprehension.
> (Steiner, 1981, p. 44)

The tape of Karin and Randy was used in a study by Gottman and Levenson; it was lent to me by Robert Levenson (personal communication, 1986). I have little background information on this couple. What I gathered from their conversation is that they are both in their 30s, he is a college student, an artist and sculptor, and she is employed as a manager. They are white and appear to be lower middle-class.

Both Randy and Karin are unhappy with their relationship; each is destructive toward the other. Many external pressures affect their relationship, but they are unable to work on the problems as a team. In the videotaped interview Karin comments on their relationship: "can't handle much more devastation in our relationship." Some of the recent disasters include the deaths of two babies (Karin says Randy "semiblames" her for the deaths in a subtle way), the recent death of Randy's mother, as well as a medical problem with Randy's hands that restricts him from his artwork.

They are unable to regulate the distance between closeness and isolation. This couple is isolated, from each other and from themselves. Even during the positive interaction they were unable to support each other socially or emotionally. Randy seemed to have little interest in what Karin had to say. Karin advised and lectured Randy.

Of the four couples examined in this volume, Karin and Randy have the bitterest quarrel. It is characterized by hostile criticism on both their parts. Karin's anger is subtle, emerging in disguised forms, such as innuendo that Randy is sexist. Randy's hostility is very overt, emerging as "character assassination," seen in such comments as "you look . . . you have the same silhouette as a sixty-five year old broad" (10:48.57). Their quarreling is characterized by innuendo, name-calling, blaming, demeaning criticism, interruptions, and other tactics.

The focal point of the quarrel is the weight that Karin has gained: "Since the death of the last baby alone I've gained 80 pounds." Although on the tape Randy appears also to be quite overweight, little mention is made of his weight. During the 15-minute quarrel, they move from topic to topic: who gave whom support, their sex life, Randy's friends, and Karin's father. Each blames the problems they have on the other; neither takes responsibility for the part he or she plays. The bond between them seems to be quite fragile, and their manner of communicating grievances damages it further. This quarrel escalates 8 times in 15 minutes, ending with cursing and a very high level of anger between them.

The quarrel is already in process from the beginning of the mention of the topic. This seems to be the type of quarrel in which each knows what the other will say, and knows that it will be futile, but neither can stay out of it. Nine excerpts are included to show the patterns at points of escalation; three excerpts are broken down by cues (the transcript in ordinary English appears in the Appendix). The quarrel begins with Randy cautiously bringing up the topic:

Excerpt 1

05:10.60 a R: So yer brother Joseph ( ) was gonna talk to me at one
         b   point in time *(3.75) ya-remember* you were gonna tell
 21.63 c   me that *uh (2.60)* he's saying that *um (1.25)*
         d   men in ( ) *what S::amoa or something*
 26.35 e K: **Jamaica**
         f R: In Jamaica ( ) would prefer ( ) overweight women
 30.65 g K: **they-don't preFER-it they jist accEPT it** (1.69)

The feelings are high at the start of the quarrel. Karin is
fidgety (frequent gaze aversion, directing attention to a dog
lying on the floor)—behavior she did not display while discussing events of their day; she is uneasy with the topic of her
weight. Randy displays covert feelings, seen in the many cues:

WORDS: Randy 1a-d

CUES:
  (1a) *averts gaze   lean away   hesitation   triangle   pause*
  (1b) *lean away   long pause*
  (1c) *filler   long pause   filler   averts gaze   long pause   hesitation*
  (1d) *averts gaze   pause   hesitation   mitigation   generalize*

FEELINGS:
  shame state

EXCHANGE:
  cautious avoidance, triangulation, maintain bond

Randy starts by bringing up a third person, Karin's brother;
triangling is used as a diversion to avoid feelings, increasing
the distance between them. Instead of talking about what is
going on with each other, they focus on third parties. By avoiding being direct, Randy seems to be maintaining the bond at a
certain distance, a tactic in which Karin colludes. He pauses
after he says "one point in time," giving Karin a cue to speak.

Karin ignores the cue, closes her eyes, shakes her head affirmatively, but subtly, and averts her gaze; she relinquishes her turn, avoiding the topic and possibility of changing the emotional distance.

Randy's first utterance gives no clues for anger, but there is hiding behavior: caution, hesitation, and attempt at casualness or indifference. Indifference is a state of bypassed shame, "it succeeds in warding off feelings of humiliation in the self and it can succeed in evoking them in others" (Lewis, 1981a, p. 12). Randy also denies responsibility for his involvement in their problems. They had discussed this topic previously and they both knew what Karin's brother said to Randy about other cultures' perception of *overweight women*. Randy also knows the potential unpleasantness involved.

As Randy speaks (1a-d, and during the 3.75-second pause) Karin displays much emotion. She does not take the cue Randy gives to her to speak, although she nods her head slightly. She gives up her turn and relinquishes control. Refusal to engage and withdrawal from interaction are accompanied by hiding behavior, which lasts the entire duration of Randy's speaking turn: gaze aversion, false smiling, fidgeting, vertically wrinkling forehead. To be overweight in our culture (particularly for women) is often stigmatized. We can assume that Karin is already in a state of shame about being overweight; the topic serves to intensify this state. Her silence and withdrawal not only mark shame, but shows anger and disrespect. Withdrawal can be interpreted as passive aggressive and hostile; she leaves Randy hanging with the immediate responsibility for the discussion.

After the long pause Randy continues to speak, cuing her further: "ya-remember . . ." (2.60); Karin looks down and smiles tightly, avoiding involvement, even visual involvement, with Randy. Randy pauses and stalls as he tries to engage Karin in the topic of weight. Karin continues to avoid bringing up the topic. Karin is already affected before she begins to speak; anger first appears in Karin vocally as she corrects Randy's error (1e-f):

WORDS: 1e-f

CUES:
  Karin
    (1e) *averts gaze* **whine** **other correction** *minimal response*
       withdrawal *fidgets* **tight mouth**
  Randy
    (1f) *pause hesitation pause question/statement indifference*

FEELINGS:
  K: alternating shame-anger
  R: shame

EXCHANGE:
  K: increases distance
  R: attempt to repair bond, cautious, avoiding

Karin whines the word "Jamaica," which is indicative of "helpless anger" (Labov & Fanshel, 1977). Anger is present in her correction: *"You are mistaken—it was not Samoan women, but Jamaican." One implication of Karin's correction might be *"I am correct, you are wrong," or one-upmanship (she imparts an air of moral superiority over Randy throughout the interview). She averts her gaze as she corrects Randy. Karin helps damage the bond by showing disrespect in her matter-of-fact correction with the tone *"Any fool would know it was Jamaica and not Samoa."

Randy attempts to repair the bond as he readily corrects himself, completing his idea with attempted indifference. He pauses before he says the word "overweight"; he ends his sentence with a question, as if asking for a go-ahead, or reassurance about discussing the issue. Karin does not give either, looks away while he speaks, and corrects Randy's error again, displaying increased anger cues:

WORDS: Karin 1g

CUES:
  averts gaze **other correction** staccato heavy emphasis <u>whine</u>
  heavy emphasis *long pause* *averts gaze*

FEELINGS:
  shame-rage alternation

EXCHANGE:
  triangle

In Excerpt 1g Karin and Randy are not talking about "other" women. She digs into Randy, implying that *he* doesn't accept her weight gain—not that he should prefer it but *he* should accept her despite the weight. She strikes out by correcting Randy at each opportunity, as if attacked by him. Karin is disrespectful toward Randy, as if he were putting her down in some way in the present. She appears to be acting in accordance with past experience and future expectations, rather than in the present interaction.

Although Randy does *not appear* to be showing hostility in Excerpt 1 (and in fact *appears* to be polite), later in the interview he blatantly denies responsibility and puts Karin down in the most hostile and demeaning ways. Each seems to know what the other will say, and how the other will respond, but cannot keep from quarreling. Even though neither party seems to want to quarrel, it is almost uncanny how they are drawn into it. Karin continues putting Randy down in a disguised way:

Excerpt 2

```
05:35.00  a  K:  jis-tryin-tu-say-that Madison avenue type (.85)
          b      stereotype ( ) of what American women should look
   40.49  c      like (2.00) I mean-jis ALL
          d  R:  umhm
   46.90  e  K:  right now (1.8) (inaud) what Madison avenue thinks
          f      women should look like-hhh I mean not all women are
          g      ( ) five ( ) feet six inches high ( ) I-mean tall an
```

	h		*you know* weigh 123 pounds (1.10) there's a lot of
	i		women because they weigh 160 or because *they weigh*
59.60	j		*250 are not acceptable* because they're overweight ( )
06:03.00	k		but *society doesn't accept them (1.05) yer not*
	l		*accepted on job interviews yer not accepted*
	m		*(1.06) you know with MO::ST ( )* **so called**
	n	R:	*umhm* [*uhm*]
11.20	o	K:	**elitist-type men** *an stuff so (1) who-***who needs it**
	p		*(1.3) an if yu* happen tu have gained weight because
	q		*you've* got problems in *yer* life then *yu* gain weight
	r		because *you* got problems in yer life *that-doesn't-*
	s		*mean-yer any less of-a-person ( )*

Karin is off in a frenzy of feeling as soon as "overweight" is mentioned. She seems to know that the quarrel will take a nasty course, how it will proceed, and that she will be blamed. By briefly moving into future excerpts it becomes clearer why Karin attacks Randy. Just 8.3 minutes later, Randy completely denies any responsibility for their problems, assuming that the responsibility lies entirely with Karin:

13:53.00	K:	. . . that sex isn't the greatest,, could any of it
		be your fault
	R:	NO
56.62	K:	NONE of it
	R:	uhuh
	K:	none of it in BED was your fault it was all my
		fault that it wasn't the greatest (1.8) ya see
		what yer saying
	R:	ya I do ( ) and that's what I'm saying
		. . .
14:10.00	K:	wel-I mean but let's be honest about it ( ) I'm
		THAT horrible in bed tha-and yer that exciting
		( ) is that what yer saying
	R:	umhmm

Randy's self-righteous attitude may help account for Karin's behavior in Excerpt 2. He assumes that if only *she* would just lose weight *everything* would be better:

15:00.52 K: [cause all that stuff] (their problems) would
disappear? yer gonna care more if I weighed
a hundred an twenty-five
03.92 R: [HELL:: YA]

Returning to Excerpt 2a, Karin now includes "Madison Avenue" stereotypes, society not accepting overweight, job inter-
viewers, elitist men; she also uses second person ("you") rather
than first person in her description. These are all important
social issues about the stigmatization of overweight people that
need to be addressed. But at least for the moment there is also
a subtle world of gestural interaction occurring between Karin
and Randy that is being ignored: Their manner toward each
other and their emotions are not being addressed. Karin's message reveals isolation and intense emotion:

WORDS: Karin 2a-s

CUES:
- (2a) *mitigate avert gaze rapid/condensed triangle pause*
- (2b) **hostile** *pause avert gaze lean away fidget triangle*
- (2c) *long pause justify mitigate* **emphasis** <u>expansion</u>
- (2e) *avert gaze fidget fragmentation long pause inaudible lax articulation triangle*
- (2f) *avert gaze* **forced outbreath** *justify generalize pause*
- (2g) *pause avert gaze pause self-correction avert gaze filler*
- (2h) *long pause fidget avert gaze generalize triangle*
- (2i) *avert gaze fidget wrinkle forehead*
- (2j) *wrinkle forehead pause ideation isolation*
- (2k) *wrinkle forehead ideation isolation pause avert gaze ideation isolation emphasis*
- (2l) *avert gaze ideation of isolation*
- (2m) *long pause filler avert gaze* **heavy emphasis** *pause* **hostile implication**
- (2o) **heavy emphasis** *avert gaze generalize filler pause oversoft repetition denial pause*
- (2p) *avert gaze denial* **blame**
- (2q) *avert gaze* **heavy emphasis**

(2r)   *avert gaze*
(2s)   *ideation of being insignificant   pause*

FEELINGS:
shame-rage alternation (shame prominent)

R: becomes very uncomfortable as K begins to talk about rejection

EXCHANGE:
triangles, avoidance, blame

Excerpt 2a-s provides a massive constellation of cues (visual, paralinguistic, and verbal), with the ideation of being "less of a person" and "unacceptable." Excerpt 2 also points to increasing anger. Karin insults Randy by implying that he is like "elitist-type men" (she looks directly at him as she says this). Anger cues include whining, heavy emphasis, and implication (Randy is one of them).

Karin's anger is covert. She is not direct; she does not level with Randy. She acts as if she is not talking about Randy, but about everyone else. Karin continues with an air of moral superiority. She does not prepare or warn Randy that she is going to change the subject from Jamaican men to Madison Avenue women, but springs it on him, like an act of guerrilla warfare. This marks flagrant disrespect and hostile, covert anger.

During Karin's long vocalization Randy's response becomes minimal, as if he is politely listening to her (he is not a person who is at a loss for words). Visually he becomes uneasy: He scratches his chin, covers his mouth (28.84), leans away, and averts his gaze until the end of Karin's exchange. Randy has a strong emotional reaction in Excerpt 3.

Excerpt 3

06:25.87 a R: *(4) YA we::ll ( ) (long sigh) (8.26)*
  34.38 b K: **ya-well-wha** *(3.70)*
       c R: *ya but I hesitate ta get into this at all I ( )*

```
         d  K:  well
42.30    e  R:  ([AHH!] -guttural noise) (  ) cause I (3)
         f      you know I don't wanna (  ) get into yer (  )
         g      character assassination but I usually do (3.20)
58.80    h  K:  you-don't-have-tu say anything SUPER personal
                but
```

Randy becomes more hesitant, Karin challenges him, and he explains his hesitance, displaying a constellation of cues:

WORDS: 3a-b

CUES:
Randy
  (3a) *hand over mouth avert gaze long pause hesitation mitigation
  pause avert gaze* **long sigh** *long pause*
Karin
  (3b) **tight eyes/mouth challenge direct gaze** *wrinkle forehead
  rapid/condensed words avert gaze fidget long pause*

FEELINGS:
  R: shame
  K: anger-shame alternation

EXCHANGE:
  avoidance, challenge

In Excerpt 3a Randy no longer tries to repair the bond, but hesitates about getting into battle. There is a sigh that seems to be a precursor to going into the battle he knows is inevitable. There is an unusually long silence (8.3 seconds) that conveys reluctance.

As Randy speaks in 3a, anger flashes across Karin's face as her eyes and mouth tighten, followed by a gaze aversion a fraction of a second later, followed by another anger expression 1 second later as she begins to speak (3b). Karin has taken more than 8 seconds to respond to Randy's last utterance. When she finally does respond she challenges him. As she speaks she displays a constellation of anger and shame cues. They both hesitate as Randy explains his reluctance (3c, e, f, g).

WORDS: 3c-h

CUES:
  Randy
    (3c) *avert gaze* **whine** *pause*
  Karin
    (3d) *false smile* ⎫
         lick lips ⎬ sequence
         avert gaze ⎭
  Randy
    (3e) *avert gaze* **harsh sound** *pause* *long pause*
    (3f) *filler* *pause* *pause*
    (3g) **violent image** *long pause*
  Karin
    (3h) *false smile* *wrinkle forehead* *ideation of exposure* *mitigation* *fidget* *avert gaze*

FEELINGS:
  R: shame-rage alternation
  K: shame

EXCHANGE:
  reluctance, avoidance, indirect, alienation

Until now Randy has not displayed anger cues. They begin to appear as Randy explains why he does not want to argue: He already thinks he knows what will happen—he will assassinate Karin's character. Karin also hesitates, displaying a sequence of cues for shame, one following and blending into the previous. Karin tries to diminish the threat of getting too personal (3h). Randy pays no attention to her suggestion. In Excerpt 4 Randy reacts to what Karin said in Excerpt 2 and explains his grounds. (Excerpts 1-3 gave the gist of the analysis; Excerpts 4 to 9 will not be broken down by cues, but accentuated only through use of boldface and italics.)

Excerpt 4

```
        R:                          [but] ya have
                    tu understand that-*ah um (2.40) if-uh-you-know-*
07:02.00            *tha-tha I mean* yer living with one of the most anti-
                    social men in the world (1.50) that anything that
                    society would do I would AUTOmatically try to find
                    a a completely different way tu go about anything
   13.30 K: **but NOT when women are concerned**
        R:                    [but you also] *we-* **that's not true**
   17.50 K: **ya it is**
```

In Excerpt 4 Randy interrupts Karin, showing disrespect. He has taken what Karin said in Excerpt 2 personally. Randy is insulted by Karin's implication that he is an "elitist-type man," like the rest of society in how he treats overweight people. Randy tries to explain his grounds and that he is antisocial; he defends himself. Karin challenges Randy further (07:13.30); they are off, tit for tat. Randy attempts to maintain the bond at a distance; Karin continues to attack.

Even though Randy said he did not want to get into Karin's "character assassination," he cannot stay out of it. Excerpts 5-9 are episodes of angry escalation, each more intense than the preceding one. In Excerpt 5, Randy bursts into a furor of anger:

Excerpt 5

```
        R: **it's not true** *I mean* (  ) I think *every* man has their
07:21.29    dream woman (  ) *every* man has th-their dream nuh
            silhouette (  ) dream (  ) shape (  ) *you know uh* dream
            eyes *uh:: you know* **whatEVER (2.35) and um (3.15)**
            **an I I hate tu put it you this uh you know I hate**
            **tu (2.62) to always harp on the same stuff but-tuh**
            **(2.75) I mean** at your weight now: *(2.35)* **you're**
   50.36    **just not doin-it for me** *(2.50) and uh (4) I know*
            *that it's been really shitty* of me *to (2.10)* **not**
```

```
08:00.00      touch you and not be romantic with you an not
              (2.50) sometimes even be kind to you (2.10) but uh
              (3) I don't-know-yu-know it started out about
   15.50      about a year ago that uh (  ) yu know I I suddenly
              felt very very hemmed very frustrated by it
              (3.53) and tu begin with if (  ) we're both down to
   33.17      our proper weights (2.59) sex would be much better
```

Cues for anger multiply and are now alternating rapidly with shame. A characteristic feeling associated with shame-rage is that the situation is endless or hopeless. At 4 minutes and 18 seconds into the quarrel Randy expresses this feeling: **"this one seems like a never-ending one (2.75)"** (09:17.51). The quarrel continues to escalate in intensity. The level of anger is high (boldface) in Excerpt 6:

Excerpt 6

```
09:39.03  R:  you have you you have tu lose some weight
   41.30  K:  I agree but the support from you should come=
          R:                                            =I gave
              you five years of support=
   46.31  K:                                   =can't say that
              because I mean obviously
          R:      [with every damn diet]
   48.40  K:  I wasn't getting ENOUGH support or I wouldn't have
              gained all this weight
   51.90  R:                      [well] then you would need to have
              married FIFTY men and had them all sort of u u u
   55.50  K:  that's not fair <softly)
          R:  telling you that "you kin do it, you kin do it" the
              support doesn't necessarily jus come from without (  )
              there' a million
10:03.90  K:  [I wouldn't]
          R:  times you walked up to the corner tu Swensen's an I
    8.20      asked you (  ) leave the damn ice cream alone (  ) an
              you would get an ice cream cone tu spite me
   13.50  K:  ya but the support doesn't come in telling me not
              what tu eat but realizing that I have some problems
              an I'm internalizing em is where the support an YOU
              should come in
```

23.34 R: *ya but I can't get into yer mind*
      K: *well I-I you know I ( )* **fairly read you well**
29.52 R: *well* **I fairly read you well** *too* and *it it and I*
          don't know I don't know what's going on it seems
          like ( ) I mean **we're both gonna be sixty-five**
          someday *( )* an **I'm not going** *to you know* I'm not
          gonna *( )* **mind livin with a sixty-five year-old**
          broad when I'm sixty-five ( ) but we're in our
          thirties
48.57 K: *I don't think I look like I'm sixty-five*
      R: *(clears throat)* **you have the same silhouette as**
          a sixty-five-year-old broad
53.71 K: that doesn't matter

Randy and Karin argue about where the weight problem originated. She complains that it stems from lack of support; he claims that he has given her support. Complaints and countercomplaints are exchanged; each sees the problem as the fault of the other person. They are in a blame-blame cycle.

At 10:23.34 intense escalation occurs in less than a minute as Randy responds to Karin's complaint: *"ya but I can't get into yer mind"* (ideation of separation)—they are alienated. Karin responds with one-upmanship *"well I-I you know I ( )* **fairly read you well."** She starts out with repetition, hesitation, pausing, but finishes with a comparison between herself and Randy in which he comes out deficient. She says that she is *able* to do something he is *unable* to do—she can understand and he can't.

This seems to affect Randy intensely, because his next response (10:29.52) is defensive and dense with shame cues: gaze aversion, repetition, fragmentation, and self-interruption—all indicative of disorganized thought processes involved in shame states. Escalated anger rapidly follows, as he ups the ante by saying Karin looks like a "sixty-five-year-old broad." His intense verbal attack is preceded by a constellation of shame cues, as it is in each instance of escalation. His words and manner humiliate Karin, who responds defensively, and so on. In Excerpt 7 they blame each other further:

Excerpt 7

14:21.61 K: *(laugh)* yu see yer not even FACING the problem
             an maybe that's where the problem lies
   24.78 R: [what do you mean] not no
             no see the problem is (1.63) jis-visualize ( )
             you at a hundred and twenty-five
   31.59 K: EVEN IF I WEIGHED a hundred
             and twenty-five we'd still have a problem in bed
   32.63 R: [wait a second I'm not finished talking] that's
             not true ( ) <u>what kind of a problem would we have</u>
   38.40 K: the same problem we have NO::W because of the way
             you ARE
         R: what do you mean that I don't kiss you
   43.97 K: <u>you don't yer not really</u>
         R: [that I] don't that I don't get
   46.21   <u>into</u> foreplay that I don't get into um:: being kind
             an an <u>um being uh</u> ( ) watchful for your own *um* ( )
         K: *[laugh]*
         R: *yu know* climaxes an yer own ( ) *uh*

Their quarrel is out of control. Overt anger now predominates, whereas earlier unacknowledged shame was in the fore.
Each blames the other for the problem. Randy continues claiming that the problem is Karin's weight. Karin now says that
Randy doesn't face the problem, which will not end if she loses
weight because it is Randy's denial that causes the problem.
They begin to interrupt and criticize each other more frequently
and vehemently, both showing greater disrespect than previously. Randy has become unnecessarily personal, publicly
revealing details of their sex life. Neither person levels, and
neither comments on the manner or the state of the bond. The
tactics they use erode the bond between them. Another episode
of escalation occurs a minute later:

Excerpt 8

16:40.49 R: . . . simply because **I don't want tu kiss you or spend
             time kissing you** *doesn't mean* **I don't like YOU** ( ) *yu
             see* **you got that backwards**
   50.06 K: [yes it does]=

```
        R:                        =no you got that backwards ( )
                    what that means is ( ) is that I don't like yer FACE
54.40               ( ) right now ( ) I mean it used tu be that had some
                    actual lips ( ) NOW::yer there's-ther there's very
17:01.31 K:                        [you don't have any upper lip]
        R:  little definition
        K:  don't talk about my lips
```

The topic is seemingly trivial, but the argument is expressed with great vehemence. They continue to interrupt each other, showing increased signs of anger. They use tactics that humiliate and blatantly insult the other. Their defensiveness turns to offensiveness.

The quarrel escalates to include Randy's friend (e.g., K: "look at Kevin and his relationship . . . he's entering his fourth marriage; his ideal of women is only looking through the magazines and not caring about their character") and Karin's father, putting the friend and father down in demeaning and hostile ways:

Excerpt 9

```
19:57.12 R:  I don't know how the hell you were raised that way
             I mean your father is the mo-is the biggest liar ( )
             I mean you could ask yer father what day it was . . .
```

Third-party involvement (triangle) draws them further from each other and away from the source of the problem. The manner each uses toward the other is never addressed—each is isolated in thought and feeling. If the actual outside parties were to get involved personally, polarization could build into tribal warfare (Neuhauser, 1988).

The level of anger and hostility became very high as the 15-minute session came to a close. When a timer signaled the end of the session, Randy could not stop; he finally ended with the line, "**GOD DAMN KARIN** *I'm jis gonna go the rest of my life with* . . . ," indicating that shame-rage is still present, and demonstrating the hopelessness and helplessness about the situation that these kinds of feelings can bring.

Each incident of escalation brings the quarrel to an increased level of anger; the increase in anger parallels the increase in shame. Anger and disrespect serve as a defense against vulnerability. As long as they both continue to deny their own part, their own responsibility, and try to change the other, the situation will feel hopeless.

Summary

Randy and Karin's conflict clearly characterizes the escalation phenomenon: Their conflict escalates out of control; anger increases rapidly in intensity, frequency, and duration. Although the quarrel begins with Karin's weight, it moves rapidly from topic to topic; each new topic follows an increase in shame and precedes increased anger. The rapid change of topics shows disrespect; it is used to blame, to overwhelm the other, and serves to avoid feelings and connection with each other.

Although anger is readily visible and increases rapidly, this quarrel began with manifestations of shame rather than anger. Initially cues for shame increased while the anger was held under control. But with increasing shame and no acknowledgment, disrespect increased. If we trace sequences of events within and between persons, certain patterns emerge: Alienation and unacknowledged shame preceded disrespectful anger.

Throughout the quarrel the bond is being damaged. Except for the start of the quarrel, there are no moments of repair. Their is a great gap of emotional distance between Karin and Randy. Perhaps Karin uses her weight to avoid closeness with Randy, to keep him at a distance. The weight may be an indirect way for Karin to express anger, to "fluff her feathers," because she feels so powerless in the face of their recent tragedies and lack of support. Each party is unable to acknowledge feelings. Both lack ability to talk about relationship issues.

Randy and Karin's quarrel is the bitterest of the four presented here. Randy's anger is overt, marked by demeaning criticism and put-downs of Karin; Karin's anger is covert. Karin and Randy's use of triangles keeps them at a distance from each other. Putting the distance of a third person or object between them can be seen as an attempt to reduce the amount of feeling and to avoid closeness.

This particular couple had a large constellation of shame cues preceding the escalation, more than the other couples. Randy's demeaning outbursts are proportional to the amount of shame prior to the outburst. As he displays shame, so does Karin. Both Randy and Karin are very vulnerable in their relationship. Both seem to be uncomfortable with the expression of feelings: Randy displays emotions in disguised verbal statements and in paralanguage, while Karin is mainly visual—neither is respectfully direct.

Randy and Karin's conflict appears to be the type that could lead to physical violence: Their bond is fragile. As shame increases and is not acknowledged, anger increases proportionally, expressed as demeaning criticism aimed at the other. Max Scheler (1961) notes in *Ressentiment* that "a hatred that cannot content itself with revenge . . . seeks its satisfaction in the deeper injury of making the enemy blush with shame" (p. 71). This seems to characterize Randy and Karin's relationship. Under these conditions outbursts become quite intense.

Neither party acknowledges feelings in a constructive way; the two are alienated from each other and unable to regulate the distance between them. Randy creates distance by withdrawing affection. Karin does not acknowledge her shame about being overweight and, degraded by her husband, instead separates herself emotionally from Randy, perhaps by gaining excessive weight. They are both in a state of unacknowledged shame, and both express their anger in ways that destroys the bond further: through blame, demeaning criticism, and withdrawal of affection. Their attacks serve only to reinforce each other's isolation.

PART THREE

The Social Bond

8 Repairing the Bond

> Given the universality of the emotions
> of shame and anger, and the part that
> rituals of respect play in personhood,
> the need for loving respect . . . is a key
> feature of all social interaction. (Scheff,
> 1987, p. 146)

This chapter examines episodes of deescalation and bond repair. If protracted conflict stems from damaged bonds and
unacknowledged shame, is it possible to resolve conflict by
reversing this process? If so, how can damaged bonds be repaired? Instances of deescalation will be used to examine the
reduction of conflict; this will be dealt with from two points of
view: two-party systems and third-party intervention. In a
two-party system repairs can be made by the participants themselves. A third party can also introduce tactics that help the
disputing parties reduce conflict.

The earlier chapters explored emotional communication
and how interaction can go wrong. By implication, interaction can go right by reversing the dynamics that lead to conflict. Repair of damaged bonds involves processes opposite
those that cause damage to bonds: (a) face-saving (respectful

tactics); (b) acknowledgment of feeling and the state of the bond; (c) awareness of interacting systems—within persons, between persons and social networks; (d) understanding the source of impasse by tracing sequences of emotion; (e) establishing a secure base for exploration—an intact bond.

The conventional term for conflict reduction is *resolution*; rather than this usage, I prefer *repair of the bond*. While resolution can take place in the moment and agreement can be reached, the underlying patterns at the source of the conflict may remain unchanged. Repairing the bond involves broadening the framework of communication between persons. When bonds are intact, conflict can be dealt with constructively by changing the system.

I examine two types of repair: spontaneous deescalation in two-party systems and deescalation as a result of third-party intervention. In two-party systems there is no intervener; the course of the conflict changes spontaneously or through conscious effort on the part of the interacting parties. A spontaneous moment of deescalation occurred in David and Colleen's quarrel, and the anger was reduced. Although it was short-lived, there was a dramatic change in mood.

Third-party intervention is explored using three cases from several sources: self-viewing, psychotherapy, and mediation. Rosie and James gained insight by viewing themselves on tape; Mariel and Anna, a violent couple in psychotherapy (Lansky, 1980), and Joan and Paul, a couple in mediation (Saposnek, 1983) are used to show some components of deescalation. In each case conflict is reduced as a result of intervention. These episodes involve heated quarrels that are abruptly reduced— the mood changes considerably.

I begin the discussion with a comparison of David and Colleen with Roxanne and Brian that shows the role of poorly differentiated selves in conflict. The comparison illustrates how each couple copes with the balance between togetherness and separateness. This balance plays a significant role in the perpetuation of conflict because it can be a source of strong emotion. What is it that kept Roxanne and Brian's quarrel from escalating, while David and Colleen lost control?

A BRIEF COMPARISON OF TWO CASES

I suggest that the bonding system between Roxanne and Brian is more flexible than that between David and Colleen because Roxanne and Brian have more clearly defined selves (see Figures 2.1 and 2.2 in Chapter 2); they are able to regulate the distance more flexibly. In other words, Roxanne and Brian are more differentiated, and are able to tolerate differences without losing their bearings. David and Colleen have little tolerance for differences and are unable to move between closeness or separateness; they are either in a state of engulfment or in isolation. Unlike David and Colleen, neither Roxanne nor Brian feels ruined by disagreement.

It happened that in both marriages, as the couples were discussing what they enjoy doing together, each wife said to her husband that she liked to go out for dinner, and each husband opposed this idea. Just before the discussion of eating out, both couples had been discussing their enjoyment of nature and the outdoors, which both husbands supported. Both couples have the 1960s ideal that nature takes precedence over material values. The couples took distinct courses in how they dealt with their differences. Roxanne and Brian:

```
 1  R:  (clears throat) um (  ) I like going out to dinner::
 2      (laughs)
 3  B:  see look that's civilized that's civilized comforts again=
 4  R:                                                          =w-
 6      well it's not we don't do it that often so I enjoy it
 7      when we do
 8  B:  [inaud] great (  ) where ya taking me out-tu dinner
 9      tonight
10  R:  the Thai foods (  )
11  B:  goo::d OK=
12  R:             =OK
13  B:  yer treat
14  R:  yep
```

Although Roxanne seems a little embarrassed (she clears her throat, laughs, and looks sheepish) about bringing up the topic, she and Brian maintain eye contact and an even tone of voice as they speak. Eating out was not one of Brian's favorite things to do, but he was not rigid about it (line 3). Roxanne sticks to her position with an assured tone (lines 6 and 7); she likes to eat out, regardless of Brian.

Neither Roxanne and Brian's bond nor their identities are completely dependent on agreement; they are not engulfed. Their self-boundaries and bond are intact enough that they are able to negotiate differences—he is willing to have Thai food, especially if she treats. Differences in one party do not threaten the other, which shows their ability to cope with separateness without feeling destroyed. Their bonding system is flexible, they are somewhat differentiated. Roxanne and Brian were able to find a solution to their difference.

Roxanne and Brian deal well with the separate aspect of their relationship, but do have difficulty with the together aspect. Roxanne reported that it was rare for her and Brian to talk about positive events in their relationship (a topic that brings them too close for comfort), but she had enjoyed the positive interaction so much in the laboratory that she had tried to get Brian to repeat this exercise at home; Brian would not cooperate. One of their complaints as a couple is not showing enough affection.

David and Colleen are unable to work out a solution to a similar problem; Colleen appears to be ruined by opposition from David:

```
1  C:  (inaud) (L) I enjoy going out to dinner you know (  ) nice
2       romantic dinners (  ) or (  ) breakfast or (L) um (inaud)
3  D:                                          [not so much]
4  C:  yes <oversoft—almost inaudible)
5  D:  no I wouldn't say so
6  C:  yeah (  ) we like going out for dinners
7  D:  yeah we might like going out well I mean but that's not
8       something that we both really (L) enjoy doing a lot
9  C:  well (  ) doesn't have to be a lot but (  )
10 D:  (sniff)
11 C:  I mean I-I like going out (  ) to nice places (  ) but you do
12      too you like going out (  ) (inaud) maybe not as much as me
```

13   (inaud)
14 D: I don't ( ) as I look back I don't recall ( ) going
15   out to dinner and having real great times ( ) I don't *(L)*

Like Roxanne, Colleen begins with her enjoyment of eating out, displaying signs of discomfort (many pauses, inaudibility, and filler words). Unlike Brian, who makes direct eye contact, David averts his gaze as Colleen speaks, cutting her off visually; he also interrupts her in his disagreement (line 2), his voice harsh, his face wrinkled in disgust and anger. Colleen opposes David's "no" with a soft "yes" (line 4), her voice is barely audible, her face long and sullen; as early as line 4 she appears upset. They go back and forth as to whether they both like eating out (lines 1-6); she insists that they both like eating out (line 6). She is unable to separate her likes and dislikes from David's—in fusion there is no separate self.

Colleen is attempting to maintain a together identity with David; her sense of self seems to be dependent on him. He at the same time is attempting to maintain his separateness. In lines 7-9 they each mitigate: David gives a little toward togetherness (7-8), qualifying his argument with ideation of separateness (*"We may like it, but we both don't really enjoy it"); Colleen mitigates by saying it doesn't have to be a lot (line 9).

In line 11 Colleen declares her separateness by stammering, "I-I like going out," pausing frequently, then drawing David back into her likes in line 12, ending with a further mitigation and ideation of the separateness of her and David. Lines 14 and 15 are further indication of David's separateness.

David and Colleen's bond is fragile and easily damaged. Separateness, even in the form of different likes and dislikes, is experienced as isolation for Colleen; David seems unable to tolerate togetherness. Colleen's identity is rooted in agreement with David, she does not have a solid sense of self; David uses individualism—isolation—as a defense. So they dance together but to different beats—she moves toward engulfment, he toward isolation. David and Colleen have a rigid bonding system;

they are unable to balance the distance between togetherness and separateness. They are unable to negotiate differences in a constructive way.

These brief exchanges by the two couples illustrate the problems associated with a low level of differentiation when differences arise in relationships. The less differentiated, the more emotionally reactive persons (and relationships) become, the less each is able to distinguish his or her own thoughts and feelings from the other person's, and the more ruined each will feel over disagreement. Identity is lost to togetherness for Colleen, and the relationship is lost in favor of separateness for David; each is alienated. Like David and Colleen, in many marriages, when one party moves in one direction, the other party moves in the other direction. The issue at hand in such a relationship is not the topic of conversation, but the balance of distance.

In order to negotiate differences, parties need to have a sense of self and at least a fragment of a bond, either between the disputing parties or with a third party helping in the negotiations. An undifferentiated self is inversely related to the ability to steer clear of protracted disputes. Poorly differentiated persons have insufficient self boundaries, and are unable to balance the distance between togetherness and separateness. They are shame-prone.

The less differentiated the person, the more shame-prone, increasing the likelihood of destructive disputes. Undifferentiated persons are more likely to be easily insulted and to see the source of the problem as coming from the other. The more shame-prone an individual is, the more difficult it is for him or her to acknowledge shame, because feeling ashamed in itself is a source of shame. Inability to differentiate between self and other and unacknowledged shame go hand in hand. The more differentiated a person, the more intact the boundaries, the less shame-prone he or she will be. A highly differentiated self is associated with the ability to acknowledge shame without emotional reverberations.

SPONTANEOUS DEESCALATION

David and Colleen

The following episode, taken from David and Colleen's quarrel, is an instance of deescalation. It illustrates how repair of the bond occurs. Although the mood change is dramatic, this moment is brief and the couple quickly resume their quarrel.

David and Colleen's argument has shifted from topic to topic. In this passage it concerns whether or not David has been speaking up about his grievances. David argues that he has been complaining for the last 15 years, but nothing has changed. The following episode directly follows the episode presented in Chapter 5 (see the Appendix for the excerpt in everyday language):

Excerpt A

```
32:31.11  C:  if you speak up I would be
          D:  I HAVE been speaking up ALL along
   35.05  C:  well no (inaud)
          D:          [all] along
          C:  um um ( ) um umm (L)
   42.06  D:  well we could get into another subject if=
          C:                                      =hee
              heehee=
   46.25  D:         =we wanted to ( ) I guess (clear throat) ( )
          C:  ok alright so you say you've been speaking up
              an=
   55.21  D:    =I think I have pointed out the problem uh ( )
              hhh with how our environment is crowded ( ) with
              ( ) just JUNK an uh its not satisfactory to me an
              I've been complaining about it an there's no
              change it's continuous an it has been for fifteen
              years ( )
33:16.20  C:  but you haven't been complaining about that for
              fifteen years= <very soft)
          D:                =ya for fifteen-well not for
              fifteen years but (inaud) located
```

33:21.29 C: **[I heard about it in the] last** (1.47) I've
25.00   heard about it in the last *(1.28)* three years ( )
            D: *(2.06)* **well that would be enough I would think**
               wouldn't it? (1.80)
            C: hm <*very slight laugh*) ( ) *well?*

Again David and Colleen argue back and forth, and the
conflict increases progressively. Although topics change,
the emotions remain the same; as shame increases, anger increases. Both exhibit visual signs of shame (gaze aversion, lick-
ing/biting tongue and lips), while words and paralanguage
reflect anger (heavy emphasis, complaints, derogatory terms).
Each is disrespectful toward the other. The argument shifts to
a further oscillating series: the amount of time the complaining
has occurred (3 or 15 years). Colleen displays a lengthy facial
expression of anger (33:25.00), but ends in a sequence of shame
behaviors: She bites her lips and smiles falsely.
   After a long pause David continues with a further angry
complaint in the form of a question: "Well that would be
enough I would think wouldn't it?" Colleen appears embarrassed as she slightly laughs. David and Colleen both show
visual signs of shame: David covers his face with his hand as
he finishes his sentence, Colleen exhibits shame by biting her
lips, false smiling, and covering her face with her hand. It
appears that the quarrel between David and Colleen will continue in much the same way, when David throws in a new twist:

Excerpt B

33.12 D: **three years (2.85)** HEY WOULD YOU PASS THE BUTTER
          I REA::LLY NEED THE BUTTER ( ) **three years**
                  later I get the butter passed
        C: [. . . . . laugh . . . .]
        D: (laugh) ( )
47.17 C: sorry (laugh) ( )
        D: (sniff) *well (1.91) I-uh (3.05)*

The quarrel begins to take a turn at this point; the mood
begins to shift. David draws an analogy of his needs to having

butter passed. Colleen laughs hard. More laughter occurs here than anywhere else during their quarrel; Colleen's exceeds David's in exuberance—it is extended and hearty. After the laughter Colleen apologizes, but with an air of submissiveness. David is at a loss for words; the mood changes further as Colleen apologizes a second time:

Excerpt C

58.03	C:	I'm sorry <very gently) *(2.95)*
34:01.10	D:	I know (15.10) I-feel-like-this is all the stuff ( )
		that we're learnin about life *(2.00)*
21.15	C:	an who we are <soft)
22.06	D:	an who we are an (1.15) stuff that we didn't learn
40.10		earlier (15.25) (sniff) (9.85)

The mood shift is dramatic: from angry quarreling to reflection. The quarrel vanishes, as if they had forgotten the fight. Colleen's second apology is not submissive, but strong and sincere; she looks directly at David when she speaks. Her apology reflects her separateness and willingness to take responsibility. They engage in a long mutual gaze. David acknowledges her apology, maintaining eye contact as he does; a very *long* pause (15.10 seconds) follows. Both look down, their facial expressions are sad. They seem to be attuned in sadness.

David continues after the pause by reflecting on their relationship. He includes both of them ("stuff that we're learning"), something he had not done previously—he is no longer forcing separateness. They are in the boat together: They use "we" rather than "I" and "you." "We," at least on a cognitive level, is a shared state; "you," during blame, is a state of isolation and a source for shame. In this segment neither party blames the other for the state of the relationship; instead, they discuss their shared state of ignorance about relationships.

They acknowledge *their* situation, and all they didn't learn earlier. Colleen acknowledges their joint condition, and David affirms the position. They level with each other rather than blame, withdraw, placate, interrupt, and so on. Each uses first-person plural: They are in this learning situation together.

Acknowledging the fact that there has been so much they didn't know is getting close to acknowledging their feelings of inadequacy (shame), rather than blaming. Shane (1980) posits that learning cannot begin to take place until the shame of not knowing is admitted; this is what David and Colleen seem to be doing. Together they acknowledge the inadequacy of their "sorry" state.

Cues for shame and anger have virtually disappeared at this point and are replaced by facial expressions of sadness. Excerpt C lasts only about 42 seconds; the conversation then quickly regresses. David reverts back to asking Colleen questions, but with an important difference:

Excerpt D

	D:	*so um (2.15) what ARE we going to be doing (1.75)*

   D: *so um (2.15) what ARE we going to be doing (1.75)*
   with **all the STUFF** at the house *(2.50)* one thing I
35:01.00   need tu know (1.15) cause as I finish up the living
   room an dining room which are empty now *(2.10) u::m*
   ( ) an the upstairs ( ) which will be finished=
08.05 C: =**its good**
   tu empty it out like that *ya know*

David continues by stating his request as a need: "I *need* to know." Talking in terms of one's own needs, rather than blaming or triangling onto a third person or thing, points toward respectful communication. Stating needs rather than blaming the other puts a person in a vulnerable state (susceptible to further shame) when there is not a secure base. Studies have shown that self-disclosure can make a person more vulnerable to threat and further shame, which leads to angry aggression (e.g., Green & Murray, 1973).

In their joint state of momentary awareness and sadness, David may have felt vulnerable and felt a loss of the bond. When one is open to vulnerability and alienated from the other simultaneously, further shame and retaliation come easily. Stating one's needs may be felt as deeply wounding, particularly when the other person does not respond or acknowledge the vulnerability being expressed.

Colleen ignores David's need to know (she doesn't have to fulfill it, but it would have been courteous to acknowledge his statement of feeling). Although her words are affirmative ("its good"), she shows disrespect by withdrawing and changing the topic; she does not respond to the relationship aspect of his statement, but focuses only on another topic (emptying out the cupboards). Not surprisingly, the quarrel escalates approximately a minute and a half later, with even more vehement anger. Their quarrel expands to how the cupboards were done incorrectly and whose fault that was. Anger continues to increase until they are shouting at each other, and Colleen threatens to walk out. The quarrel ends only when the interviewer returns to the room, restoring order.

Summary

The main ingredients in spontaneous deescalation are (a) respect, (b) acknowledgment of feelings, and (c) a state of momentary connectedness (Colleen moves toward separateness, David toward togetherness), seen in language of connection (we/us versus I/you) and long mutual gaze. Connectedness is a balance between separateness and togetherness.

The missing components are (a) understanding the sources of impasse, (b) knowledge of their own family system, and (c) a secure base for exploration. The third missing component is particularly important. It seems unlikely that a couple immersed in past grievances would be able to untangle the knot alone. A secure base—therapist, mediator, or the like—may be needed; someone who could form a bond with each party, support each in vulnerable feelings, and help each identify past and present patterns in his or her communication style. An elastic system can then develop that would enable each party to tolerate differences without triggering an immediate emotional reaction.

THIRD-PARTY INTERVENTION

Rosie and James

The case of Rosie and James illustrates the importance of acknowledgment. As a courtesy, couples were invited to view their tapes at a later date; the tape was paused on emotion cues. Each person was asked to explain what was occurring in him- or herself at particular moments. Nothing about specific emotions was mentioned. Rosie and James were able to view their relationship from the outside, gaining insight into their own behaviors.

Most of Rosie and James's comments and interpretations reflected their own behaviors, rather than their partners'. James commented to Rosie, while looking at his own facial expressions: "Now I can see what you've been so upset about all these years, I never knew I looked like that." Rosie also commented on seeing herself: "That's one angry woman!" (she had not known that she was angry before viewing the tape).

During the viewing, when James was asked what it was like for him when Rosie expressed anger directly, rather than withholding anger (which was her normal style), he commented that a clear anger message is "like being at a great distance apart." He said the withholding was a mixed message, and was "like having a wall between us; I don't like either, but prefer the former." The session lasted three hours. Many issues, particularly about feelings, were discussed (e.g., how James felt when Rosie called his airplane a toy—he felt diminished and trivialized). Both realized that they did not like indirect forms of anger.

Rosie and James are a couple who were basically isolated; there was not much togetherness in their relationship, particularly in sharing their feelings. What they gained in their viewing was a sense of togetherness through the shared expression of emotion in a safe context (the interviewer was present). By the time the viewing had ended both were crying; Rosie went to James and sat on his lap, and they hugged.

The relationship between Rosie and James changed as a result of the viewing. A year later both James and Rosie reported, "We are getting along better now than we ever have." They said that they had reunited and that their marriage was improved. Follow-ups two and three years later found them living together and reporting greater satisfaction with their relationship than ever. There has been no further talk of separation or divorce. James is building a new airplane, and Rosie just graduated from a master's program. The plane is no longer an issue; instead, they have been directing their discussions to the relationship between them. They have learned to talk about their feelings with each other. Acknowledgment of shame and anger, in a safe context (free of shame), allowed then to explore their feelings, breaking their impasse.

Shaming transactions, such as interpreting a spouse's behavior, rarely work for gaining insight. Observation from an intervener—even a skilled therapist—can also be interpreted as shameful. Self-viewing can be used as a technique for reducing shame; when an interpretation comes from the self it is rarely shameful. Although a person might be ashamed of him- or herself for behaving in a certain manner, any insight about that behavior is self-generated and more readily incorporated.

Skill and tact are necessary in helping people view themselves on videotape, because self-viewing can be a potential source of shame. First-time viewers need to adjust to seeing themselves from the outside; any interpretations they make are their own, and should be treated with respect. Each needs to focus on his or her own behavior rather than on that of the spouse; the therapist should guide each toward viewing self, otherwise the viewing will become a further source of blame and shame.

People are going to see only what they are ready to see. They need to progress at their own rates. Rosie and James were prepared to see the hurt and anger in themselves and the way they felt when they were put down. Viewing themselves from the outside allowed them to change their own behaviors toward each other.

Mariel and Anna

Conflict between "Mariel" and "Anna" was described by Lansky (1980). They were in family therapy because of Mariel's physical violence toward Anna. The therapy session began with a temper tantrum by Mariel because Anna was late for the session. Apparently there had been some misunderstanding as to where they were to meet; Mariel had been left waiting for Anna, and was powerless to do anything about it. Being left suggests abandonment.

Also inherent in the situation was disrespect: Anna leaving him waiting is a message to Mariel that he and his time are unimportant—*"You don't matter to me." Both disrespect and separation (physical separation as well as ideation of emotional separation, seen in his comment about Anna's fear of being alone) are in the context preceding Mariel's angry outburst. Acknowledgment by the therapist and reduction of anger are illustrated in the following excerpt (Dr. T = therapist; M = Mariel):

```
 1  T:  boy you sound angry
 2  M:  I am GODDAMN angry (shouting)
 3  T:  What are you angry about?
 4  M:  at this unreliable (inaud. . . . . . . . .)
 5  T:  unreliable (inaud)
 6  M:  ASSHOLE (shouting) (4.30)
 7  T:  unreliable asshole
 8  M:  exactly
 9  T:  What makes you so angry about that? I'm missing
10      what you're angry about
11  M:  I come up here (  ) depending on her being here at a
12      certain time (1.20) and she ain't there (  ) she's (1)
13      off doing her own thing (1.90) like this ain't the
14      first time this's the story of her life (1) I cannot
15      depend on her to-to do a simple little function (  )
16  T:  I cannot depend on her is really (inaud)
17  M:                      [I get the-the short] end of the
18      stick
19  T:  It happens over and over again (  ) from your experience
20  M:  (  ) yes (softly) (5.30)
```

Dr. T not only acknowledges Mariel's anger (line 1 and 9) but asks about the context for the anger (line 3). Mariel (line 2) acknowledges his anger, describing a shame context (lines 11-15): (a) Mariel in relation with Anna, not being able to depend on her; (b) Anna is off on her own—symbolic of abandonment; (c) not only does Mariel get less than deserved ("short end") (see Tables 2.1 and 2.2, in Chapter 2), but his self boundaries are weak (he has difficulty with differentiation). His self is not intact, which makes it difficult for him to tolerate separateness; like Colleen, he is engulfed. Dr. T comments on the intensity of the shame context in a gentle and respectful way (lines 16 and 19); Mariel's anger decreases dramatically, heard in the calmness of his affirmation—"yes" (line 20).

Because Mariel is so engulfed, the boundaries between self and other so fragile, he is prone to shame. A third party was needed to help him become aware of his feelings and his relationships with others. In this case, a temporary bond is formed between Dr. T and Mariel; Dr. T shows respect in his manner, which is soft and gentle. Dr. T helps Mariel regain composure, allowing him to restore lost face. Dr. T is able to help Mariel acknowledge some of his feelings without further loss of face. Acknowledgment of hidden shame for the patient by the therapist, and then by the patient, seems to have reduced Mariel's anger.

In this interview most of the components of repair are visible in the dialogue: (a) some exploration of the source of impasse, tracing sequences of emotion and social events; (b) face-saving (respect tactics); (c) acknowledgment of feeling; and (d) a secure base for exploration. Although exploration of interacting systems (present and in family of origin) did not occur in this excerpt, it was a component in the intervention as a whole (Lansky, 1980).

Joan and Paul

Face-saving is illustrated by an incident reported by Saposnek (1983) involving the couple "Joan" and "Paul," in mediation of a custody dispute: "In the middle of a heated exchange, a wife said to her ex-husband, 'You never paid any attention to the children, then you left me, and you're *not* getting the children now or ever' " (p. 185).

Joan does not discuss her feelings directly, but they are implied. In her one sentence there are three statements that show a sequence of perceived insults and humiliations leading to angry revenge. First, Joan complains about and blames Paul, implying that he is an inadequate father; then she reveals a context for intense humiliation, "You left me" (he severed the bond between them). The third breath is a threat of angry revenge—to withhold the children from Paul. All three statements are potentially humiliating for Paul—he is the one at fault with the children, the marriage, and a threat to separate him from his children (as he has separated himself from Joan). There is a mountain of both anger and shame. At this point, the mediator intervened before Paul had a chance to reply, saying:

> The anger and hurt you feel right now is not unusual, and it is very understandable. It is also not unusual for a parent who was not involved with the children before a divorce to decide to become sincerely involved after the divorce. Allowing that opportunity will give your children a chance to get to know their father in the future in a way that you wanted in the past. But give yourself plenty of time to get through these difficult feelings. (pp. 185-186)

This is a crucial moment for intervention: The mediator acknowledges and reframes for both parties in a way that helps them to begin building a new bond—that of coparents. At the same time the intervention deflects potential humiliation, the mediator interprets vulnerable feelings for both parents, justifying their anger and hurt.

The mediator interrupted the cycle in which the disputants had been entangled, but in a way that did not further humiliate either party. The intervention was paradigmatic; even though it saved face, it did not endorse the position of either party. The mediator was able to remain neutral; he did not become enmeshed in the family conflict. Saposnek describes the effects of the intervention:

On hearing this the husband kept quiet, for he knew that the mediator's remark implied support for his continuing relationship with the children, yet presented it in a way that allowed both him and his wife to save face. He then tearfully expressed his sincerity in wanting to become more involved with the children. The wife cried and was able to constructively express her hurt feelings at being left by the husband. Negotiations then became possible. (p. 186)

By interrupting the quarrel cycle, and by expressing shame and hurt for the clients, the mediator appears to have avoided further escalation.

This incident illustrates repair in several ways. First, it suggests that in order to build a new bond between the disputants, the mediator must be continuously active, rather than passive. *Social bonds are at risk in all encounters*; if they are not being built, maintained, or repaired, they are being damaged. A fallacious result of "cathartic" theories has been the unfortunate notion that a passive mediator is allowing the parties to "blow off steam." There can be little benefit from contempt, disgust, or ridicule. On the contrary, these types of emotional expression are harmful to the point that they should usually be interrupted, because they further damage bonds, perpetuating the quarrel system.

The mediator's intervention exactly illustrates key components of repair, which is also seen in Lansky's (1980) case, and in the cases of spontaneous repair: saving face (avoiding further shaming transactions) and helping clients to acknowledge their "hurt." In the case of Joan and Paul, the mediator appears to have detected the potential for humiliation of the husband in the utter rejection implied in the wife's comment: *"You don't count; it doesn't matter to me what you say, think, or feel." The old bond between wife and husband has been broken; if the mediator allowed this comment to pass, it would become more difficult for them to form a new bond as coparents.

Most of the components for repairing the bond are present in this single intervention: (a) the source of impasse, seen in sequences of Joan's first utterance; (b) face-saving (respectful tactics); (c) acknowledgment of feeling and the state of the bond; (d) knowledge of interacting systems; and (e) a secure base for exploration, provided by the mediator.

DISCUSSION

Repairing the bond involves five major components: face-saving, acknowledgment, understanding emotion sequences, complex systems, and establishing a secure base for exploration. Each is discussed below.

Face-Saving: Respect

Self-perpetuating cycles of shame-rage are implied in the work of Saposnek (1983) and Johnston and Campbell (1988), in terms of loss of face. In the present scheme, loss of face is one of many metaphors for damaged bonds, loss of self-identity, and unacknowledged shame. Goffman (1967) has dealt with face-saving extensively. Social behavior is motivated by the maintenance of social bonds—to look good, to present oneself in a favorable light to significant others. All members of all groups attempt to protect and repair their images—to maintain or repair bonds.

Many of the disparaging tactics used in marital quarrels can be seen as attempts to save face at the expense of the other; often they are revengeful. In blaming transactions, the implication is "I don't want to look (and feel) like I'm wrong (or bad)"; instead, the other is sacrificed. Blaming the other is a clumsy attempt to maintain one's own sense of worth. Anger and rage can be seen as attempts to avoid humiliation (loss of face). It may be more comfortable to use the inadequacies of a spouse as a rationalization than to acknowledge the part played by self, *particularly if the bond is already damaged or threatened.*

A key is to help both parties restore, maintain, and save face. Several studies of conflict resolution have stressed the importance of maintaining and repairing face (Brockner & Rubin, 1985; Folger & Poole, 1984; Johnston & Campbell, 1988; Saposnek, 1983). Face-saving and respect go hand in hand:

> The point of departure for intervening with narcissistically vulnerable parents is to help them save face. This involves repairing their wounded self-esteem and preventing further attacks on their sense of self-worth. . . . The counselor demonstrates respect for the parents . . . (. . . avoiding labeling, blaming . . .). . . . Indeed, successful mediation, especially for deeply mortified parents . . . , often hinges on the respect shown them. (Johnston & Campbell, 1988, p. 95)

Narcissistic (shame-prone) relationships can be repaired by maintaining respect. With respect, face can be saved and the bond rebuilt, repaired, or maintained. When both parties are shame-prone, the intervener must be particularly sensitive to shame and shaming transactions. In two-party interaction, tactics that do not contribute to loss of face are necessary to begin bond repair.

Respect is central. Respectful tactics help all parties save, maintain, or repair lost face. Respect involves use of tactics that do not shame others. Face-saving tactics prepare the foundation for the repair of damaged social bonds—loss of face and loss of bond are interconnected; we lose face not in isolation, but in the eyes of another.

Acknowledgment and Leveling

Acknowledgment and leveling are further ingredients in repair. Although shame is easily detected once it is understood, it is difficult to acknowledge (Lewis, 1971a; Lynd, 1958). According to Lynd (1958), because shame involves threat to identity and loss of trust in self and another, and because shame is so painful, it is extraordinarily difficult to communicate. Lewis (1971a) describes how easy it is to become ashamed of being ashamed: "One is often ashamed of being or having been ashamed . . . because it feels like so primitive and 'irrational' a state, shame is connected with the specific defense of hiding or running away" (pp. 37-38). A characteristic response to shame is to hide; shame is connected with all forms of hiding behavior (see Chapter 3).

Acknowledgment is essential for the reduction of conflict, but the risk of acknowledgment often feels immense. To acknowledge would mean not only facing shame, but the possibility of bondlessness. But acknowledgment can lead to bonding: "The very fact that shame is an isolating experience also means that if one can find ways of sharing and communicating it this communication can bring about particular closeness with other persons" (Lynd, 1958, p. 66). Lewis (1971a, 1981a, 1983, 1987), like Lynd, points to the acknowledgment of shame as a vehicle for constructive personal and social change. Although experiences of shame are painful, they reveal unrecognized aspects of self and society. If shame can be experienced instead of denied, it becomes a powerful agent for change.

While unacknowledged shame is an isolating experience and contributes to alienation and increased anger, the opposite occurs with acknowledgment.

Lack of a language contributes to the sense of estrangement. If, however one can sufficiently risk uncovering oneself and sufficiently trust another person, to seek means of communicating shame, the risking of exposure can in itself be an experience of release, expansion, self-revelation . . . , of belief in oneself, and entering into the mind and feeling of another person. (Lynd, 1958, p. 249)

Respectful acknowledgment can lead to the restoration of bonds. A secure bond—a base for exploration—is necessary for acknowledgment. Questions to explore in any conflict include these: What is the state of the bond—is it being built, maintained, repaired, or damaged? Is the bond intact or threatened? Does a secure bond exist for any party involved? What are the feelings being displayed? Is there denial? What are the tactics being used?

Communication tactics that show respect, acknowledge feelings, and build bonds include reframing, summarizing, encouraging, validating, normalizing, empathizing, and acknowledging. Tactics that communicate disrespect generate alienation and strong emotions, leading to protracted and destructive conflict: ordering, preaching, lecturing, judging, threatening, manipulating, labeling, distracting, blaming, and disrespectful interpreting.

Use of communication tactics that involve *leveling*—rather than those that blame, distract, withdraw, or placate—help build, maintain, and repair bonds. Leveling may be necessary for constructive social change (Satir, 1972).

Tracing Sequences of Emotion

It is not always easy to know when someone is losing face, or whether what one person experiences as respectful is felt as disrespect by another. Cues are emotional indicators as to how communication tactics are received; they help identify the state of the bond before conflict escalates or positions become polarized.

Once conflict occurs, tracing sequences of emotion back from the point where anger first occurred usually reveals a context where bonds have been damaged and shame evoked. By recognizing when shame occurs in the present, while discussing social sequences, parties can save face, acknowledge feelings, and begin negotiation. Tracing sequences is a complex process. Sequences occur not only within persons, but between persons; they often involve extended social networks (kin, attorneys, therapists, past histories, and so on).

Complex Systems

Three interrelated systems are involved: the self system (within—includes social-emotional history), interpersonal systems (between persons, especially interpersonal communication), and extended family and social networks, which involve complex webs of subsystems of the first two systems. Change on any level will begin change on other levels, since they are all interdependent.

The extended network can involve others who are not directly disputing but who help maintain or decrease conflict. Entanglement of networks is evident in child custody disputes. Parents are willing to make agreements that seem satisfactory to them, but that are unsatisfactory to lawyers, grandparents, friends, or siblings. As more people become involved in the conflict, the more polarized the battle becomes; the system is no longer able to differentiate the members—it is engulfed within networks and isolated between them.

The absence of supportive networks, isolation as well as engulfment, can also contribute to protracted conflict. When the only source of support has been someone who has abandoned or betrayed another, conflict can continue indefinitely as a way of maintaining the relationship (Johnston et al., 1984). Humiliation and anger are particularly high in these cases. The only bond is with the deserter; if the conflict ended, there would be complete absence of bonds. Because bonds are so important, people sometimes prefer destructive conflict over no bond.

Summary

Repairing bonds is a crucial first step in resolving conflict. The bonding process particularly involves manner and communication tactics: respect and acknowledgment. Respect on the part of the mediator requires tactics such as having an open agenda (i.e., explaining all activities to the parties, laying out the whole process) and interrupting interpretations of one party by the other, which can be a source of shame—used to subtly humiliate the other person.

It is crucial to respect parties' distance from each other; too much closeness or distance can lead to further shame and can intensify destructive tactics. Disputing parties need to find a range in which both are comfortable. The mediator should respectfully point to each person's different requirements for distance, making clear that no judgment is involved—differences are not right or wrong, but simply requirements.

Mediators can take the following steps. Begin by focusing on the details of shaming transactions (bonding issues). Comment on what is occurring in the present. Help each party to save, restore, or maintain face. Explore the extended network (i.e., intergenerational processes, social networks, and the like) as a way to reduce shame. Assist parties in observing patterns. Explore feelings about being in the presence of a third party.

The mediator can assist parties in tracing sequences of emotion, looking for shame behind rage, guilt, hostility, withdrawal, and other nonleveling tactics. He or she can help persons identify recurring cycles (feelings, events, communication patterns, and so on), linking past events and feelings to the present situation. Satir (1972) could tell whether a family had a closed or open system by the way she felt in their presence. The mediator must use his or her own feelings as a guide, checking them with concrete evidence. Parts I and II of this book provide a map for tracing sequences.

It is important to note that shame should not be treated as guilt, or ignored in favor of guilt. Although remorse has its place, it can also serve as a defense against shame; guilt is often used as a way to deny the shame at the root of the problem. Recall that guilt is usually about specifics; shame is about the entire self and its important bonds. It rarely helps to argue about or dismiss shame as trivial, which is likely to be experienced as disrespect or abandonment; in narcissistic persons shame can be associated with loss of self boundaries and inability to balance distance. The basis for shame feels real to the person experiencing it; shame should be treated as having a realistic base.

It is no surprise that shame has been the focus in recent books and articles by psychiatrists, psychoanalysts, psychologists, and sociologists. Unacknowledged shame has been proposed to play a role not only in protracted conflict, but in depression (Lewis, 1981a), narcissistic disturbances and vulnerability (Lansky, 1985; A. Morrison, 1989), schizophrenia (N. Morrison, 1987; Retzinger, 1989), anorexia (Scheff, 1989), addictive and codependent relationships (Bradshaw, 1988; Cavanaugh, 1989; Kaufman, 1989), crime and violence (Braithwaite, 1988; Johnston et al., 1984; Katz, 1988; Lansky, 1987; Retzinger, 1991b; Scheff, 1987; Scheff, Retzinger, & Ryan, 1989), dysfunctional families (Fossum & Mason, 1986), and tension in medical encounters (Lazare, 1987).

The shame concept has been applied to therapy by Lewis (1971a, 1981a, 1987), Lansky (1987), Wurmser (1981), and N. Morrison (1987), and its practicality has been demonstrated by Scheff (1987, 1989), and Retzinger (1989). In her work, Lewis has dealt particularly with the shame patients feel about revealing their inadequacies to the therapist. If shame is not dealt with in the therapy session, Lewis proposes, the therapeutic process is impaired. Symptoms remain the same or become worse as a result of unacknowledged shame.

Studies of mediation have dealt indirectly with shame through the concept of face management: helping disputing parties to save face or to restore lost face—that is, to avoid excess shame (Johnston & Campbell, 1988; Saposnek, 1983; Volkema, 1988). Narcissistic injury is about shame-proneness. Repair of the bond has been of interest to psychologists, particularly developmental psychologists, such as Bowlby (1988).

CONCLUSION

Not all conflict is destructive; conflict can be instructive and positive—reestablishing boundaries, leading toward effective problem solving. By learning to identify potentially humiliating exchanges, we will be better equipped to use strategies that will break impasse. If shame is acknowledged, negotiation, readjustment, and change can occur. By identifying shame, it is possible to get beneath the topic to the basic issue, alienation. If bonding issues can be found and discussed respectfully, impasse can be broken.

An important factor in impasse involves the manner of disputing parties; the content of a dispute is often less important than the manner in which it is conducted. Content and manner need to be weighed and balanced carefully. By analyzing words, manner, and implication, sequences of emotion can be traced back to when anger first appeared; there is likely to be an incident of humiliation or shame (*hurt* is a code word). The implication here is that somehow the person cares about the other in such a way that separation is profoundly wounding. Commenting on this level, by using the person's own metaphors and vocabulary, rather than on the anger level, is usually productive.

These findings have implications for both research and clinical practice. If a dispute or impasse is not getting resolved, that is, if anger continually arises, the chances are that there is some humiliation that is being hidden on one or both sides. The bond is being continually damaged.

A primary goal in resolution or deescalation of conflict is repairing damaged bonds. Repair of bonds can occur in all areas of society, not just in marriages. Respectful and disrespectful tactics are employed between factions in corporations and communities and between nations. By understanding innuendo and implication in communication, we can optimally monitor social distance, avoid escalation, and resolve conflict.

9 Emotional Communication and the Social Bond

> Since the language of intimacy will always be to a large extent a language of gesture, facial expression, and touch, it should be important to enlarge the possibilities of verbal language for such communication. (Lynd, 1958, p. 249)

Our society faces vast amounts of conflict and violence, from large-scale warfare and community conflict to intimate violence behind closed doors. We need to learn more about the underlying dynamics of escalating conflict. Little is known about escalation; attempts to identify the dynamics of conflict using aggregate data have only skimmed the surface. Although conflict theorists have touched on important issues, they have not discovered the dynamics of escalation. The preceding chapters have given a glimpse of the forces behind conflict escalation in terms of the social bond and emotions.

This chapter summarizes the preceding chapters and develops propositions about protracted conflict. It also addresses the ambiguity of human communication and the problem of translation, and finally suggests implications for the study of shame and the social bond.

COMMON PATTERNS

All four of the cases presented in this book show similar patterns beneath surface differences. After a brief review of major differences—children versus no children, external stressors, economic backgrounds, emotional expression (verbal, visual, paralinguistic), and dispute style—similarities are reviewed that may serve as universal keys to understanding protracted conflict.

The two couples with children, Roxanne/Brian and Randy/Karin, have more external pressures than do the two childless couples. Roxanne and Brian have financial difficulties and conflicts with ex-partners and with stepchildren. Randy and Karin have had recent major losses: the death of two babies, the death of Randy's mother, and impairment of Randy's hands. Roxanne and Brian cope adequately; they are able to hold their relationship together under stress, and often enjoy each other's company. Randy and Karin seem to fall apart; they find little enjoyment in each other.

The couples are also different in how they express emotion (visual, verbal, paralinguistic). Roxanne and Brian are the only couple who strongly express emotion in all three areas, giving them the appearance of being highly emotional. The other couples display emotions primarily in paralanguage, but also used code words and phrases. One interpretation of this is that each couple, with the exception of Roxanne and Brian, is engaged in hiding behavior at all times; they have all learned not to display emotions visually. Instead, emotion cues leak out in the more disguised forms of paralanguage, code words, and innuendo. The wives also all display more emotion cues than their husbands, with the exception of David, who displays more cues than Colleen.

The dispute styles of the couples are overt or covert, chronic or acute. Rosie and James's style is particularly characteristic of silent impasse; this couple have gone 11 years without overt quarrels. The other three couples quarrel overtly, but impasse also occurs. Although all couples have chronic conflict, Randy and Karin's is acute. The proportional differences of shame to anger seem to reflect the chronicity of the conflict, particularly when shame is high at the onset of the quarrel. This is the couple who had the most shame at the start of their quarrel, and the highest level of anger as the quarrel progressed.

All the couples show signs of both isolation and engulfment, with the exception of Rosie and James, whose styles are both primarily isolation. Within the couple, Colleen's style is more engulfed than David's, whose style is mostly isolation; David/Colleen and Randy/Karin are most easily hooked by the other's behavior (engulfed and emotionally reactive). Randy and Karin both go from isolation to engulfment to isolation and so on, without being able to regulate distance constructively. Roxanne and Brian, although often becoming entrenched and isolated, are able to regulate distance better than the other couples. Optimal regulation of distance leads to emotional attunement and solidarity. Some couples are more comfortable being at a greater emotional distance than others, who prefer more togetherness (see Fitzpatrick, 1988).

Randy/Karin and David/Colleen's quarrels are most suppressed initially; both have high proportions of shame to anger cues as the quarrels begin. The anger of these couples reaches the highest level. Randy and Karin's quarrel is the bitterest. The high frequency of shame and little display of anger at the start of the quarrel represents alienation, and may account for the high intensity of anger when it finally does emerge. Coser (1956) conjectures that greater intensity of conflict can be expected in relationships where hostile feelings are suppressed. Shame is one of the greatest inhibitors of anger. When shame is intense but not acknowledged, the situation is ripe for intense anger. The high proportion of shame to anger seems to have laid the foundation for the frenzied anger that follows.

Rosie and James also have a high proportion of shame to anger cues at the start of their quarrel. Although there is rapid escalation in the first 34 seconds, their quarrel takes the form of an impasse. In this case, bypassed shame served to suppress anger. This couple have a great wall of unspoken feelings between them; they have fallen out of love.

Roxanne and Brian are the only couple for which anger occurs at the same frequency as shame (they are also the only couple who expresses happiness with their relationship). Their style is quarrel/impasse, marked by a rapid alternation of shame and anger in relatively equal proportions. Conflict reaches a certain intensity, then submerges into impasse, where anger is held in check until it emerges in another outburst. Roxanne and Brian have more clearly defined selves than do the other couples. Although they are more separate than together, they are better equipped to regulate the distance between togetherness and separateness.

All the couples are alike in that they are white, middle-/lower-middle-class, and in their 30s. Rosie and James have the highest income, Roxanne and Brian the lowest; Rosie/James, David/Colleen, and Roxanne/Brian are homeowners; it is not clear whether or not Randy and Karin own a home. But there are also deeper similarities involving etiology, high densities of shame cues, alternation of emotions within and between spouses, and disrespect (manner), each of which plays a role in the escalation of anger.

Etiology

Etiology embodies alienation, as suggested by Simmel (1955); it is complex in that it involves both the self system and the social system. To the degree that a person is alienated from self, he or she is unable to regulate distance with others; the individual is either isolated or engulfed. To the degree that a person's social bonding system is inflexible, he or she will be alienated. Alienation is complex in that it comes in two major forms: engulfment and isolation (see Chapter 2). The question of etiology becomes: To what degree are couples alienated? Are couples able to regulate involvement and detachment? What are the signs of alienation?

Each conflict began with alienation:

(1) ideation of separation
(2) differences in power positions
(3) language of disconnection
(4) use of triangles and other nonleveling responses
(5) lack of acknowledgment or response
(6) withdrawal
(7) lack of eye contact and other hiding behaviors
(8) de-selfing
(9) threats of abandonment

The initial topic in Roxanne and Brian's quarrel is Brian's ideation of isolation: "It's the times when *you feel like you're the only soldier on the field.*" He uses language of disconnection and displays hiding behavior. The disparaging manner that follows generates overt conflict. Rosie and James are emotionally alienated from the start. Their quarrel begins with hiding behavior; there are unequal power positions between them as Rosie plays the role of the mother, treating James as if he were a child; James withdraws.

David and Colleen's alienation is seen in ideation of separation at the start of their quarrel, shown by hiding behavior before anger emerges. Throughout their quarrel David and Colleen use language of disconnection much more than language of connection. In one 63-second period (32:17.00-33:22.00) they use language of connection ("we") twice and language of separation ("I," "you") 20 times. David and Colleen also use threats of abandonment.

Throughout their quarrel Randy and Karin also show ideation of separation. They begin their quarrel by focusing on third persons, separating themselves from the issues that divide them, instead focusing on distant and abstract topics. The triangling is surrounded by numerous hiding behaviors. The more entrenched Randy and Karin become, the more they use language of separation.

Randy and Karin also separate themselves from each other through an air of moral superiority, particularly on Karin's part: She is self-righteous, implying that Randy is morally deficient. Karin uses moral superiority as an attack and as a defense against Randy. He is reduced to a morally inferior position by implication. He responds by being emotionally violent. Moral superiority is also evident in David's self-righteous style of behavior toward Colleen.

Katz's (1988) work shows how violent persons may believe they are upholding the moral good. In some of his cases, the morally self-righteous person resorted to homicide to uphold the good. Unlike in Katz's findings, however, it is Karin who acts morally superior but who ends up abused, not physically but emotionally. One individual's sitting on a high moral horse can be a source of shame for others because it reduces them to an inferior position—emotional abuse, in this case, was the response to moral superiority in the other.

Roxanne and Brian appear to have the most secure bond. They are better able to move between togetherness and separateness than the others, and anger is not outweighed by shame cues, as with the other couples. Their selves are more clearly defined, although they also get caught in isolation and engulfment. Perhaps marital happiness is related to the ability to regulate involvement and detachment in a way that does not elicit excessive shame, and that allows for the shame that does arise to be acknowledged.

David and Colleen have the least flexible bond. Colleen's sense of self is extremely fragile—it is dependent on engulfment with David. In response, David isolates himself, which causes Colleen to become more desperate, which in turn causes David to pull back further. Rosie and James are the most isolated of all the couples; each is an emotional island.

The tactics Rosie and James use, withdrawal and computing, further isolate them from each other. Randy and Karin move between isolation and engulfment; they cut off, then are violently drawn into the quarrel system, and distance themselves further from each other. The key is that both engulfment and isolation are forms of alienation; the bond is vulnerable in either form. Shame appears to be the key emotion in the social distancing mechanism, signaling that one is too far away or too close for comfort.

Prominence of Shame

Each conflict is marked by a high density of shame cues; unacknowledged shame is present within and between persons. There are many more cues for shame than for anger, particularly at the start of the quarrel. Shame is consistently high across all persons and relationships, while anger is not. In an earlier pilot study I found that in a small group unable to resolve resentment (shame + anger), the occurrence of shame was 90% greater than anger, whereas in the group that resolved resentment, shame was only 9% greater than anger (Retzinger, 1987). The implication is that anger is bound by shame. If shame is high, when anger does emerge it can become savage.

Disrespectful Manner

Manner involves communication tactics, both verbal and nonverbal. Subtle nonverbal cues can create havoc in a relationship when they are not congruent with the words spoken, because the message is ambiguous and open to more interpretations. Any nonleveling tactic is apt to arouse emotion. In all four quarrels, each spouse showed disrespect toward the other, either subtly or vehemently. Disrespect by one party was followed by shame cues in the other party, which were followed by anger and reciprocation of disrespect.

Roxanne and Brian call each other names, blame, interrupt, and exaggerate. Randy and Karin use triangles that carry a world of hostile implication; they put each other down in demeaning ways. David and Colleen blame, interrupt, placate, and interrogate; questioning is used as an attack and a defense. Rosie and James appear polite on the surface—they don't yell and scream, interrupt each other, or call each other names. Instead, there is hostile innuendo, disguised with fixed smiles.

It is important to look closely at questioning as a form of defense and attack. David's questioning puts Colleen in a bind, because she is unable to step out of the frame and comment on it. Rather than being real requests for information, David's questions defend him from his own feelings and at the same time covertly attack Colleen. Behind the questions is a statement about his feelings of powerlessness.

The manner of a dispute is important because it is a major source of intense emotion. Disrespectful manner damages the bond, perpetuating alienation, shame, and anger. Disrespectful communication is opposed to the building and repair of bonds, just as respectful tactics can repair and build bonds. *Disrespect is the medium for exchange of shame-rage between partners,* particularly when the message is subtle and ambiguous, and/or parties are lacking the ability to comment from another frame of reference. Disrespectful tactics can be viewed as fruitless attempts to repair the bond and/or maintain self-esteem.

Alternation of Emotions

When shame occurs and is not acknowledged, anger is quick to follow, which generates further shame, anger, and disrespect in the other. Rapidly alternating sequences of shame and anger were found in each case. Often the two emotions were so brief they could be detected only in slow motion, since each emotion can be evident as briefly as a single second. Alternation occurred with all couples. Often when one party expressed anger, the other simultaneously displayed cues for shame; when the other party began his or her turn to speak, the words showed angry disrespect.

Alternation occurs *within* when a person is humiliated or shamed, and then becomes angry, and then ashamed for being angry, and so on. The clearest example of alternation among the couples discussed here occurs when Rosie tries to pull back what she said to James (22:42.14-49.00: **"I-I sacrificed a LOT for you to have toys ( )** *but you-didn't-ask-for-it-***an-Iresent-***later-an-an-we're-still-going-over-it* **( )** *ok"*). Rosie's emotions alternate between shame and rage six times in 6.5 seconds:

(1) **eyes widen**
(2) *stammers, tight smile, vertical wrinkling in forehead*
(3) **heavy emphasis, anger expression**

(4) *smile fades, long pause*
(5) **complaint, condescending**
(6) *tight laughter, rapid, condensed speech*

The clearest example of alternation *between* parties occurs in Roxanne and Brian's quarrel: Brian vocalizes (a) ideation of separation, and (b) makes a long, demeaning complaint about Roxanne's behavior, (c) showing disrespect; Roxanne displays (d) shame cues, and then (e) anger, which is communicated (f) disrespectfully. When Roxanne finally begins to complain about Brian, he displays shame cues, followed by anger and disrespect toward Roxanne, and so on. A triple shame-rage spiral (Scheff, 1987) has six component parts: (1-2) shame in each party, (3-4) anger in each party, and (5-6) mutual disrespect between parties.

Escalation

Alienation and shame were not only involved in etiology and alternation with anger, but *in all cases they preceded each episode of angry escalation*. As shame increased and was not acknowledged, anger and disrespect appeared. Tactics became disrespectful, views polarized.

The most dramatic illustration of escalation occurs between Randy and Karin. The start of the quarrel is rampant with shame, before anger is visible: lack of eye contact, fidgeting, avoidance, frequent pausing, mitigation, whining, defensiveness, and vagueness. Each moment of escalation (seven instances in 15 minutes) shows the same pattern.

Intense verbal attack is preceded by ideation of separation and constellations of shame cues. Words and manner are rejecting; the other responds defensively by rejecting back. None of the couples steps out of the frame or comment on what is going on between them; they're caught in a frenzy of feeling. Each point of escalation follows the same pattern, not only with Randy and Karin, but with all the couples.

PROPOSITIONS

Seven propositions seem central to destructive conflict. Propositions 1 and 2 are implicit in the prior work discussed in Chapters 1 and 2. The other five propositions provide links among alienation, unacknowledged emotions, and conflict.

- *Proposition 1:* Human behavior is primarily social; everywhere, and at all times, human beings have been organized into groups that reflect their social nature.

Developmental studies as well as sociological studies describe the results of alienation and demonstrate the signal function of emotions: Shame and anger signal damaged bonds; pride and joy signal intact bonds.

The new surge of infant-caretaker research has demonstrated the social nature of human beings from the earliest moments of life. A primary motive of human behavior is to stay connected with significant others. Each person monitors his or her behavior in relation to other, and makes adjustments accordingly. Human culture also reflects the social nature of human beings: Always and everywhere human beings have been organized into groups governed by moral law. Violation of moral law activates shame and guilt.

- *Proposition 2:* Conflict is latent in the very elements that hold the group together.

Kerr and Bowen (1988) call human beings "proximity-seeking animals"; a relationship must meet appropriate conditions of distance to survive. Well-defined self boundaries are necessary for an individual to regulate social distance and maintain secure bonds; secure bonds are needed for the development of well-defined self boundaries. An inflexible bonding system implies a narrow range of distance between engulfment and isolation; there is little room to maneuver, increasing the potential for strong emotion.

Shame signals violation of the boundaries that protect relationships; it generates the rhythm of social interaction. That is, *shame signals the state of the bond*, enabling self to move smoothly through transactions; in this way it functions as a means by which we continue to stay connected with others. The elicitation of shame brings into focal awareness both self and other, enabling persons to readjust their behavior in relation to others—that is, to move closer or further apart.

Shame acts as a thermostat. It registers when the self becomes alienated from important others (either engulfed or isolated). If the self-monitoring mechanism fails to function, regulation of the bond becomes difficult. With intense sequences of emotion generated by unacknowledged shame, it becomes excessively difficult to regulate self in relation to other, leading to dysfunctional behavior—violent conflict.

Optimal social distance is not identical for everyone. Depending on the culture, class, or family, people require different levels of distance between togetherness and separateness. Japanese culture leans toward engulfment, whereas American culture leans toward isolation. But across cultures, races, genders, and classes, human beings need both separateness and togetherness in some combination to stay emotionally attuned with other persons. When regulation is lost, intense and protracted emotions occur.

- *Proposition 3:* Social bonds are being built, maintained, repaired, or damaged at each moment.

Regulation of the bond occurs at all times in face-to-face interaction, and is largely dependent on gestures. A world that focuses on symbols may lose touch with gestures basic to regulating bonds.

Bonds are built, maintained, and repaired in part by optimal regulation of distance, or at least distance with which interactants are comfortable. If early socialization is in a sea of engulfment or isolation, a person may feel comfortable only in one or the other of these states. Inability to regulate distance at an optimal level may help explain the development of pathological relationships. If the bond is build around alienating patterns, the relationship may be destructive.

Unacknowledged alienation may help explain violent relationships; battered persons continue to stay with their batterers because the partners are bound by mutual symbiosis and the inability to regulate distance. When distance cannot be regulated, persons may be in a constant state of alienation and shame, leading to destructive outcomes. When persons cannot regulate distance, they can move neither one way nor another to escape entanglement. In Bowlby's (1988) terms, a secure base is needed for an individual to explore beyond a state of symbiosis. Where persons are unable to regulate distance there can be no secure base. Bondability (in a secure base) is largely dependent on the abilities to maintain self boundaries and to regulate social distance. Whether the bond is being built, maintained, repaired, or damaged can be observed in the communication process by focusing on emotions.

Quarrels are not the only direction couples take when bonds are damaged. When self-monitoring systems fail, there are many directions behavior may take: conflict, aggression, overconformity, mental illness, silent impasse (persons separated by a wall of indifference), or withdrawal.

- *Proposition 4:* Conflict follows from separation, rather than separation following from conflict.

"When we have tried in vain to gain a person's love and respect, we are likely to find in him ever new negative qualities" (Scheler, 1961, p. 73). Traditional studies have pointed toward the importance of alienation. Alienation from others violates the social nature of human beings, in which a major motive is to maintain bonds with those we care about. When there is no adequate means for expressing the experience, persons are isolated further.

- *Proposition 5:* Threat to social bonds (alienation) is the primary context for shame.

Alienation and shame are inseparable. In itself, unacknowledged shame creates a form of self-perpetuating entrapment in one's own inner experience of isolation from the other; if one hides this sense of isolation from the other, it creates a further sense of shame, which creates further alienation. The association between shame and alienation is crucial in that it appears to be at the root of destructive conflict. *When shame and alienation are denied, it is almost impossible to repair the bond.*

- *Proposition 6:* Shame and anger have a powerful affinity. When shame is evoked but not acknowledged, anger is quick to follow.

"Without expression . . . shame cannot be expiated, and reality cannot be confirmed. Shame festers without communication. When it festers, anger grows" (Cottle, 1980, p. 254).

The self-other involvement in shame is complicated. If shame is denied, the other can be perceived as the source of hostility; anger almost inevitably follows. Anger can be seen as a protective measure and represents an attempt to repair the bond. One function of conflict is to reinstate bonds. The bond may or may not be reinstated, depending on how signals are taken and the ability of interactants to communicate effectively.

Anger is an assertive emotion—it moves forward/toward. Shame is an emotion that is represented by implosion, hiding, or turning away. Here we have two forces acting in opposition, one pushing toward assertion, the other pressing toward withdrawal. Usually the person is not aware that he or she is in a state of shame or even that he or she is angry; his or her behavior is disrespectful, no matter how subtle. As one spouse shows disrespect, the other responds with shame, then attack. This in turn causes the other shame, which then remains unacknowledged, which leads to a counterattack.

When alienation and shame are not acknowledged, ambivalence is created, which can drive people up the wall. When acknowledged, emotions can be powerful forces for constructive social change. If shame is acknowledged, negotiation, readjustment, and change can occur. When shame is denied, rigidity, resistance to change, rapidly rising anger, and the possibility for destructive conflict are generated.

Shame and anger have important functions: They provide signals that may help readjustment in the relationship (if anger is not bound by shame) and ward off destructive conflict. They are messages that someone is "hurt"; something in the relation-ship is not right—needs are not being met, a spouse is being taken for granted, someone is giving more than he or she is comfortable with. Anger provides a clue to a deeper message—shame. To cut off or deny anger is to shut down communication lines; to act out anger in behavior also shuts down those lines—both avoid deeper feelings of alienation and shame.

- *Proposition 7:* Functional conflict reaffirms the bond; dysfunctional conflict alienates. Conflict is functional or dysfunctional, depend-ing on the ability to acknowledge feelings that signal the state of the bond.

This proposition perhaps most clearly illustrates Bowlby's (1973) idea of functional and dysfunctional anger; one serves to reinstate the bond, the others damages it further: "Dysfunc-tional anger occurs whenever person . . . becomes so intensely angry with his partner that the bond between them is weak-ened . . . and the partner is alienated" (pp. 248-249). When separation is temporary, persons are not alienated, and shame is acknowledged, anger has the goal of "assisting a reunion and discouraging further separation . . . although expressed toward a partner, such anger acts to promote, and not disrupt, the bond" (Bowlby, 1973, p. 248).

Conflict escalates when alienation and shame remain unac-knowledged. Both positive and negative emotions are equally geared to affectional maintenance; they are the means by which we monitor ourselves in relation to others. In each of the cases presented here, shame and alienation play an important role not only in etiology, but in escalation.

Denial of shame leads to the rigidity found in destructive conflict. The intensity of the conflict is related to the rigidity of the system. It is the rigidity and not the conflict that threatens the equilibrium of the system; rigidity permits hostilities to accumulate. Rigidity in families and social structures is a seri-ous problem. Rigid families are intolerant of individuality, leading to pathological behavioral patterns. Rigid social struc-tures have the greatest risk of destruction.

TRANSLATION/AMBIGUITY

Human beings are the only creatures on earth able to use a complex system of symbols as well as gestures. All human language is therefore ambiguous. With its common surface and private base, language can make it difficult for people to understand one another. Each is involved in a constant process of translation between one mode of communication and the other: "To talk about relationships requires adequate translation from the analogic into the digital mode of communication" (Watzlawick, Beavin, & Jackson, 1967, p. 66). This translation process is problematic.

Steiner (1981) demonstrates this in his analysis of translation of poetry from one language to another; much of the emotional impact of the poetry is lost. Translation poses a problem not only between cultures, but between sexes, races, classes, and generations. Steiner suggests that language was developed as much to conceal from outsiders as it was to reveal to insiders.

Translation involves communication between and within persons. That is, the dialogue between the "I" and the "me" involves translation from physiological impulse into culturally learned modes of communication. Ability to regulate distance is dependent on translation both within and between. The task of translation is constant; each message must be weighed and balanced in terms of gestures and symbols. In order to comment on a relationship, one must move back and forth among impulse, gesture, and symbol. When a particular culture (individual, gender, family, race, class, or whatever) is impoverished in use of symbols that represent emotional states and relationships, accurate translation is difficult—communication lines are weak and communion between persons easily threatened.

While emotional gestures are universal, symbols for describing emotions are culture specific. In this view, under the vast differences in class, race, or gender, human beings are the same; we all speak an emotional language, but are often poor translators when it comes to cultural symbols for the emotions. Chapter 3 provides a map of the passions, the beginning of a common language to connect people in solidarity rather than isolate by differences.

Without a map, persons different from oneself may be misunderstood and rejected. Differences are necessary; they provide variety and color. But without a common base, differences cannot be celebrated. The notion of differences and similarities is an extension of the idea of separateness and connectedness. Even though each human being is different (separate), all humans are also similar (together). The study of translation, then, needs to be enlarged to include a universal language of gestural communication.

IMPLICATIONS AND FUTURE DIRECTIONS

This book began with macrotheories, applying them to microsituations, noting parallels between marital conflict and conflict in the larger social order. Marital conflict not only parallels those on a macro level, but the microroots of domination are also manifested in the interactions between spouses, giving a glimpse of how patriarchy may be maintained on macro and micro levels.

Although structures of domination often involve overt coercion, there may be only very subtle emotional coercion. Structures of domination, like other human systems, involve regulation of social distance. Both the dominating husbands and the dominated wives seem to be imprisoned by an invisible world of discourse tactics. In the cases presented in this book, domination, like escalation, seems to be a joint accomplishment.

Domination is usually a system where all members play a part; it involves the subtle forces of human interaction as much as the overt macroforces. The sole focus on patriarchy as a male problem is similar to the problem of couples who complain that one nags because the other withdraws. Whether females submit because males dominate or males dominate because females submit may be arbitrary. The problem of domination can be solved only by looking at the ways in which all members participate, the regulation of closeness and distance, the nature of the feelings involved, and the nature of the bonding systems.

Given that gender is one of the most important ways that the self is organized, relationships between the sexes make an excellent place to observe tolerance of differences, regulation of distance, and emotional exchange. At present, change is occurring at a rapid rate, from traditional to contemporary gender roles. In resisting change, shame is often used as a powerful form of social control (Scheff, 1988). Wherever change occurs at a rapid rate, shame can be found. For example, a man who shows tender feelings—weeps in public, for example—is likely to be ridiculed or shamed; women in the same situation are more likely to be given sympathy. Men may refuse to acknowledge tender feelings because their display may elicit ridicule and threaten their gender identity.

In the same way, women may cling to traditional roles for fear of appearing unfeminine (or, more accurately, for fear of the shame they would feel if they were seen as unfeminine by others). Women who behave according to the cultural patterns for male behavior are no closer to being liberated than if they clung to traditional female roles: Both maintain the status quo by holding on to what is defined as having the most value in a patriarchal system. Without secure bonds, constructive social change is difficult.

The maintenance of the status quo, whether in a conflictful relationship, a litigious family court, or a patriarchal system, is mutually and reciprocally achieved by all members. Each party is partially responsible, but each perceives the problem as existing only in the other. Neither steps out of the frame to acknowledge feelings or otherwise comment on the relationship between them. Each stays on a topic level. Both persons, in ignoring the manner between them, play roles in maintaining the quarrel system.

When shame is not acknowledged, persons cling to old patterns and beliefs—gender, racial, class, or religious stereotypes. In a rigid system, innovation and shame are experienced as threats. There is the threat of being unloved, unacceptable, ridiculed for being different, laughed at—alone, isolated, and separated from the group.

Rigidity is reflected in the communication patterns between spouses. As they quarrel nothing new is said; the same patterns of dispute continue, often for years. Many of us look at the other and say, "They never change," their behavior is rigid. Perhaps it might be better to ask, How do I deal with emotions? Do I acknowledge shame? To what extent am I alienated from others? It is relatively easy to see what is going on in other people; it is more difficult to see ourselves. Each of us first learned how to communicate from our parents (who learned from their parents, who learned from theirs). Some aspects of communication are invisible, like the air we breathe; we take it for granted. The ubiquity of communication makes the patterns difficult to change. It is far easier to focus on topics, ignoring the manner and tactics.

In contemporary society shame is denied, its importance played down; but we can no longer negate the role of shame in human behavior. When social structures are intolerant of fundamental human behaviors, a form of rigidity exists in itself. Although patterns of communication are virtually invisible, video recordings have opened up a new world for investigating social interaction (like the microscope opening up the world of microorganisms). It allows us to see patterns we never noticed before.

More generally, the concept of shame-rage alternations may be crucial not only in marital quarrels, but in conflict at all levels. Issues of bonding and shame-rage may provide insights into domestic violence, homicide, and the conflict between nations. Durkheim (1966) found that cultures that were alienated were more prone to suicide. It may be that such societies are prone not only to suicide but to violence and conflict of all kinds. Investigating the microroots of conflict opens new possibilities for conflict management, mediation, and resolution— social change.

Many conflict theorists have posited that conflict is functional, that it plays an important role in social change. But while some conflict resolves differences and has positive outcomes, all conflict is not constructive. Social change is necessary, but not all change is desirable. Change can be damaging for individuals, couples, and society at large, as in the cases of spouse abuse, homicide, riots, and nuclear war. Conflict is destructive or constructive depending on the management of shame. Shame can exclude others, leading to alienation, or include them, leading to solidarity.

When persons are in a state of unacknowledged shame it is almost impossible for them to take personal and social responsibility. In his tour de force, Braithwaite (1988) shows what might happen if communities took responsibility for their own problems. Shame can be a powerful force in criminal justice and the reintegration of offenders.

Braithwaite describes two types of shaming practices, one that stigmatizes and separates people from others, and one that integrates. He has shown how the shaming of white-collar criminals works to deter crime, and how this technique is used in Japan (where there is a very low rate of crime). The main argument against Braithwaite's work has been that it may not work with blue-collar offenders or in a culture like our own.

One way to look at a solution to this problem is to look at blue- and white-collar crime in terms of togetherness and separation and the role shame plays. White-collar criminals are usually integrated: There is much togetherness, but no shame. Shame plays a role in deterring crime on this level by adding a component of separation: publicly shaming the offender in the eyes of significant others.

Blue-collar criminals are separated from the mainstream; they are shamed but not integrated. Further shame may serve to isolate them further. These people need to have more togetherness (i.e., to have shame reduced) in order to be reintegrated. One way to reduce shame is by acknowledging it in a safe context, or by involving the punished in the negotiation of their own punishment. Use of shaming techniques is like walking a tightrope; care must be taken in dealing with reintegration and use of shaming. Using these practices in the context of criminal justice would require extensive knowledge of shame and how to reduce it.

Two organizations that have been successful in the practice of reintegrative shaming are Alcoholics Anonymous and Al-Anon. Shame and denial of human dependency, rather than guilt, are seen as lying at the root of alcoholism. Alcoholics

Anonymous can be seen as a form of shame therapy: Acknowledgment of one's shame and dependency on other people play an important role in recovery. The meetings involve a supportive network in which people acknowledge their lack of control, powerlessness, and shame. Through this process persons are helped to be able to function at a higher level, to differentiate themselves from other family members in a way that changes the family system and reduces alienation.

For constructive social change to occur, a first step is to repair damaged bonds. A key step in rebuilding or repairing the bond is to abide by rituals of respect. Encompassed in respect and acknowledgment is the idea of differentiation—for instance, entering the other's space only with permission to do so. By acknowledging the state of the bond, shame, and feelings of vulnerability, repair can begin. If an individual denies feelings, he or she is necessarily isolated; when he or she acknowledges bond and associated feelings, the experience can be profoundly connecting (Lynd, 1958). With acknowledgment, quarrels can take a dramatic turn, as illustrated in Chapter 8.

Changing old habits involves conscious and sustained effort, as well as many mistakes (and shame); they are seldom easy to change. Like music, theory provides only an abstract foundation. To be a pianist, one must practice. To change communication patterns, one must not only learn new skills, but unlearn old patterns—ways in which we communicate with self and with others.

CONCLUSIONS

Very little is known about the role of emotions in human actions. The study of conflict among interactionists has been weak in the area of emotion. The theory presented in this book places primary emphasis on the experience and display of emotion. My findings reveal dynamics of conflict between couples, shedding light on etiology, escalation, and possibilities for resolution.

While the study of symbolic interaction has substantially advanced knowledge of human interaction, the study of emotional interaction may be a further step in understanding relationships. By identifying emotions in discourse, new information can arise, such as the role of emotion in state of the bond between persons. Although case studies cannot demonstrate structure or prevalence, they can tell much about the microfoundations of conflict.

The method presented here differs from other methods for studying conflict in that it focuses on emotion and is multilevel and interdisciplinary. While most studies on emotion use survey or field methods, I use sequential analysis of discourse as it occurs in interaction. This method of analysis may lend itself well to expanding studies of emotion, in addition to, or in conjunction with, other types of research methods. Studies of this kind have important implications for theory and hypothesis building because they can lead to new ways of viewing the social world.

Escalation can be explained at a specific point in time, as well as conflict-habituated marriages, and proneness to dysfunctional forms of conflict. Proneness to engage in conflict is not only a psychological phenomenon but social psychological, based on damaged early bonds; it is relationship based. Families with secure bonds have less severe conflict than families with damaged and threatened bonds. An alienated society has conflict that is more widespread and damaging than does a society with secure bonds.

The patterns described in this book suggest the crucial importance of shame in human bonding. By focusing on the role of emotions and threatened bonds, an alternative view of conflict appears: Conflict and aggression are reactions to threats to the social bond. My analysis parallels earlier approaches and integrates them in a new way. What leads to escalation and interminable conflict is not anger as such, or even differences between people, but the absence of a secure bond between persons or groups.

Many dysfunctional communication patterns have their roots in shame and shame-rage; the amount of unacknowledged shame during a quarrel seems to reveal the level of destructiveness. It must be remembered that shame in itself is not destructive. Shame is a normal and necessary part of human social organization. The way it is managed is the source of concern.

This book is a beginning. My analysis is as yet tentative and exploratory; further steps are needed to test my conclusions. As yet, the extent to which the procedures I use may cause shame is not known. This is an exploratory study in which I develop a testable theory. The actual testing will require studies in a wide variety of contexts, using several kinds of methods. I describe a new method for inferring causal sequences second by second. This method does not strip away context, but instead relies on contextual understanding. A definitive answer to the reliability of these findings can come only with further use and testing.

Attempts to generalize the results at this early date can be risky, unless further studies give independent testimony. The work of Lansky (1987), Katz (1988), and Scheff (1987) provides support for my finding about the role of shame in destructive conflict. Additional cases are needed that specify the presence or absence of concrete emotions such as shame, guilt, contempt, or disgust, using a method similar to mine. Both internal arousal and the communicative aspects of specific emotions need to be assessed as they occur in conflict situations. Ultimately, the role of shame in conflict can be tested with large numbers of cases using survey data. Perhaps shame and anger scales could be used. Before this is done, more work on particular cases may be needed to specify causal processes and identifying cues.

The shame-rage construct may be helpful in explaining many puzzling phenomena. First, the concept of chain reactions of emotion (or spiraling) may explain both acute and chronic anger and how anger is exchanged between spouses. When shame serves as a stimulus for anger (which serves as a stimulus to further shame), arousal can last indefinitely and increase without limit. When emotions are not acknowledged, each person's response is a stimulus for the other's response, which in turn becomes a stimulus.

Second, the idea of shame-bound conflict can help distinguish normal from pathological conflict. Normal conflict can be instructive and positive—reestablishing boundaries leading toward effective problem solving. Pathological conflict is interminable, confusing, painful, and destructive, marked by rigidity, resistance to change, and rapidly rising anger. Shame helps explain why it is so easy to blame or criticize the other, and how some quarrels never end. To the extent that a society is alienated, marked by inadequate bonds and unacknowledged shame, there is increased risk of destructive conflict.

Alienation is a disease of insecure bonds and inability to repair damage; it seems easier to reject the rejector—the need for other human beings—maintaining a distorted individualism. "The recovery of a proper sense of shame would go hand in hand with our acknowledgment of radical sociality" (Schneider, 1977, p. 136). The presence of shame symbolizes (and reminds us of) our mutual social involvement and the alienation and estrangement that characterize modern Western society. Society and human dependency are treated as if they were enemies; we protest being members, and pretend to be independent pillars—in need of no one. In reality it may not be dependency that we protest, but being members of an *alienated* society.

The question each might begin with is this: What is it to be a human being? Many have placed shame and shame concomitants at the heart of human nature and morality (Darwin, 1872/1965; Ellis, 1900; Nietzsche, 1878/1910, 1886/1954; Soloviev, 1918). These writers have realized that human beings are the only creatures that blush; shame distinguishes human beings from other animals—that shame is at the root of morality. It is interesting that these ideas were prominent before World War I, with almost no further interest in shame for nearly 50 years—until only recently. Just as the 1970s were the decade of anger research and therapies related to anger, the 1990s are likely to be the decade of research on shame.

Social life is the unique way in which human beings have adapted for survival. Shame is an inevitable and auspicious part of the moral system that governs the human world. Human beings are creatures conscious of self—seeing self as others do, vicariously and symbolically. Self-other involvement is essential to human existence. Shame is the price human beings have paid; we are the only species whose behavior is fundamentally determined by an ethical code, and whose lives are regulated by a series of profoundly felt rules.

As social creatures we have been given the burden of being social and autonomous simultaneously. How do we, as human beings, balance the needs for both independence and autonomy? Inability to regulate these phenomena leads to social alienation, strong emotion, particularly shame, and conflict. I suggest that a healthy sense of shame and acknowledgment can help balance these forces, bridge the gaps between persons, and reduce conflict at all levels.

Appendix

ROSIE AND JAMES

22:23.25	R:	so what aspect of the plane do you want to talk about?
	J:	oh just airplanes in general it doesn't have to be
	R:	oh
	J:	specifically the one we have now (laugh)
30.09	R:	no I wanna NARROW it RIGHT down TO that one
34.15	J:	because I don't plan on it being the last the end of the line
37.07	R:	NO well I don't either not for you
	J:	Oh good
40.28	R:	no I wouldn't take your toy from you
	J:	all right
42.14	R:	I I sacrificed a LOT for you to have toys (1.79)

(both laugh tightly)

49:00	R:	but you didn't ask for it and I resent later and we're still going over it ok
	J:	Yeah it (3)

. . .

31:30.10	J:	what do you mean opted out
32.00	R:	well to go to school and to be away from like the house and everything and and working towards (1.34) the relationship and the house and

38.20		everything (2.44) you know, I'm not really in
		I can't do much there I'm here (2.75) so (3.56)
53.28		(laugh) isn't it great I get totally blank
	J:	(laugh)
	R:	(laugh) repression's a marvelous defense
		mechanism
	J:	(laugh)
	R:	it saved me more than once OK
32:05.20	J:	anyway we got off the airplane

. . .

32:08.20	R:	. . . yeah it (1.75) you know I resent it I
16.25	J:	yeah I know
32.04	R:	you know I feel like I've had to bail it out
		a couple of times, and bailed out the first
		airplane I feel like I bailed out this one
		financially when it needed a thousand dollars
		for its taxes and I resent it cause I really try
		to live very (1.06) cheaply and not spend money
		(1) and then to see, you know money go for THAT
		which is something I resent, hate, despise,
48.26		loathe, (2.28) just really negative emotions
		towards (1) it it really causes me a lot of pain
		(1) I'm feeling like I'm scrimping on myself to
		save money but then if the airplane needs it
		then it's gone to the airplane (2.22)
33:01.20		and that's real painful (3.22)
33:08.20	J:	(laugh)
	R:	(laugh)
10:05	J:	yeah we well I feel (1.91) feel you know
		different from that
	R:	umhm

. . .

34:04.10	R:	but to you it's not it's it's means something to
		you
08.01	J:	yeah (1.13) it makes it it makes it for me it
		makes it real difficult (1.78) it's not (2.10)
		you know it's not not PLEASANT owning it (3.25)
		in that respect in that, you know that it does
20.16		(1.53) cause you so much grief (Laugh)
34:29.10	R:	(laugh) yeah no I resent it I honestly don't
		like it, I resent it, I hate it (1.34) I have a
		lot of negative emotions attached to it, I I

38.25   think I taken maybe a lot of what with our
          relationship and life in general and put it
          just done a great projection job on the old
          airplane and
49.20 J: yeah
      R: cause it's safe to get mad at the airplane and
      J: yeah
53.15 R: won't get rejected or anything (2.59) and that's
          part of me and there's another part of me that
          understands that, you know, that's a dream of
35:01.10 yours and we're all entitled to dreams

DAVID AND COLLEEN

25:01.00 C: ok I'll go first
         D: all right
06.08 C: Well, I've taken your criticism and unhappiness
          about the house hard because my natural tendency
          is to decorate to you know, with whatever I've
29.00   got and I've been with whatever I have whether
          we were living on the beach you know, in a shack
          I'd decorate with seashells or something to
          make it comfortable but if I had umpteen million
34.14   dollars then I would decorate differently
55.05   there's certain inclines that carry through and,
26:01.10 but in general I think what I'm comfortable with
          is not what you're comfortable with
03.20 D: are you comfortable with the the concept of
          quote-unquote whatever's there? In other words
          decorate with whatever material is available if
16.11   it's bottles, OR if it's seaweed,
      C: umhm
22.20 D: just decorate with whatever's there
      C: umhm
25.00 D: what would you really like to decorate with if
          money weren't an object? I mean is there a style
          that you have in your head that you would say,
      C: yeah
34.12 D: Oh, if I had money to decorate any way that I
          could I would prefer to use SHELLS and BOTTLES?
          and

```
   43.00  C:  umhm, well I'm very eclectic I like all
   45.20      different kinds of things I like high class,
              high tech, velvet, chrome, glass
          D:  uhm
   51.28  C:  and things
          D:  uhu
          C:  I like things that are a very natural and warm,
   57.25      and and relaxing, pleasing, you know, wood and
              grasses and
27:01.20  D:  but what I'm getting at is it
          C:      inaudible
   09.25  D:  I was, what I'm getting at is it you're going
              to implement your desire to decorate
          C:  umhm
   16.15  D:  participation in the house was the aspect of
              participating in the house is the need to
              decoRATE
          C:  umhm
   24.10  D:  I mean there's definitely a need once you have
              the bare walls all done and the floors and
              ceiling finished
          C:  umhm
   29.24  D:  you're going to decorate the inside
   31.04  C:  so you're talking about mood or attitude
   33.13  D:  I'm just saying it it do you KNOW what you WANT?
              Cause you can't GET there if you don't know
              what you WANT
   40.11  C:  right, yeah
          D:  and the other part is why after fifteen years if
              you KNOW what you want if you can desCRIBE it
   45.25      or visualize it in your head
          C:  hm
   50.24  D:  why you haven't implemented it?
          C:  umhm
   53.09  D:  and if the money wasn't there that's just an
              excuse, it's just a roadblock
          C:  umhm
   57.01  D:  to overcome
          C:  umhm
   58.05  D:  why didn't you do something to get the money
              together to decorate just the way that you
```

28:01.07   wanted?
        C: Yeah, ok so what I've done and it's to
07.00   decorate just with what I've got
        D: right and that's satisfactory?
10.20   C: well, it's been practical
13.10   D: and that's satisfactory?
        C: uhhu, I mean yes and no.
18.00   D: it hasn't been for me.
        C: like, it's like making do with what I've got
21.12   D: it hasn't been for me
22.15   C: that's not it hasn't been ok with me to spend
            money that I didn't think was there
        D: umhm
35.15   C: like if I if I envisioned it, the feeling is if
            I let my imagination run as to how I wanted to
            decorate something
        D: umhm   umhm
45.29   C: just tons of money would be spent on all these
            external things,
        D: umhm
51.18   C: and my thought was that that that was a waste of
            money, that there wasn't that money there and I
            might spend foolishly and so I'll just do the
29:00.24   best with what I've got
        D: how much is a ton of money?
. . .
29:58.12 C: . . . to me the way that I decorate is not I'm
            gonna go out I'm gonna (2) you know throw all my
            (1.2) (1.9) history away
        D: umhm
        C: things that are meaningful to me and just start
            new (4.4)
30:15.20 D: has it been satisfactory to you all this time to
            decorate with your history instead of making
            your history? (1.70)
24.19   C: I'm making my history all the time I decorate
            with new things as they come in (4.31) it's only
            just beginning (1.35) to
30:34.21 D: do you know what I'm saying do you understand
            what I'm saying?
37.20   C: yeah (2.77) that you want to start new
        D: NO! I'm suggesting I'm I'm (2.71) one of the

30:50.17		(1.95) bones of contention has been for me
		anyway (1) between us (1.12) from my point of
		view has been that there's just chachkas
		everywhere all around the house there's hardly
31:01.00		a surface to put anything down and there's no
		place where the eye can rest (3.06) and (4.87)
		not only that but every little cubbyhole has
15.01		been just stuffed with stuff from
	C:	you think it's because that stuff?
19.25	D:	hoarded with stuff of your history
	C:	uhhu
21.25	D:	the stuff from your past that you've hauled
		all over the different places we've been
	C:	umhm
31:25.23	D:	because it's mementos that mean every little
		(1.69) gnat and butterfly and everything
33.10	C:	right so they're not they have no meaning to you?
31:33.10	D:	it's not that they don't have meaning to me,
		yes they have meaning to me
38.05	C:	I mean that's ok if they don't if they're my
		history
	D:	yeah
40.20	C:	they don't have to have any meaning to you and I
		can see
31:40.20	D:	well the thing is I have to take care of (1)
		and have had to take care of providing a storage
		facility for all this stuff and it happened to
		be in the environment
	C:	(laugh)
50.18	D:	where I also abide (1.79) and that's very
		unsatisfactory to me (1.53) and since I'm having
		to be the one that has gone out and had to make
		the money, in order to buy (1.81) the material
32:02.13		things, provide the material things, I would
		have thought that my partner my mate would have
		been sensitive to me in what I would require to
17.00		make a comfortable environment (1.82) would of
		been just if I gave the money and bringing it
		(2.25) that I would think that you would be
		responsive (1.37) to my needs, cause I'm trying
		to be responsive to yours.
32:31.11	C:	If you speak up I would be.

	D:	I HAVE been speaking up ALL along.
35.05	C:	Well no.
	D:	All along.
	C:	umum, umumm (L)
42.06	D:	well we could get into another subject if
	C:	(laugh)
46.25	D:	we wanted to, I guess
	C:	ok, all right so you say you've been speaking up and
55.21	D:	I think I have pointed out the problem with how our environment is crowded with just JUNK, and it's not satisfactory to me, and I've been complaining about it, and there's no change, it's continuous and it has been for fifteen years
33:16.20	C:	but you haven't been complaining about that for fifteen years
	D:	yeah for fifteen, well not for fifteen years but (inaudible) located
33:21.29	C:	I heard about it in the last (1.47) I've heard
25.00		about it in the last (1.28) three years
	D:	(2.06) well that would be enough I would think wouldn't it? (1.80)
	C:	hm (slight laugh) well?
33.12	D:	three years (2.85) HEY WOULD YOU PASS THE BUTTER I REALLY NEED THE BUTTER three years later I get the butter passed
	C:	(. . . . . laugh . . . .)
	D:	(laugh)
47.17	C:	sorry (laugh)
	D:	well (1.91) I (3.05)
58.03	C:	I'm sorry (2.95)
34:01.10	D:	I know (15.10) I feel like this is all the stuff that we're learning about life (2.00)
21.15	C:	and who we are
22.06	D:	and who we are and (1.15) stuff that we didn't
40.10		learn earlier (15.25) (sniff) (9.85)
	D:	So (2.15) what ARE we going to be doing (1.75) with all the STUFF at the house (2.50) one
35:01.00		thing I need to know (1.15) cause as I finish up the living room and dining room which are empty now (2.10) and the upstairs which will be finished
08.05	C:	it's good to empty it out like that you know

ROXANNE AND BRIAN

16:17.05 B: It's the times when you feel like you're the only
soldier on the field and you come I come home
   26.20 B: and you're going OH MAN I've done EVERYthing
today I've just done everything I've dealt with
this and that and this and that and now it's
        R: laugh   ah
        B: YOUR TURN to DEAL with it, and here take
        R: (cough)
   36.05 B: Christopher, and here change his diaper, and let
me eat, and give me two minutes of peace, and
I'm burned out (2.85)
   43.15 R: OH I do that every day (2)
        B: More often than not
   48.05 R: Bull shit (1.75)
        B: More often than not
        R: uhuh
   52.05 B: You're tired you don't wanna deal with it
        R: yeah I am tired
        B: you don't wanna deal with Christopher, you
        R: no, not all the time
   58.28 B: feel like YOU'VE had to do everything in the
house and pick up everything
        R: hhhhhhh
17:02.00 B: and clean everything and you SAY!
        R: YEAH I got to PICK up AFTER YOU ALL THE TIME
you're such a SLOB you just take your clothes
off in the middle of the floor
  05.22d B: and you say that I don't do anything
  09.09 R: You don't if I don't move your shoes out of the
middle of the living room they just stay there,
if I don't pick up your clothes in the middle of
the floor they'll stay there. You'll walk all
  17.06   over them. You'll walk over them when you get
home from work. Your mess in the closet, it's
still there you don't put ANYTHING away. I fold
your laundry, I wash it and put it some where
  28.05   where you can put it away and you don't put it
away. It's more work for me
  38.08 B: I NEVER put it away.

R: WELL, before OUR parents come you usually tidy
up a little.
45.00   B: it's not the only time
R: and once in a blue moon, when you get the urge
to of pick up your things and you need laundry
and you're looking for something under the piles
B: yeah
R: yeah
58.13   B: yeah. I put it away when it bothers me.
18:02.05   R: Once in a BLUE moon.
B: hn, there's a lot of blue moons these days, you
R: No
08.16   B: know, it's because of the pollution
R: (tight laugh)
13.06   B: No come on, you feel like the only soldier
fighting the battle
R: No Brian, more often than not I clean up after
you make food

. . .
22:47.10   B: No this is (inaudible) sometimes I feel like I'm
the only soldier going out there and doing
battle with the world
R: And working making money; I just had a baby do
you WANT me to GO GET a job and waitress and pay
a babysitter to take care of Christopher and
23:00.15   come back with zero
. . .
29:44.17   R: OK it's resolved (laugh)
B: ok let's, that that's inside the house what
about outside
47.20   R: I'm ALWAYS cleaning up and picking up and
sweeping and raking the front yard, what? do I
54.10   leave laying around it's YOUR tools and your
stuff that you can't find that you leave
58.27   B: like the bunkbeds and after you took the car and
30:01.00   R: where am I going to put them dear, sweetheart,
where
05.25   B: who does all the weed cleaning and carrying the
weeds away
R: who's going to
B: who does the (inaudible) cleaning

08.20 R: who helps you I helped you last time but I
started choking and gagging and sneezing
B: uhhu
13.00 R: you know I can I'm going to kick you
B: uhhu, I have to do everything outside the house
19.08 R: bull shit
B: just everything (laugh) well
R: I help you
26.17 B: I, see if I want, if I wanted to build a a case
R: I took wheelbarrow loads to the pile
B: like that
30.17 R: all right you made your point
B: I could BUILD a case but I don't want to build a
case, I don't want to RAG on anybody, I don't
like it when somebody rags on me so I don't
37.06 wanna rag on anybody
R: OK fine
43.08 B: well so it's unfair, unjust for me to put up
with ragging that I receive when I don't give
it that much
52.22 R: YOU'RE SARCASTIC and that's worse than ragging on
B: no no no my sarcasm has valuable social merit
31:01.17 R: Brian if you were nice to me you wouldn't
believe what you'd get
B: I am nice
R: NO
08.24 B: I'm only sarcastic to people that I'm nice to
R: I can't handle it all the TIME you got to give
me at least a few days of a break

RANDY AND KARIN

05:10.60 R: So your brother Joseph was going to talk to me
at one point in time (3.75) you remember you
were going to tell me that (2.60) he's saying
21.63 that (1.25) men in what Samoa or something
26.35 K: Jamaica
R: In Jamaica would prefer overweight women
30.65 K: they don't prefer it they just accept it (1.69)
05:35.00 just trying to say that Madison Avenue type
(.85) stereotype of what American women should

40.49   look like (2.00) I mean just all
     R: umhm
46.90 K: right now (1.80) what Madison avenue thinks
       women should look like, I mean not all women are
       five feet six inches high, I mean tall, and you
       know weigh 123 pounds (1.10) there's a lot of
       women because they weigh 160 or because they
       weigh 250 are not acceptable because they're
59.60   overweight but society doesn't accept them
06:03.00   (1.05) you're not accepted on job interviews,
       you're not accepted (1.06) you know with MOST so
       called
     R: umhm uhm
11.20 K: elitist-type men and stuff so (1) who needs it
       (1.3) and if you happen to have gained weight
       because you've got problems in your life then
       you gain weight because you got problems in your
       life that doesn't mean you're any less of a
       person
25.87 R: (4) yeah well (long sigh) (8.26)
34.38 K: yeah well what (3.70)
     R: yeah but I hesitate to get into this at all I
     K: well
42.30 R: AHH! cause I (3) you know I don't want to get into
       your character assassination but I usually do (3.20)
58.80 K: you don't have to say anything SUPER personal
       but
     R: but you have to understand that (2.40) if you
       know, that I mean your living with one of the
07:02.00   most antisocial men in the world (1.5) that
       anything that society would do, I would
       automatically try to find a completely different
       way to go about anything
13.30 K: but NOT when women are concerned
     R: but you also—that's not true
17.50 K: yeah it is
     R: it's not true I mean I think every man has their
21.29   dream woman every man has their dream
       silhouette dream shape you know dream eyes you
       know whatever (2.35) and (3.15) and I I hate to

		put it you this, you know I hate to (2.62) to
		always harp on the same stuff, but (2.75) I mean
		at your weight now (2.35) you're just not doing
50.36		it for me (2.50) and (4) I know that it's been
		really shitty of me to (2.10) not touch you and
08:00.00		not be romantic with you and not (2.50)
		sometimes even be kind to you (2.10) but (3) I
		don't know you know it started out about about a
15.50		year ago that, you know I I suddenly felt very
		very hemmed very frustrated by it (3.53) and to
		begin with if we're both down to our proper
33.17		weights (2.59) sex would be much better

. . .

09:39.03	R:	you have you you have to lose some weight
41.30	K:	I agree but the support from you should come
	R:	I gave you five years of support
46.31	K:	can't say that because I mean obviously
	R:	with every damn diet
48.40	K:	I wasn't getting ENOUGH support or I wouldn't
		have gained all this weight
51.90	R:	well then you would need to have married FIFTY
		men and had them all sort of telling you that
55.50	K:	that's not fair
	R:	"you can do it, you can do it" the support
		doesn't necessarily just come from without
		there's a million
10:03.90	K:	I wouldn't
	R:	times you walked up to the corner to Swensen's
8.20		and I asked you leave the damn ice cream alone
		and you would get an ice cream cone to spite me
13.50	K:	yeah but the support doesn't come in telling me
		not what to eat but realizing that I have some
		problems and I'm internalizing them is where the
		support and YOU should come in
23.34	R:	yeah but I can't get into your mind
	K:	well I I you know I fairly read you well
29.52	R:	yeah I fairly read you well too and it it and I
		don't know I don't know what's going on it seems
36.49		like I mean we're both gonna be sixty-five
		someday and I not going to you know I'm not
		gonna mind living with a sixty-five-year-old

broad when I'm sixty-five but we're in our
thirties

48.57 K: I don't think I look like I'm sixty-five

       R: you look you have the same silhouette as a sixty-
           five-year-old broad

53.71 K: that doesn't matter

. . .

14:21.61 K: you see you're not even FACING the problem and
              maybe that's where the problem lies

24.78 R: what do you mean not no no see the problem is
           (1.63) just visualize you at a hundred and
           twenty-five

31.59 K: EVEN IF I WEIGHED a hundred and twenty-five we'd
           still have a problem in bed

32.63 R: wait a second I'm not finished talking that's
           not true what kind of a problem would we have

38.40 K: the same problem we have NOW because of the way
           you ARE

       R: what do you mean that I don't kiss you

43.97 K: you don't, you're not really

       R: that I don't that I don't get into

46.21   foreplay that I don't get into being kind and
           being watchful for your own you know

       K: . . . laugh . . .

       R: climaxes and your own

. . .

16:40.49 R: . . .simply because I don't want to kiss you or
              spend time kissing you doesn't mean I don't like
              YOU, you see you got that backwards

50.06 K: yes it does

       R: No, you got that backwards; what that means is is
           that I don't like your FACE right now, I mean

54.40   it used to be that had some actual lips NOW
           your there's there's very little definition

17:01.31 K: you don't have any upper lip, don't talk about
              my lips

. . .

19:57.12 R: I don't know how the hell you were raised that
              way I mean your father is the is the biggest
              liar I mean you could ask your father what day
              it was . . .

References

Adamson, L., Als, H., Tronick, E., & Brazelton, T. B. (1977). The development of social reciprocity between a sighted infant and her blind parents. *Journal of American Academy of Child Psychiatry, 16*, 194-207.

Adamson, L., & Bakeman, R. (1982). Affectivity and reference: Concepts, methods, and techniques in the study of communication development of 6-to-18-month-old infants. In T. Field & A. Fogel (Eds.), *Emotion and early interaction*. Hillsdale, NJ: Lawrence Erlbaum.

Ainsworth, M. (1989). Attachment beyond infancy. *American Psychologist, 44*, 709-716.

Ainsworth, M., Bell, S., & Stayton, D. (1974). Infant-mother attachment social development: "Socialization" as a product of reciprocal responsiveness to signals. In M. Richards (Ed.), *The integration of the child into a social world*. New York: Cambridge University Press.

Allport, G. (1937). *Personality: A psychological interpretation*. New York: Henry Holt.

Archer, D., & Akert, R. M. (1977). Words and everything else: Verbal and nonverbal cues in social interpretation. *Journal of Personality and Social Psychology, 35*, 443-449.

Averill, J. R. (1982). *Anger and aggression: An essay on emotion*. New York: Springer-Verlag.

Bach, G. R., & Wydens, P. (1968). *The intimate enemy*. New York: Morrow.

Bakan, D. (1966). *The duality of human existence*. Chicago: Rand McNally.

Bales, R. (1950). *Interaction process analysis: A method for the study of small groups*. Reading, MA: Addison-Wesley.

Barnett, L. R., & Nietzel, M. T. (1979). Relationship of instrumental and affectional behaviors and self-esteem to marital satisfaction in distressed and non-distressed couples. *Journal of Consulting and Clinical Psychology, 47*, 946-957.

Barrett, K., & Campos, J. (1987). Perspectives on emotional development II: A functional approach to emotions. In J. D. Osofsky (Ed.), *Handbook of infant development* (pp. 555-578). New York: John Wiley.

Bateson, G. (1972). *Steps to an ecology of mind.* New York: Ballantine.

Bateson, G., Jackson, D., Haley, J., & Weakland, J. (1956). Toward a theory of schizophrenia. *Behavioral Science, 1,* 251-264.

Baxter, L. (1988). A dialectical perspective on communication strategies in relationship development. In S. Duck (Ed.), *Handbook of personal relationships* (pp. 257-273). New York: John Wiley.

Beck, A. (1976). *Cognitive therapy and the emotional disorder.* New York: International University Press.

Benedict, R. (1946). *The chrysanthemum and the sword.* New York: Houghton Mifflin.

Berkowitz, L. (1983). Aversively stimulated aggression: Some parallels and differences in research with animals and humans. *American Psychologist, 38,* 1135-1160.

Berscheid, E. (1983). Emotion. In H. Kelley, E. Berscheid, A. Christensen, J. Harvey, T. Huston, G. Levinger, L. Peplau, & D. Peterson (Eds.), *Close relationships.* New York: W. H. Freeman.

Birchler, G. R., Weiss, R. L., & Vincent, J. P. (1975). Multimethod analysis of social reinforcement exchange between maritally distressed and nondistressed spouse and stranger dyads. *Journal of Personality and Social Psychology, 31,* 349-360.

Blumer, H. (1936). Social attitudes and nonsymbolic interaction. *Journal of Educational Sociology, 9,* 515-523.

Boulding, K. (1962). *Conflict and defense: A general theory.* New York: Harper.

Bowen, M. (1978). *Family therapy in clinical practice.* New York: Jason Aronson.

Bowlby, J. (1963). Pathological mourning and childhood mourning. *Journal of American Psychoanalytic Association, 11,* 500-541.

Bowlby, J. (1969). *Attachment and loss* (Vol. 1). New York: Basic Books.

Bowlby, J. (1973). *Attachment and loss* (Vol. 2). New York: Basic Books.

Bowlby, J. (1988). *A secure base: Parent-child attachment and healthy human development.* New York: Basic Books.

Bradshaw, J. (1988). *Healing the shame that binds you.* Dearfield Beach, FL: Health Communications.

Braithwaite, J. (1988). *Crime, shame and reintegration.* Cambridge: Cambridge University Press.

Brazelton, T. B. (1982). Joint regulation of neonate-parent interaction. In E. Tronick (Ed.), *Social exchange in infancy.* Baltimore: University Park Press.

Brazelton, T. B., Koslowski, B. V., & Main, M. (1974). The origins of reciprocity: Early mother-infant interaction. In M. Lewis & L. Rosenblum (Eds.), *The effect of the infant on its caregiver.* New York: John Wiley.

Brockner, J., & Rubin, J. Z. (1985). *Entrapment in escalating conflicts.* New York: Springer-Verlag.

Brown, D. E. (1991). *Human universals.* New York: McGraw-Hill.

Buck, R. (1984). *The communication of emotion.* New York: Guilford.

Burgess, E., & Cottrell, L. (1939). *Predicting success and failure in marriage.* New York: Prentice-Hall.

Burrell, N., & Fitzpatrick, M. A. (1990). Psychological reality of marital conflict. In D. Cahn (Ed.), *Intimates in conflict* (pp. 167-185). Hillsdale, NJ: Lawrence Erlbaum.

Campos, J., & Stenberg, C. (1981). Perception, appraisal and emotion: The onset of social referencing. In M. Lamb & L. Sherrod (Eds.), *Infant social cognition.* Hillsdale, NJ: Lawrence Erlbaum.

Cavanaugh, E. (1989). *Understanding shame.* Minneapolis: Johnson Institute.

Coleman, J. (1957). *Community conflict.* New York: Free Press.

Collins, R. (1975). *Conflict sociology: Towards an explanatory science.* New York: Academic.

Condon, W. S., & Ogston, W. D. (1971). Speech and body motion synchrony of the speaker-hearer. In D. L. Horton & J. J. Jenkins (Eds.), *Perception of language.* Columbus, OH: Charles E. Merrill.

Cooley, C. H. (1962). *Social organization.* New York: Schocken. (Original work published 1909)

Cooley, C. H. (1964). *Human nature and the social order.* New York: Schocken. (Original work published 1902)

Coser, L. A. (1956). *The functions of social conflict.* New York: Free Press.

Cottle, T. J. (1980). *Children's secrets.* Garden City, NY: Anchor.

Cuber, J. F., & Harroff, P. B. (1965). *Sex and the significant Americans.* Baltimore: Pelican.

Dahrendorf, R. (1965). *Gesellshaft und demokratie in Deutschland.* Munich: Piper Verlag.

Darwin, C. (1965). *The expression of the emotions in man and animals.* London: John Murray. (Original work published 1872)

DeCasper, A., & Fifer, W. (1981). Of human bonding: Newborns prefer their mothers' voices. *Science, 208,* 1174-1176.

Deutsch, M. (1969). Conflicts: Productive and destructive. *Journal of Social Issues, 25,* 7-41.

Dewey, J. (1922). *Human nature and conduct.* New York: Modern Library.

Dewey, J. (1958). *Experience and human nature.* New York: Dover. (Original work published 1925)

Dodds, E. (1951). *The Greeks and the irrational.* Oxford: Oxford University Press.

Donohue, W., Lyles, J., & Rogan, R. (1989). Issue development in divorce mediation. *Mediation Quarterly, 24,* 19-28.

Duck, S. (Ed.). (1988). *Handbook of personal relationships.* New York: John Wiley.

Duncan, S., Jr., & Fiske, D. W. (1977). *Face-to-face interaction: Research, method and theory.* Hillsdale, NJ: Lawrence Erlbaum.

Durkheim, E. (1964). *The division of labor in society.* New York: Free Press. (Original work published 1893)

Durkheim, E. (1966). *Suicide.* New York: Free Press. (Original work published 1897)

Edelmann, R. J., Asendorf, J., Contarello, A., Zammuner, V., et al. (1989). Self-reported expression of embarrassment in five European cultures. *Journal of Cross-Cultural Psychology, 20,* 357-371.

Ekman, P., & Friesen, W. (1975). *Unmasking the face.* Englewood Cliffs, NJ: Prentice-Hall.

Ekman, P., & Friesen, W. (1978). *Facial action coding system.* Palo Alto, CA: Consulting Psychologists Press.

Ekman, P., & Friesen, W. (1982). Felt, false and miserable smiles. *Journal of Non-verbal Behavior, 6,* 238-252.

Ellis, H. (1900). *The evolution of modesty.* Philadelphia: F. A. Davis.

Erikson, E. H. (1963). *Childhood and society.* New York: W. W. Norton.

Feshbach, S. (1956). The catharsis hypothesis and some consequences of interaction with aggression and neutral play objects. *Journal of Personality, 24,* 449-462.

Field, T., Woodson, R., & Cohen, D. (1982). Discrimination and imitation of facial expression by neonates. *Science, 218,* 179-181.

Fitzpatrick, M. A. (1988). *Between husbands and wives: Communication in marriage.* Newbury Park, CA: Sage.

Fitzpatrick, M. A. (in press). Sex differences in marital conflict: Social psychological verse cognitive explanations. *Text.*

Fitzpatrick, M. A., & Wamboldt, F. (1990). Where all is said and done: Toward an integration of intrapersonal and interpersonal models of marital and family communication. *Communication Research, 17,* 421-431.

Folger, J., & Poole, M. (1984). *Working through conflict.* Glenview, IL: Scott, Foresman.

Fossum, M., & Mason, M. (1986). *Facing shame: Families in recovery.* New York: W. W. Norton.

Freud, S. (1959). Inhibitions, symptoms, and anxiety. In S. Freud, *Standard edition* (Vol. 20, pp. 87-172). London: Hogarth. (Original work published 1926)

Freud, S., & Breuer, J. (1961). *Studies on hysteria.* New York: Avon. (Original work published 1896)

Funkenstein, D. H., King, S., & Drolette, M. (1957). *Mastery of stress.* Cambridge, MA: Harvard University Press.

Gaylin, W. (1979). *Feelings.* New York: Harper & Row.

Gaylin, W. (1984). *The rage within: Anger in modern life.* New York: Simon & Schuster.

Gaylin, W., & Person, E. (1988). *Passionate attachments.* New York: Free Press.

Gelles, R. J. (1987). *Family violence.* Newbury Park, CA: Sage.

Gelles, R. J., & Straus, M. A. (1979a). Determinants of violence in the family: Toward a theoretical integration. In W. Burr, R. Hill, F. I. Nye, & I. Reiss (Eds.), *Contemporary theories about the family.* New York: Free Press.

Gelles, R. J., & Straus, M. A. (1979b). Violence in the American family. *Journal of Social Issues, 35,* 15-39.

Giddens, A. (1989). Paper presented at a colloquium, University of California, Santa Barbara, Department of Sociology.

Goffman, E. (1959). *The presentation of self in everyday life.* Garden City: Doubleday.

Goffman, E. (1967). *Interaction ritual.* Garden City, NY: Anchor.

Gottman, J. M. (1979). *Marital interaction.* New York: Academic Press.

Gottman, J. M. (1990). How marriages change. In G. Patterson (Ed.), *Depression and aggression in family interaction* (pp. 75-102). Hillsdale, NJ: Lawrence Erlbaum.

Gottman, J. M., & Levenson, R. (1986). Assessing the role of emotion in marriage. *Behavioral Assessment, 8,* 31-48.

Gottman, J. M., Markman, H., & Notarius, C. (1977). Topography of marital conflict: A sequential analysis of verbal and nonverbal behavior. *Journal of Marriage and the Family, 39,* 361-377.

Gottschalk, L. A., Winget, C. N., & Gleser, G. C. (1969). *Manual of instruction for using the Gottschalk-Gleser content analysis scales: Anxiety, hostility, and social alienation-personal disorganization.* Berkeley: University of California Press.

Green, R., & Murray, E. (1973). Instigation to aggression as a function of self-disclosure and threat to self esteem. *Journal of Consulting and Clinical Psychology, 40,* 440-443.

Groen, J. J. (1975). The measurement of emotion and arousal in the clinical psychological laboratory and in medical practice. In L. Levi (Ed.), *Emotions: Their parameters and measurement.* New York: Raven.

Gross, E., & Stone, G. (1964). Embarrassment and the analysis of role requirements. *American Journal of Sociology, 70,* 1-15.

Hall, S. (1899). A study of anger. *American Journal of Psychology, 10,* 506-591.

Hansburg, H. (1972). *Adolescent separation anxiety: A method for the study of adolescent separation problems.* Springfield, IL: Charles C Thomas.

Harlow, H. F. (1962). The heterosexual affectional system in monkeys. *American Psychologist, 17,* 1-9.

Harrington, C. L. (1990). *Emotion talk: The sequential organization of shame talk.* Unpublished doctoral dissertation, University of California, Santa Barbara.

Heritage, J. (1985). Recent developments in conversational analysis. *Sociolinguistics, 15,* 1-19.

Hess, R. D., & Handel, G. (1959). *Family worlds: A psychosocial approach to family life.* Chicago: University of Chicago Press.

Holtzworth-Munroe, A., & Jacobson, N. S. (1985). Causal attributions of married couples: When do they search for causes? What do they conclude when they do? *Journal of Personality and Social Psychology, 48,* 1398-1412.

Horowitz, M. J. (1981). Self-righteous rage and the attribution of blame. *Archives of General Psychiatry, 38,* 1233-1238.

Izard, C. (1971). *The face of emotion.* New York: Appleton-Century-Crofts.

Izard, C. (1977). *Human emotion.* New York: Plenum.

Jackins, H. (1965). *The human side of human beings.* Seattle: Rational Island.

Jackson, D. D. (1957). The question of family homeostasis. *Psychiatric Quarterly Supplement, 31,* 79-90.

Jackson, D. D. (1965a). Family rules: Marital quid pro quo. *Archives of General Psychiatry, 12,* 589-594.

Jackson, D. D. (1965b). The study of the family. *Family Process, 4,* 1-20.

Jacobs, S. (1988). Evidence and inference in conversation analysis. In J. A. Anderson (Ed.), *Communication yearbook 11* (pp. 433-443). Newbury Park, CA: Sage.

Jacobson, N. S. (1977). Problem solving and contingency in the treatment of marital discord. *Journal of Clinical and Consulting Psychology, 45,* 92-100.

Jacobson, N. S., McDonald, D. W., Follette, W. C., & Berley, R. A. (1985). Attributional processes in distressed and nondistressed married couples. *Cognitive Therapy and Research, 9,* 35-50.

James, W. (1910). *Psychology.* New York: Henry Holt.

Janov, A. (1970). *The primal scream.* New York: Dell.

Johnston, J., & Campbell, L. (1988). *Impasses in divorce.* New York: Free Press.

Johnston J., Campbell, L., & Tall, M. (1984, April 7-11). *Impasse to the resolution of custody and visitation disputes.* Paper presented at the 61st Annual Meeting of the American Orthopsychiatry Association, Toronto.

Kahn, M. (1966). The physiology of catharsis. *Journal of Personality and Social Psychology, 3,* 278-286.

Kaplin, R. (1975). The cathartic value of self-expression: Testing catharsis, dissonance, and interference explanations. *Journal of Social Psychology, 97,* 195-208.

Katz, J. (1988). *Seductions to crime.* New York: Basic Books.

Kaufman, G. (1989). *The psychology of shame: Theory and treatment of shame-based syndromes.* New York: Springer.

Kelley, H. H., Berscheid, E., Christensen, A., Harvey, J. H., Huston, T., Levinger, G., Peplau, L., & Peterson, D. (Eds.). (1983). *Close relationships.* New York: W. H. Freeman.

Kendon, A. (1967). Some functions of gaze-direction in social interaction. *Acta Psychologica, 29,* 22-47.

Kerr, M., & Bowen, M. (1988). *Family evaluation.* New York: W. W. Norton.

Klinnert, M., Campos, J., Sorse, J., Emde, R., & Svejda, M. (1982). The development of social referencing in infancy. In R. Plutchick & H. Kellerman (Ed.), *Emotion: Theory, research and experience: Vol. 2. Emotion in early development.* New York: Academic Press.

Kohut, H. E. (1971). Thoughts on narcissism and narcissistic rage. In H. E. Kohut, *The search for the self.* New York: International University Press.

Kreisberg, L. (1973). *The sociology of social conflicts.* Englewood Cliffs, NJ: Prentice-Hall.

Labov, W., & Fanshel, D. (1977). *Therapeutic discourse.* New York: Academic Press.

Laing, R. D. (1965). *The divided self.* Baltimore: Penguin.

Lansky, M. (1980). On blame. *International Journal of Psychoanalytic Psychotherapy, 11,* 409-425.

Lansky, M. (1985). Preoccupation as a mode of pathologic distance regulation. *International Journal of Psychoanalytic Psychotherapy, 11,* 409-425.

Lansky, M. (1987). Shame and domestic violence. In D. Nathanson (Ed.), *The many faces of shame*. New York: Guilford.

Lazare, A. (1979). Unresolved grief. In A. Lazare, *Outpatient psychiatry: Diagnosis and treatment*. Baltimore: Williams & Wilkins.

Lazare, A. (1987). Shame and humiliation in the medical encounter. *Archives of Internal Medicine, 147*, 1653-1658.

Lewis, H. B. (1958). Over-differentiation and under-individuation of the self. *Psychoanalysis and the Psychoanalytic Review, 45*, 3-24.

Lewis, H. B. (1971a). *Shame and guilt in neurosis*. New York: International University Press.

Lewis, H. B. (1971b). Shame and guilt in neurosis. *Psychoanalytic Review, 58*, 434-435.

Lewis, H. B. (1976). *Psychic war in men and women*. New York: New York University Press.

Lewis, H. B. (1979). Using content analysis to explore shame and guilt in neurosis. In L. A. Gottschalk (Ed.), *The content analysis of verbal behavior*. New York: Halstead.

Lewis, H. B. (1981a). *Freud and modern psychology* (Vol. 1). New York: Plenum.

Lewis, H. B. (1981b). Shame and guilt in human nature. In S. Tuttman, C. Kaye, & M. Zimmerman (Eds.), *Object and self: A developmental approach*. New York: International University Press.

Lewis, H. B. (1983). *Freud and modern psychology* (Vol. 2). New York: Plenum.

Lewis, H. B. (1985). *Some thoughts on the moral emotions of shame and guilt*. In L. Cirillo, B. Kaplin, & S. Wapner (Eds.), *Emotions in ideal human development*. Hillsdale, NJ: Lawrence Erlbaum.

Lewis, H. B. (Ed.). (1987). *The role of shame in symptom formation*. Hillsdale, NJ: Lawrence Erlbaum.

Lindsay-Hartz, J. (1984). Contrasting experiences of shame and guilt. *American Behavioral Scientist, 27*, 689-704.

Locke, H. J. (1951). *Predicting adjustment in marriage: A comparison of a divorced and a happily married group*. New York: Holt.

Longley, J., & Pruitt, D. (1980). Groupthink: A critique of Janis's theory. *Review of Personality and Social Psychology, 1*, 74-93.

Lynd, H. (1958). *On shame and the search for identity*. New York: Harcourt.

Mace, D. R. (1976). Marital intimacy and the deadly love-anger cycle. *Journal of Marriage and Family Counseling, 2*, 131-137.

Mahler, M., & McDivitt, J. (1982). Thoughts on the emergence of the sense of self, with particular emphasis on the body self. *Journal of the American Psychoanalytic Association, 30*, 827-848.

Margolin, G., & Wampold, B. E. (1981). A sequential analysis of conflict and accord in distressed and non-distressed marital partners. *Journal of Consulting and Clinical Psychology, 49*, 554-567.

Markman, H. (1981). The prediction of marital distress: A five-year follow-up. *Journal of Consulting and Clinical Psychology, 49*, 760-762.

Markman, H., & Notarius, C. (1987). Coding marital and family interaction: Current status. In T. Jacobs (Ed.), *Family interaction and psychopathology: Theories, research and methods* (pp. 329-390). New York: Plenum.

Marx, K. (1964). *Economic and philosophic manuscripts of 1844.* New York: International Publishers. (Original work published 1844)

Massie, H. (1982). Affective development and the organization of mother-infant behavior from the perspective of psychopathology. In E. Tronick (Ed.), *Social interchange in infancy.* Baltimore: University Park Press.

McDougall, W. (1908). *An introduction to social psychology.* New York: University Paperbacks.

Mead, G. H. (1934). *Mind, self, and society.* Chicago: University of Chicago Press.

Mead, G. H. (1964). *Selected writings.* Indianapolis: Bobbs-Merrill.

Mehrabian, A. (1972). *Non-verbal communication.* New York: Aldine.

Mishler, E. (1986). *Research interviewing: Context and narrative.* Cambridge, MA: Harvard University Press.

Mishler, E., & Waxler, N. (1968). *Interaction in families.* New York: John Wiley.

Morrison, A. (1989). *Shame, the underside of narcissism.* Hillsdale, NJ: Analytic Press.

Morrison, N. (1987). The role of shame in schizophrenia. In H. B. Lewis (Ed.), *The role of shame in symptom formation.* Hillsdale, NJ: Lawrence Erlbaum.

Neuhauser, P. (1988). *Tribal warfare in organizations.* Cambridge, MA: Ballinger.

Nichols, M. P., & Zax, M. (1977). *Catharsis in psychotherapy.* New York: Gardiner.

Nietzsche, F. (1910). Human, all-too-human. In O. Levy (Ed.), *The complete works of Friedrich Nietzsche.* London: T. N. Foulis. (Original work published 1878)

Nietzsche, F. (1954). *Beyond good and evil: The philosophy of Nietzsche.* New York: Modern Library. (Original work published 1886)

Nietzsche, F. (1967). *Genealogy of morals.* New York: Vintage. (Original work published 1887)

Noller, P. (1984). *Nonverbal communication and marital interaction.* New York: Pergamon.

Noller, P., & Fitzpatrick, M. A. (1990). Marital communication in the eighties. *Journal of Marriage and the Family, 52.*

Notarius, C., & Johnson, J. (1982). Emotional expressions in husbands and wives. *Journal of Marriage and the Family, 44,* 483-489.

Notarius, C., & Markman, H. (1981). The Couples Interaction Scoring System. In E. E. Filsinger & R. A. Lewis (Eds.), *Observing marriages: New behavioral approaches.* Beverly Hills, CA: Sage.

Olson, D. (1986). Circumplex model VII: Validation studies and FACES III. *Family Process, 25,* 337-351.

Olson, D., Lavee, Y., & Cubbin, H. (1988). Types of families and family response to stress across the life cycle. In D. Klein & J. Aldous (Eds.), *Social stress and family development* (pp. 16-43). New York: Guilford.

Olson, D., & Rider, R. (1970). Inventory of Marital Conflict (IMC): An experimental interaction procedure. *Journal of Marriage and the Family, 32,* 443-448.

Parsons, T. (1949). *The structure of social action.* New York: Free Press.

Parsons, T., & Bales, R. F. (1955). *Family, socialization, and interaction process.* New York: Free Press.

Patterson, G. (1982). *Coercive family process.* Eugene, OR: Castalia.

Perls, F. (1969). *Ego, hunger and aggression.* New York: Random House. (Original work published 1947)

Peterson, D. R. (1979). Assessing interpersonal relationships by means of interaction records. *Behavioral Assessment, 1,* 221-236.

Peterson, D. R. (1983). Conflict. In H. Kelley, E. Berscheid, A. Christensen, J. Harvey, T. Huston, G. Levinger, L. Peplau, & D. Peterson (Eds.), *Close relationships.* New York: W. H. Freeman.

Piers, G., & Singer, M. (1953). *Shame and guilt.* New York: Charles C Thomas.

Pittenger, R., Hockett, C., & Danehy, J. (1960). *The first five minutes.* New York: Paul Martineau.

Pruitt, D. G., & Rubin, J. Z. (1986). *Social conflict.* New York: Random House.

Quanty, M. B. (1976). Aggression catharsis: Experimental investigations and implications. In R. G. Geen & E. C. O'Neal (Eds.), *Perspectives on aggression.* New York: Academic Press.

Rank, O. (1968). *Will, therapy and truth and reality.* New York: Knopf. (Original work published 1936)

Raush, H., Barry, W., Hertel, R., & Swain, M. (1974). *Communication, conflict and marriage.* San Francisco: Jossey-Bass.

Raush, H., Greif, A., & Nugent, J. (1979). Communication in couples and families. In W. R. Burr, R. Hill, F. I. Nye, & I. L. Reiss (Eds.), *Contemporary theories about the family* (pp. 468-492). New York: Free Press.

Reiss, D. (1981). *The family's construction of reality.* Cambridge, MA: Harvard University Press.

Retzinger, S. M. (1985). The resentment process: Videotape studies. *Psychoanalytic Psychology, 2,* 129-151.

Retzinger, S. M. (1987). Resentment and laughter: Video studies of the shame-rage spiral. In H. B. Lewis (Ed.), *The role of shame in symptom formation.* Hillsdale, NJ: Lawrence Erlbaum.

Retzinger, S. M. (1989). A theory of mental illness: Integrating social and emotional aspects. *Psychiatry, 52,* 325-335.

Retzinger, S. M. (1991a, Spring). Mental illness and labeling in mediation. *Mediation Quarterly.*

Retzinger, S. M. (1991b). The role of shame in marital conflict. *Perspectives on Social Problems, 3.*

Retzinger, S. M. (1991c). Shame, anger and conflict: Case study of emotional violence. *Journal of Family Violence, 6*(1), 37-59.

Rheingold, H. (1969). The social and socializing infant. In D. Goslin (Ed.), *Handbook of socialization theory and research.* Chicago: Rand McNally.

Robson, K. S. (1967). The role of eye-to-eye contact in mother-infant attachment. *Journal of Psychology and Psychiatry, 8,* 13-25.

Roloff, M. E., & Miller, G. R. (Eds.). (1987). *Interpersonal process.* Newbury Park, CA: Sage.

Rosenstock, F., & Kutner, B. (1967). Alienation and family crisis. *Sociological Quarterly, 8,* 397-405.

Rubin, L. (1983). *Intimate strangers: Men and women together.* New York: Harper.

Rubin, T. I. (1970). *The angry book.* New York: Collier.

Ruesch, J., & Bateson, G. (1951). *Communication: The social matrix of psychiatry.* New York: W. W. Norton.

Saposnek, D. (1983). *Mediating child custody disputes.* San Francisco: Jossey-Bass.

Satir, V. (1967). *Conjoint family therapy.* Palo Alto, CA: Science & Behavior.

Satir, V. (1972). *Peoplemaking.* Palo Alto, CA: Science & Behavior.

Scheff, T. J. (1983). Toward integration in the social psychology of emotion. *Annual Review of Sociology, 9,* 33-54.

Scheff, T. J. (1986). Toward resolving the controversy over thick description. *Current Anthropology, 27,* 408-409.

Scheff, T. J. (1987). The shame-rage spiral: A case study of an interminable quarrel. In H. B. Lewis (Ed.), *The role of shame in symptom formation.* Hillsdale, NJ: Lawrence Erlbaum.

Scheff, T. J. (1988). Shame and conformity: The deference emotion system. *American Journal of Sociology, 53,* 395-406.

Scheff, T. J. (1989). Cognitive and emotional conflict in anorexia: Re-analysis of a case. *Psychiatry, 52,* 148-161.

Scheff, T. J. (1990). *Microsociology.* Chicago: University of Chicago Press.

Scheff, T. J., & Retzinger, S. M. (1991). *Emotions and violence: Shame and rage in destructive conflicts.* Lexington, MA: Free Press.

Scheff, T. J., Retzinger, S. M., & Ryan, M. (1989). Crime, violence and self-esteem: Review and proposals. In A. Mecca, N. Smelser, & J. Vasconcellos, *The social importance of self-esteem.* Berkeley: University of California Press.

Scheflen, A. E. (1960). Regressive one-to-one relationships. *Psychiatric Quarterly, 23,* 692-709.

Scheflen, A. E. (1973). *Communicational structure.* Bloomington: Indiana University Press.

Scheflen, A. E. (1974). *How behavior means.* Garden City, NY: Doubleday.

Scheler, M. (1961). *Ressentiment.* New York: Free Press.

Schneider, C. (1977). *Shame, exposure and privacy.* Boston: Beacon.

Shane, P. (1980). Shame and learning. *American Journal of Orthopsychiatry, 50,* 348-355.

Shaver, K. (1985). *The attribution of blame.* New York: Springer Verlag.

Shaver, P. (1987). Love and attachment: The integration of three behavioral systems. In R. J. Sternberg & M. Barnes (Eds.), *Anatomy of love.* New Haven, CT: Yale University Press.

Shupe, A., Stacey, W., & Hazelwood, L. (1987). *Violent men, violent couples.* Lexington, MA: Lexington.

Sillars, A., Jones, T., & Murphy, M. (1982). Communication and understanding in marriage. *Human Communication Research, 10,* 317-350.

Sillars, A., & Weisberg, J. (1987). Conflict as a social skill. In M. E. Roloff & G. R. Miller (Eds.), *Interpersonal process.* Newbury Park, CA: Sage.

Simmel, G. (1955). *Conflict and the web of group affiliations.* New York: Free Press.

Sipes, R. G. (1973). Wars, sports and aggression: An empirical analysis of two rival theories. *American Anthropologist, 75*, 64-86.

Soloviev, V. (1918). *The justification of good: An essay on moral philosophy.* New York: Macmillan.

Sorse, J., Emde, R., Campos, J., & Klinnert, M. (1985). Maternal emotional signaling: Its effect on the visual cliff behavior of 1-year-olds. *Developmental Psychology, 21*, 195-200.

Spanier, G. B. (1976). Measuring dyadic adjustment: New scales for measuring the quality of marriages and similar dyads. *Journal of Marriage and the Family, 38*, 15-28.

Spitz, R. A. (1946). Anaclitic depression: An inquiry into the genesis of psychiatric conditions in early childhood II. *Psychoanalytic Study of the Child, 2*, 313-342.

Sprey, J. (1979). Conflict theory and the study of marriage and the family. In W. Burr, R. Hill, F. I. Nye, & I. Reiss (Eds.), *Contemporary theories about the family.* New York: Free Press.

Stechler, G., & Carpenter, G. (1967). A viewpoint of early affective development. *Exceptional Infant, 1*, 165-189.

Stechler, G., & Latz, E. (1966). Some observations on attention and arousal in the human infant. *Journal of Child Psychiatry, 5*, 517-525.

Steiner, G. (1981). *After Babel: Aspects of language and translation.* New York: Oxford University Press.

Stern, D. N. (1971). A micro-analysis of mother-infant interaction. *Journal of American Academy of Child Psychiatry, 10*, 501-517.

Stern, D. N. (1977). *The first relationship.* Cambridge, MA: Harvard University Press.

Stern, D. N. (1981). The development of biologically determined signals of readiness to communicate, which are language "resistant." In R. Stark (Ed.), *Language behavior in infancy and early childhood.* New York: Elsevier North-Holland.

Stern, D. N. (1984). Affect attunement: The sharing of feeling states between mother and infant by means of inter-modal fluency. In T. Field & N. Fox (Eds.), *Social perception in early infancy.* Norwood, NJ: Ablex.

Straus, M., Gelles, R., & Steinmetz, S. (1980). *Behind closed doors: Violence in the American family.* Garden City, NY: Doubleday.

Straus, M., & Hotaling, G. T. (Eds.). (1980). *The social causes of husband-wife violence.* Minneapolis: University of Minnesota Press.

Strauss, A. (1965). *George Herbert Mead on social psychology.* Chicago: University of Chicago Press.

Stuart, R. B. (1980). *Helping couples change.* New York: Guilford.

Stuart, R. B., & Braver, J. (1973). *Positive and negative exchanges between spouses and strangers.* Unpublished manuscript.

Sumner, W. (1906). *Folkways.* New York: Ginn.

Tavris, C. (1982). *Anger: The misunderstood emotion.* New York: Touchstone.

Terman, L. M., Buttenweiser, P., Ferguson, L., Johnson, W., & Wilson, D. (1938). *Psychological factors in marital happiness.* New York: McGraw-Hill.

Terman, L. M., & Wallin, P. (1949). The validity of marriage prediction and marital adjustment tests. *American Sociological Review, 14*, 503-504.

Tomkins, S. (1963). *Affect/imagery/consciousness* (Vol. 2). New York: Springer.

Tronick, E. (1980). The primacy of social skills. *Exceptional Infant, 4*, 144-158.

Tronick, E., Als, H., & Adamson, L. (1979). Structure of early face-to-face communicative interactions. In A. Bullowa (Ed.), *Before speech: The beginning of human communications.* New York: Cambridge University Press.

Tronick, E., Als, H., Adamson, L., Wise, S., & Brazelton, B. (1978). The infants' response to entrapment between contradictory messages in face-to-face interaction. *American Academy of Child Psychiatry, 17*, 1-13.

Tronick, E., Ricks, M., & Cohn, J. (1982). Maternal and infant affect exchange: Patterns of adaptation. In T. Field & A. Fogel (Eds.), *Emotion and early interaction.* Hillsdale, NJ: Lawrence Erlbaum.

Tucker, R. C. (Ed.). (1978). *The Marx-Engels reader.* New York: W. W. Norton.

Volkema, R. (1988). The mediator as face saver. *Mediation Quarterly, 22*, 5-14.

Wallace, L. (1963). The mechanism of shame. *Archives of General Psychiatry, 8*, 96-101.

Walters, R., & Parke, R. (1965). The role of distance receptor in the development of social responsiveness. In L. Lipsitt & C. Spiker (Eds.), *Advances in child development and behavior.* New York: Academic Press.

Watzlawick, P., Beavin, J., & Jackson, D. D. (1967). *Pragmatics of human communication.* New York: W. W. Norton.

Wurmser, L. (1981). *Mask of shame.* Baltimore: Johns Hopkins University Press.

Author Index

Cooley, C. H., 10, 11, 25, 26, 27, 28, 29,
    38, 39, 40, 47, 48, 53, 54, 63
Coser, L. A., 4, 5, 7, 18, 20, 180
Cottle, T. J., 190
Cottrell, L., 14
Cubbin, H., 15
Cuber, J. F., 14

Dahrendorf, R., xix, 4
Danehy, J., 66
Darwin, C., 37, 67, 73, 200
DeCasper, A., 27
Deutsch, M., 4, 5, 6, 7, 8, 9, 15, 20, 48
Dewey, J., 11, 28
Dodds, E., 40
Donohue, W., x
Drolette, M., 47
Duck, S., 15
Duncan, S., Jr., 10
Durkheim, E., 30, 36, 195

Edelmann, R. J., 67, 73
Ekman, P., 48, 67, 72, 74, 75
Ellis, H., 200
Emde, R., 17
Emerson, R. W., 3
Erikson, E. H., 30

Fanshel, D., 16, 63, 66, 69, 71, 72, 75, 82,
    103, 106, 136
Ferguson, L., 14
Feshbach, S., 47
Field, T., 27
Fifer, W., 27
Fiske, D. W., 10
Fitzpatrick, M., viii, x, xii, 15, 23, 30,
    31, 33, 34, 65, 180
Folger, J., 170
Follette, W. C., 18
Fossum, M., 42, 175
Freud, S., 17, 41, 47, 63
Friesen, W., 48, 67, 72, 74, 75
Funkenstein, D. H., 47

Gaylin, W., 26, 37, 38, 40
Gelles, R. J., 4, 15, 47
Giddens, A., xx
Gleser, G. C., 43
Goffman, E., 8, 11, 37, 39, 40, 42, 48, 59,
    69, 170
Gottman, J. M., xi, 16, 64, 65, 132
Gottschalk, L. A., 43, 66, 68
Green, R., 162
Greif, A., xi
Groen, J. J., 48
Gross, E., 88

Haley, J., 7
Hall, S., 47
Handel, G., 30
Hansburg, H., 54
Harlow, H. F., 26, 27
Harrington, C. L., 70, 71
Harroff, P. B., 14
Hazelwood, L., 8
Heritage, J., 63, 66, 67
Hertel, R., 4
Hess, R. D., 30
Hockett, C., 66
Holtzworth-Munroe, A., 18, 20, 56
Horowitz, M. J., 18, 48, 56

Izard, C., 48, 67, 72, 73, 74, 75

Jackins, H., 47
Jackson, D. D., 6, 7, 11, 13, 18, 19
Jacobs, S., ix
Jacobson, N. S., 16, 18, 19, 56
James, W., 26, 28, 53, 54
Janov, A., 47
Johnson, W. 14
Johnston J., 6, 42, 170, 171, 174, 175,
    176
Jones, T., 18

Kahn, M., 47

Subject Index

About the Author

Suzanne M. Retzinger received her Ph.D. from the University of California, Santa Barbara, in 1988. She is currently Assistant Research Sociologist at the Community and Organization Research Institute at UCSB, and Family Relations Mediator, Superior Court of Ventura County. She is also conducting a study of protracted child custody disputes in high-conflict families, using case history methods in combination with videotape. She is coauthor, with Thomas Scheff, of *Emotions and Violence: Shame and Rage in Destructive Conflicts* (Lexington, 1991) and has published articles on conflict, emotions, self-esteem, mental illness, and mediation.

NOTES

NOTES